Broadmoor Inmates

True Crime Tales of Life and Death in the Asylum

Nicola Sly

First published in Great Britain in 2023 by
Pen & Sword History
An imprint of Pen & Sword Books Limited
Yorkshire – Philadelphia

Copyright © Nicola Sly 2023

ISBN 978 1 39904 890 3

The right of Nicola Sly to be identified as
Author of this Work has been asserted by her in accordance
with the Copyright, Designs and Patents Act 1988.

A CIP catalogue record for this book is
available from the British Library

All rights reserved. No part of this book may be reproduced or
transmitted in any form or by any means, electronic or mechanical
including photocopying, recording or by any information storage and
retrieval system, without permission from the Publisher in writing.

Typeset by Mac Style
Printed in the UK by CPI Group (UK) Ltd, Croydon, CR0 4YY.

Pen & Sword Books Limited incorporates the imprints of After the
Battle, Atlas, Archaeology, Aviation, Discovery, Family History,
Fiction, History, Maritime, Military, Military Classics, Politics,
Select, Transport, True Crime, Air World, Frontline Publishing,
Leo Cooper, Remember When, Seaforth Publishing, The Praetorian
Press, Wharncliffe Local History, Wharncliffe Transport,
Wharncliffe True Crime and White Owl.

For a complete list of Pen & Sword titles please contact

PEN & SWORD BOOKS LIMITED
47 Church Street, Barnsley, South Yorkshire, S70 2AS, England
E-mail: enquiries@pen-and-sword.co.uk
Website: www.pen-and-sword.co.uk
or
PEN AND SWORD BOOKS
1950 Lawrence Rd, Havertown, PA 19083, USA
E-mail: Uspen-and-sword@casematepublishers.com
Website: www.penandswordbooks.com

Broadmoor Inmates

Contents

Introduction 1

John Darby Shelley: 1800–1889 3
William Hayward: 1808–1869 7
Sophia Hyson: 1810–1888 11
James Potter: 1811–1866 13
Peter Whittle: 1811–1885 18
James Stevenson: 1812–1879 23
Daniel McNaughten, McNaughton or M'Naghten: 1813–1865 26
Henry Dommett: 1813–1879 30
John Green: 1815–1876 35
Richard Dadd: 1817–1886 37
Martha Spencer Weaver: 1818–1902 39
James Senior: 1819–1893 43
Joseph Bones: 1821–1879 47
Mary Crooks (or Crookes): 1825–1874 51
Thomas Humphreys (or Humphries): 1828–1879 54
Christiana Edmunds: 1828–1907 57
John Peacock: 1829–1894 61
Mary Ann Parr: 1829–1900 63
William Thompson: 1831–1883 66
William Brown: 1832–1885 70
William Isaac Robinson: 1833–1893 71
Robert Edwards: 1834–1879 74
Frederick Crawley: 1836–1889 77
William Carew: 1838–1880 79
James Edwards: 1840–1894 81
Mary Hirst: 1845–1932 84
James Smith: 1846–1890 87
William Enoch Kirk: 1846–1916 89
James Hobbins: 1848–1875 94
Sarah Ann Bull: 1848–1884 97

Eliza Whorlow: 1848–1893	99
Sarah Ann Binstead: 1849–1919	101
Elizabeth Hammond: 1849–1933	106
Joseph Shill: 1852–1885	109
Walter Deavin: 1852–1934	114
Eliza Blanche Bastable: 1853–1880	117
Frederick Marshall: 1854–1887	119
Roderick Edward McClean (or Maclean): 1854–1921	122
Frederick Ernest Page: 1856–1886	125
Emma Jackson: (approximately) 1859–1888	128
Richard Millar Archer: 1859–1937	131
James Kelly: 1860–1927	135
George James Bland: 1860–1934	140
John Henry Lush: 1860–1936	144
John White: 1861–1933	147
Samuel Bentall Collis: 1862–1899	153
James Shaw: 1862–1947	156
Margaret Rees: 1863–1903	162
Richard Edward Goodall: 1863–1913	165
Agnes Dorcas Mould: 1866–1933	168
John James Hitchens: 1867–1938	172
Octavius Diaper: 1867–1938	175
Sidney Stuart Lockhart: 1869–1952	177
Alice Keeling: 1873–1931	181
George Scriven: 1873–1934	183
George Holland: 1876–1939	186
Hannah Griffin: 1881–1948	187
Benjamin Bradford: 1882–1958	189
John Edward Jones: 1887–1958	192
Thomas Percival Thomas: 1886–1937	195
Phillip George Dickinson: 1896–1946 and John Llewellyn Phillips: 1923–1948	198
William Jarvis Yeoman: 1896–1960	203
Harry Grice: 1898–1934	205
George Trotter: 1902–1957	207
Amilia (or Amelia) Leach: 1917–1956	210
John Lionel Raymond Rusdell: 1933–1955	213
Bibliography	216
Index	219

Introduction

Since opening its imposing gates to patients in 1863, the ethos of Broadmoor Special Hospital – formerly Broadmoor Criminal Lunatic Asylum – has been twofold. As well as protecting the general public from those judged to be too dangerously affected by mental illness to live amongst them, the hospital has sought to rehabilitate and even cure those confined within its walls. Nowadays, staff have a wide range of diagnostic, pharmaceutical and therapeutic tools at their disposal, but historically, until the 1950's, the only real treatment offered to patients was work, good food, leisure activities and abundant fresh air. Patients were encouraged to exercise

Entrance Gates to Broadmoor Criminal Lunatic Asylum. (*Author's collection*)

in the asylum's gardens and to participate in a range of organised activities, from acting and singing to playing cricket and billiards.

Although the average length of stay in Broadmoor is now said to be only five and a half years, many of those unfortunates historically judged to be criminally insane never managed to escape its confines, dying before they could be seen as cured and thus effectively serving a life sentence for their crimes, some of which were as apparently as trivial as passing counterfeit coins and killing lambs!

The first female inmates were admitted in 1863 from Bethlem Hospital, which is perhaps better known by its nickname of 'Bedlam'. Reading the tragic histories of these women, many of whom killed their own children, it is evident that they would nowadays be diagnosed with postnatal depression. Yet, without the means to offer any effective treatment, many of them spent the rest of their lives confined, away from their homes, husbands and families, with no hope of being freed. Many of the inmates were physically ill, addicted to alcohol, or suffered from delusions, which would today be treated with antipsychotic or antidepressant drugs, coupled with counselling. Before the development of such medication and therapies, confinement and containment of the protagonists was the only option.

The people within this book are the forgotten – those that died insane – who were often as much victims of their own internal demons as were those they harmed.

In writing this book, I have relied heavily on the contemporary newspaper accounts of the inmates' lives and crimes. However, as today, not everything reported in the press was entirely accurate, and there were frequent discrepancies between publications, so I have used the most commonly quoted variant. Every effort has been made to ascertain, locate and contact copyright holders. My apologies to anyone I may have inadvertently missed; I can assure you it was not deliberate but an oversight on my part.

As always, there are several people to be thanked for their assistance in compiling this book, including my Commissioning Editor at Pen and Sword, Claire Hopkins, who, along with Lucy May, guided me expertly through the whole publishing process. I must also thank Peter Lewsey and The Hadleigh and Thundersley Community Archive for supplying and allowing me to use their picture of Wittering Court in Daw's Heath. Finally, my thanks to my long-suffering husband, Richard, who proofread every word of this book and kept me well supplied with mugs of tea throughout the writing process.

John Darby Shelley: 1800–1889

From 1787, the British Government transported many of their convicts to Australia. Yet the government also had hopes of creating a stable, self-supporting community there, and, to that end, began to encourage so-called free settlers to take up residence as well as convicts.

The first free settlers paid their own passage from the United Kingdom and therefore only the wealthiest people could afford to go. Early in the 1800s, the government began to pay transport costs and also to award the settlers free land in Australia, provided that it was used for a productive purpose. For those settlers wishing to farm, the government also provided free tools and labour in the form of the transported convicts. The Industrial Revolution in Britain had left many people unemployed and consequently living in poverty, so the scheme proved very popular with those who saw it as a golden opportunity to start a new life.

One of those looking to take advantage of the allotment of land was John Darby Shelley, who set sail for Australia aboard the barque *Eliza* in October 1827. On arrival in Sydney, Shelley immediately went to pay his respects to the governor, Sir Ralph Darling, thinking that the official would be pleased and impressed to welcome such a respectable and reputable man. However, much to Shelley's disgust, he was refused an audience with the governor and told to communicate with him by letter, rather than in person.

Darling was not a popular governor – indeed in his book '*Three Colonies of Australia*', Samuel Sidney described him as 'a man of forms and precedents of the true red-tape school –neat, exact, punctual, industrious, arbitrary, spiteful, and commonplace. Impressed with a marvellous sense of his own importance, and obstinate to desperation, Sir Ralph Darling brought the severest military discipline to bear upon the social relations of governor and governed.' As instructed, Shelley wrote to Darling the following day, explaining that, in view of the British government's desire to promote respectable emigration, he had sailed to Australia at considerable personal expense, winding up his affairs and forgoing his friends and was hoping to 'receive the customary indulgence of a grant of land'. In the same letter, Shelley offered to waive his claim to land if the governor could find him employment in the public offices. Shelley was not impressed to receive a formulaic printed letter in response and immediately wrote a second letter, detailing the cost of his travel to Australia and listing the value of assets that he still retained in England. He stated that he had brought around £400 with him, the majority of which he had now spent on buying suitable clothes and personal requisites.

It was intimated that, in order to receive a grant of land, Shelley would have to prove that he had at least £500 in cash or be in possession of farming implements to that value. Shelley immediately argued that he had known other people who had been awarded their land, having little more than the clothes on their backs. However, the governor would not be budged and assured Shelley that if – and only if – he decided to grant him some land, it would be no more than a section (about 80 acres).

Shelley was outraged. He wrote to Darling stating that a single section of land would place him in the lowest scale of settlers and would be too little to support the stock he intended to purchase. If he were only offered a section, Shelley's letter concluded, then he would rather not have any land at all.

Shelley began renting a cottage, hoping that he could organise sufficient funds from England to purchase some land, rather than have it allocated to him. However, as he got to know people and explained his problems with Darling, it was widely agreed by the 'country gentlemen and magistrates of respectability' that he had been unfairly treated and he was advised to submit another application, this time agreeing to accept a single section until further funds arrived.

Now Shelley consulted Colonial Office Secretary Alexander McLeay, a man he later described as 'coarse, vulgar and morose'. A close ally of Darling, McLeay told Shelley that he would not be allocated any land, suggesting that if he wanted it, he should pay to rent it. Shelley saw no need to rent land while others received it for free, including, he suspected, several friends of McLeay, whom Shelley believed had received preferential treatment.

The following day, Shelley tried again to put his case in a letter to Darling, which was ignored. When Shelley wrote again three weeks later, he received a reply from McLeay's office stating bluntly, 'His Excellency regrets that he can only repeat that under the existing regulations which the Government have found it necessary to adopt, it is not in his power to make any other communication to you than that which you have already received.'

Shelley's influential Australian friends were too fearful of the consequences of Darling's wrath to intervene on his behalf and he was advised to submit an affidavit before magistrates. He wrote a long letter, protesting against the 'unjust, unnecessary and rigorous exercise of discretionary power' against him. 'I have been long enough in this country to enable me to prove upon the most irrefutable of evidence that grants of land are almost daily with privity of the Government both given and surreptitiously obtained.' However, the only result was a response from Alex McLeay, repeating that, when he verified that he had sufficient available capital, he would receive his land in the same proportions as any other individual.

Shelley sought an appointment with McLeay, insisting that while he only had £220 in cash, he had other assets, the value of which was more than £300. McLeay remained unbending, and when the *Sydney Monitor* newspaper got hold of Shelley's affidavit and published it in full, that marked the end of any negotiations between Shelley and the governor's office.

Shelley gave vent to his feelings, writing a letter to the governor, in which he referred to him as 'a scoundrel' and threatened to take the matter up with the British government on his return to England. With all hope now dashed of being allocated any land, Shelley returned to England. His journey took eighteen months, delayed by a shipwreck in which he lost all of his belongings, and by being abandoned by a rogue ship's captain, who took his fare and left him in Penang.

On arrival in England, Shelley immediately wrote to Viscount Goderich of the Colonial Office, detailing his problems with Darling and asking for compensation for the four years of his life and the £2,000 that the battle for land had cost him. Goderich was already familiar with the case, having been briefed by Darling and wrote back, regretting that Shelley was not entitled to a grant of land in view of his lack of capital and that there would be no compensation forthcoming.

Shelley immediately wrote back, protesting that land was being apportioned to 'menials of the household, to convicted felons and numerous other classes, without any reference to property or regulations.' According to Shelley, the treatment he had received at Darling's hands had been unduly harsh, the governor 'selecting one in my situation and circumstances upon so slight and slender a pretext for ruin and disappointment.' So dire was Shelley's financial situation that he filed for bankruptcy in the Insolvent Debtors Court in 1832 and again in 1834.

He continued to pepper the government with letters, even though it was made quite clear to him that it was not possible for anyone in England to overrule Darling's decision. On 12 August 1836 Shelley was taken to court for writing a threatening letter to The Right Honourable Charles Glenelg, the then Secretary of State for the Colonial Department. 'My Lord,' wrote Shelley, 'I request to be made acquainted with your determination without further torturing delay. Am I, my Lord Glenelg, to receive any relief at your hands or not?' Shelley ended the letter 'I have sworn to my God – I am devout and religiously intent in taking this oath – that beyond this Session of Parliament I would not for any man on earth of any station or degree submit to the insults, the cruel and bloody atrocities which have been practised upon me and it will be, I repeat, not only merciful but wise to give me some relief, that I may direct my mind to some pursuit and divert it from the pressure which it has so long sustained.'

This wasn't the first threatening letter Lord Glenelg had received from Shelley. He recognised Shelley's handwriting from his previous communications, not to mention the fact that he had also signed his correspondence. In October 1835 Shelley served four months in prison for a similar offence, released only at the personal request of Lord Glenelg on the assurance that he would desist from writing any further letters.

Before the court, Shelley seemed intent on rehashing his grievances with Darling. Justice of the Peace Sir Frederick Roe refused to listen and sentenced him to keep the peace for two years. He was offered bail, but, unable to raise the money, he launched a tirade of abuse at Roe, who promptly despatched him to Westminster Bridewell by coach.

Unable to raise sureties, Shelley was confined in Westminster but became increasingly disturbed, and on 31 July 1837, the prison governor ordered him to be placed in solitary confinement for using violent, indecent, and abusive language. As turnkey Edward Utting struggled to contain him, Shelley lay down and refused to budge. When Utting bent to pull him upright, Shelley pulled a cut-throat razor from his pocket and slashed Utting's knee. Fortunately for Utting, Shelley did not have time to open the razor fully, so the injury was not as bad as it might have been,

At the Middlesex Sessions, Shelley again tried to air his grievances with Darling and the British government but was curtailed by the magistrates. It emerged that Shelley was allowed a lot more privileges than other prisoners. He was provided with special food, a comfortable bed, and newspapers, and was said to be most kindly treated. The magistrates decided to be lenient with Shelley, in view of his excited state of mind at having been so long in prison. He was sentenced to a further two months imprisonment, but by July 1839 he was still incarcerated, being unable to raise the sureties necessary for his release.

By now, there were doubts about his sanity and an application was made to magistrates to have him medically assessed. Drs Munro and Sutherland examined him, and both agreed that Shelley was insane and that prison was an unsuitable place for him to be confined. Shelley had delusions of grandeur, and was often violent and needed to be restrained, and it was believed that the prison officers were simply unable to control him. Unfortunately, the only person who could authorise Shelley's transfer to a lunatic asylum was the Home Secretary, and, in spite of several requests, no authorisation was forthcoming.

In September 1840 Shelley was finally transferred to Bethlem Lunatic Asylum by the chairman of the Middlesex Sessions, Mr Sergeant Adams. Needing to be restrained, Shelley was apparently kept under the most appalling conditions, in solitary confinement in a dark cell. When complaints were made by Adams to the Home Secretary, the Marquis of Normanby, about this maltreatment, an official investigation was launched, but since Shelley himself had made no complaint, it was determined that Adams had simply misunderstood the situation.

Shelley was sent to Broadmoor on 16 March 1864 and remained there until his death, aged eighty-nine, on 18 September 1889. Frail and bedridden due to old age, Shelley suffered from diarrhoea and stomach pains during the week leading up to his death and died from of old age and peritonitis.

William Hayward: 1808–1869

After living in America for ten years, William Hayward returned to Compton, South Petherton, in Somerset, where he met and married his wife, Ann, who was eleven years his junior. The couple, who farmed a hundred acres, went on to have one daughter.

At Christmas 1867 William began to suffer from a number of minor health problems and consequently Ann's brother, George Best, moved in with the Haywards to help with the running of their farm. In due course, Best went on to purchase all the stock, and, for all intents and purposes, took over the farm, which remained William Hayward's in name only.

On 7 May 1868 the Haywards and Best ate breakfast together as they usually did, before George went outside to start the daily chores, leaving his sister sitting by the fire, churning butter. Less than half an hour after he had left the house, George heard a loud bang, after which William rushed into the yard and implored him 'Do'ee come in'.

'What's the matter?' asked George, but William didn't reply, turning on his heel and walking back into the house, leaving George to follow on behind.

As soon as George entered the house, he could smell burning. He rushed into the kitchen to find his sister still sitting in the same chair but with her dress on fire and blood streaming from a wound in her back. As his brother-in-law stood watching, George tried to beat out the flames with his bare hands, all the while shouting for help. Within a short while, several people who lived nearby rushed into the house, having heard the loud bang and run to investigate. Farm labourer John Garrett was one of the first to enter the house, taking one of Mrs Hayward's hands and trying to comfort her. 'You've done something now, Master,' he said to Hayward.

'Yes, I have, John and it can't be helped,' replied Hayward.

Garrett was sent to South Petherton to fetch a doctor and a policeman, while the other neighbours attempted unsuccessfully to revive Ann Hayward, who had slumped forward in her chair, insensible.

Dr Walter Harvey arrived within minutes, and on unfastening Ann's dress, discovered that she had been shot in the back, just below her right shoulder blade, leaving a gaping hole that measured almost one inch in diameter. The charge had passed through her heart before lodging in her left breast, killing her almost instantly.

William sat in the kitchen trembling violently, until Police Sergeant Ashman arrived at the house to take him into custody. When Ashman charged Hayward with his wife's murder, Hayward immediately confessed. 'Oh, dear, I done it.' He admitted. 'I loaded the gun and shot her when she was sitting in the chair. She never spoke.' He accompanied the sergeant to the lock-up at Ilminster, asking only if he might put on a better hat for the journey. When he was searched at the lock-up, his waistcoat pockets contained three percussion caps and a piece of brown paper, with which Hayward told the sergeant he had loaded the gun.

The gun with which Ann Hayward was shot was normally kept standing in a corner of the farmhouse kitchen, although with a child in the house, it was always kept unloaded. The powder and shot were kept in a drawer in the kitchen but the caps were kept in a box on a shelf in the adjoining pantry. It was obvious that Hayward had deliberately loaded the gun in order to shoot his wife, and from the position of her wounds, it was also evident that he had taken careful aim and fired the gun into her back at close range.

There seemed to be no real motive for Ann Hayward's murder, although there were widespread rumours about jealousy and property disputes. Hayward was known to be somewhat eccentric, but nobody who knew him had the slightest inkling that he might possibly be dangerous. As the news of the murder spread around the locality, people began to suggest that he might be insane, although it was pointed out that up until the very moment of the murder he had successfully managed a one-hundred-acre farm. Although he had repeatedly consulted Dr Harvey for what were described as 'sundry bodily ailments' over the past three months, it was initially reported that he had showed no signs whatsoever of insanity. However, by the time the inquest on Ann's death opened a week later, it was reported that he had shown signs of 'softening of the brain', and that his friends had been sufficiently concerned about his condition to 'have his movements watched'.

Coroner Mr W.W. Monckton presided over the inquest, while Hayward sat, looking dull and vacant, taking little interest in the proceedings beyond crying, groaning and sighing occasionally. Best was the first witness called and told the coroner that his sister and her husband had always seemed very happily married. There had been no quarrel between them that morning, although William had been particularly low and despondent for a few days, walking around the house and occasionally mumbling, 'Oh, dear. I am fit for nothing at all.'

Dr Harvey then testified to the extent of Hayward's health problems, which seemed to be mainly colic, indigestion and intermittent dizziness. Neighbour Ann Male was next to testify, confirming Best's testimony that the Haywards had always seemed a happy couple. However, Mrs Male revealed something of which Best was unaware. She told the inquest that, about six months prior to the murder, William had tried to hang himself in the outside toilet. She added that William also suffered from frequent fainting fits and her husband, John, confirmed her evidence, adding that he believed that William had spent some time in an asylum after his unsuccessful suicide attempt.

Dr Harvey was recalled and stated that around two months before the murder he had been called to attend Hayward, who appeared to be under the influence of alcohol. Hayward, who was being restrained by two people, wanted to go into the cellar, where he claimed to have hidden some money. Having persuaded him to go to bed, Harvey visited Hayward the following morning and found his behaviour normal. Although Harvey had prescribed a change of air and Hayward had spent several weeks recuperating in Lyme, he had not been sent to the asylum. 'I have never seen him in a fit and at all times he seemed to be perfectly sane and more than capable of managing his own affairs,' the doctor reiterated. George Best then told the inquest that he had handled the day-to-day running of the farm since Hayward appeared incapable of managing it himself.

John Male was then recalled and stated that he had known Hayward for almost fifty years, and that for the past six months his behaviour had been very strange, particularly around the time of the full moon. Male insisted that he had advised Ann Hayward, on more than one occasion, that her husband should be committed to an asylum. He claimed to have remarked to his wife more than once that he would 'eat his hat if there isn't something as turns out bad'.

The inquest jury eventually found a verdict of wilful murder against William Hayward, although having heard that both of his parents, his grandfather, and his sister had all spent time in a lunatic asylum, they advised the coroner that they believed he was not in his right mind at the time of the murder. The matter of Hayward's sanity would be decided at the next Assizes; he was committed on the coroner's warrant, and, on the following day, by the magistrates.

Taunton County Buildings, site of the Assizes. (*Author's collection*)

When sixty-year-old Hayward appeared before Mr Baron Channell at the Somerset Assizes in August 1968, his physical health had deteriorated to such an extent that he had to be helped into the dock by a prison warder. He appeared feeble and vacant, and his defence counsel, Mr Edlin, maintained that he was not in his right mind when he murdered his wife.

Dr Francis Henry Woodforde, the proprietor of a private asylum near Taunton, was called to give evidence about Hayward's state of mind after his incarceration in Taunton Gaol. On visiting Hayward, Woodforde found him to be in a very dull state, scarcely capable of communicating. His expression was vacant and he dribbled copiously. Woodforde described Hayward's condition as being in a state of general paralysis and had no hesitation in concluding that he was in the early stages of dementia. Over the course of fifteen or so visits by Woodforde, Hayward's condition remained unchanged. He had no idea where he was or why he was in prison. Woodforde's diagnosis was confirmed by another asylum proprietor, Dr J. D. Davey. Both men believed that Hayward was insane and had been for some time.

Assize Judge Mr Justice Channell. (*Author's collection*)

The judge told the jury that it was not sufficient for them to agree that the prisoner was in a low, melancholy and desponding state of mind at the time – they must be completely satisfied that the evidence showed that Hayward was completely incapable of distinguishing right from wrong. Citing the evidence of insanity in Hayward's immediate family, the judge noted that even the prosecuting counsels had acknowledged the idea of some mental aberration, declining the chance to address the jury.

Described in the contemporary newspapers as 'a hopeless imbecile', Hayward dozed intermittently during the judge's summing up of the case, occasionally snoring gently, and having observed his conduct in court, the jury did not find it necessary to retire, immediately finding him not guilty on the grounds of insanity.

At the conclusion of the trial, Hayward was sent to Broadmoor Criminal Lunatic Asylum, arriving there on 27 August 1868. He died, aged sixty-one, from general paralysis on 7 June 1869.

Sophia Hyson: 1810–1888

Forty-five-year-old spinster Sophia Hyson lived with her widowed mother, Eliza, at 1 Garden Walk, in Shoreditch, London. Sophia was a former domestic servant who had always sent a proportion of her wages to support her mother. However, by 1854 Sophia had not worked for many years and mother and daughter survived on the proceeds of some small annuities. Sophia had spent at least four periods detained in three different asylums – St Luke's Hospital for Lunatics, Peckham House and Hoxton House, the latter known colloquially as 'Miles's Mad House' after the former owners of the building. When Sophia was discharged from her last asylum in around 1844, she was said to be 'far from cured'. However, it was her mother's wish that Sophia should come and live with her.

Mother and daughter argued constantly – in the words of a cousin of Sophia's, they used to 'worret' each other – and Sophia was often violent towards Eliza. She would sometimes get up in the middle of the night and sing, and she once jammed a saucepan on her mother's head. On more than one occasion, the couple's landlord, Henry Page, had to physically separate the two women, when Sophia tried to strangle her mother.

Then, on 14 November 1854, Sophia walked into the apartment occupied by Henry Page and his wife, Mary, and told Mrs Page, 'I think I have given the old devil her death blow'.

'Oh dear! How came you to do so?' asked the landlady, Mrs Page.

Sophia explained that she had been busy trimming a bonnet when her mother had demanded that she make a cup of tea. When Sophia refused, Eliza began to complain vociferously, at which Sophia lashed out with the scissors she was holding, cutting her mother on the back of her hand.

Sophia picked up Mrs Page's needlework scissors and showed her landlady how she had 'scratched' her mother. Although Sophia's hands were stained with Eliza's blood, Mrs Page didn't think that the injury sounded too bad. However, the following day, Sophia again came downstairs and told her that the wound was worse.

Mrs Page asked if she had seen a doctor, but Sophia told her that she had put some dripping on the wound. Mrs Page advised her to poultice it, but Eliza continued to be in pain and the landlady told Sophia to send for a doctor the next morning.

Mrs Page saw the wound for the first time when the doctor arrived. It was on Eliza's right hand and was a deep, gaping wound down to the bones, roughly one and a half inches long. By the time surgeon Peter Lodwick Burchell saw the injury, it was already red and swollen, with signs of the bacterial skin infection erysipelas. Although Burchell visited daily and nurses were engaged to care for Eliza, the wound became gangrenous and she died on 19 December.

An inquest into Eliza's death, held by coroner Mr W. Baker, returned a verdict of manslaughter against Sophia, who was immediately arrested and taken to Newgate Prison. On 1 January 1855 she appeared before Mr Justice Crowder at the Central Criminal Court, charged with feloniously killing and slaying her mother.

Old Newgate Prison. (*Author's collection*)

Following evidence from Mary Page, and also Frances Royal and Ann Deeson, the two nurses who attended Eliza on her death bed, the court called surgeon Mr Burchell, who, having described the wound and his treatment, was asked about Sophia's demeanour at the time of the incident. 'Her conduct was so queer that it was my opinion that she was not in her right mind,' testified Burchell. Unaware that Sophia had previously been in lunatic asylums, the doctor told the court that Sophia had been very rough and violent when handling her mother's wound, pulling it about while he tried to examine his patient. She had spoken randomly about her mother, saying that Eliza was more like a beast than a person, adding that she had always believed that she would be somehow responsible for her mother's death. 'I suppose I shall be hung for it,' she had remarked casually. Burchell had eventually been so concerned about Sophia's behaviour that he ordered her removal to the workhouse and brought in nurses to care for Eliza.

Sophia was eventually acquitted due to insanity, and in February 1856 she was sent to the Criminal Lunatic Asylum at St George's Fields (Bethlem), then Fisherton Asylum, near Salisbury in Wiltshire. She was one of the first patients to be accepted in Broadmoor Criminal Lunatic Asylum when it opened in 1863. She remained there until January 1888, when she died from congestion and softening of the brain.

James Potter: 1811–1866

James Potter lived in Traffic Street, Derby, with his fifty-four-year- old wife, Sarah, and their grandchild. He worked as a sheriff's messenger and as a 'bum bailiff' – a bailiff who was authorised to both collect debts and to arrest debtors for non-payment – but, by 1864, his heavy drinking had led to him losing his job.

He and Sarah were unhappily married. James usually treated his wife well, but, when drinking, seemed to believe that he was well within his rights to beat her black and blue. Yet, in spite of the almost constant abuse she suffered at his hands, and although she was terrified of her husband, Sarah continued to live with him and tried to persuade him to treat her better by showering him with love and affection.

Towards Christmas 1864, Potter's brutality took on a new dimension when he became convinced that his wife was having an affair with their lodger, John Stone. On 22 December the violence against her finally became too much for Sarah to bear, and that night she made a complaint against her husband to Police Inspector Green. Sarah Potter arrived at the police house, her fingers bleeding. 'Oh, Mr Green. You must come and take my husband.

Look, he's been ill-using me,' she complained, holding up her injured hand. 'He's crazy. I'm sure he's crazy. You will have to take him to the Asylum,' she added, before walking briskly away.

Later still that night, Green met Sarah again, this time walking the streets near her home. 'I durst not go home,' she told the inspector. 'He swears he'll kill me. He's jealous of a lodger that I have, a tailor and has been calling me a ******* whore and I durst not go home.' In spite of her obvious terror, Sarah was reluctant to allow Green to accompany her home, fearing that it would make her husband's fury even worse. It was agreed that Green would ask the local beat policeman to keep an eye on the house and this Green did, telling Sergeant Thorpe, 'Potter's been carrying on. I believe he must be going cranky – when you go that way, just look out a bit.'

Thorpe did as he was asked. He met Potter at around eleven o'clock that night and wished him good night.

'Good night, Mr Thorpe,' replied James calmly.

Two hours later, Potter was still hanging about on the streets, now standing shivering with his hands in his pockets.

'Come on James, why don't you go home?' Thorpe asked him, adding, 'You'll be starved to death' [local dialect meaning very cold].

'I won't without you'll go with me,' replied Potter.

By now, Thorpe had formed the impression that Potter was suffering from *delirium tremens* – a severe mental disturbance due to the sudden withdrawal of alcohol in those who regularly drank to excess – so he agreed to walk him home. However, when they reached the house in Traffic Street, Potter stopped suddenly. 'The damned whore has locked me out. I can't get in,' he complained.

'Nonsense,' replied Thorpe. He tried both doors of the house, finding them locked, before noticing that one of the windows was ajar. He managed to open it, telling Potter to go inside, but Potter refused unless the policeman came with him. Potter was so insistent that he didn't want to go into the house alone that Thorpe began to be suspicious of what might await them inside. 'Go on, then, I'll follow you,' said Thorpe, waiting while Potter hauled himself into the house, before suggesting that he went and got a candle.

'I have no matches,' Potter explained, so Thorpe went to a nearby pub to ask for some. When he returned, Potter had climbed back out of the window and was awaiting him on the street.

Thorpe shepherded Potter back through the window then followed him into the house, finding a candle and lighting it. Once inside, Potter immediately went upstairs to the main bedroom. He pushed the door open and said, 'There's no one here', before continuing to the attic bedroom on the very top floor of the house, repeating, 'There's no one here'.

Thorpe tried to persuade him to get into bed, but when Potter reached his bedroom, he suddenly turned and began to open the door of a second room on that floor. 'Look in here,' he insisted.

'No, you go in,' argued Thorpe, placing his hands on Potter's shoulders, and gently but firmly pushing him forward. Potter seemed reluctant to enter the back bedroom, and when Thorpe eventually followed him in, he could immediately see why. A woman's naked leg hung out of the bed. As Thorpe stepped closer in the dim candlelight, he strongly suspected that she was dead.

'Dead, dead, dead!' exclaimed Potter, who then began to mumble 'Oh, dear, oh, dear,' repeatedly.

Thorpe searched Potter's pockets, finding a key, a wallet, a few coins and a knife. 'By God, are you going to take me?' Potter asked the policeman, as if suddenly realising the seriousness of his situation.

Thorpe led him downstairs and out into the street, where he saw two women across the road. Thorpe asked them if they would go and look at the body to confirm that she was dead. The women agreed, so Thorpe and Potter climbed back into the house, helping the two neighbours through the window and leading them back upstairs. Once the women had confirmed Thorpe's suspicions, they all trooped outside again. The two women went to fetch a doctor and the police while Thorpe detained Potter, threatening to floor him if he tried to escape.

Market Place and Town Hall, Derby, where the inquest was held. (*Author's collection*)

The doctors arrived too late to save Sarah Potter, who had suffered a single stab wound to her breast, inflicted by a sword stick that had punctured her heart. Potter was arrested. Amazingly, the Potters' lodger slept through the whole drama and only found out about his landlady's brutal murder when the police woke him.

An inquest into Sarah Potter's death was held at the Town Hall, Derby, by coroner James Vallack. Once the two police officers had testified, the Potters' married daughter, Elizabeth Clements, gave evidence. She stated that she had warned her mother time and time again that she must leave her father, before 'it all ends in something serious'. According to Elizabeth, for as long as she could remember, her father had always acted with great brutality towards her mother, continually beating and ill-treating her. On the evening of her mother's murder, Elizabeth had been at the house and had been attacked by her father, who had grabbed her by the throat and called her a 'bitch' for 'interfering' during his rages at his wife. Elizabeth had taken her mother to the safety of a nearby pub, but James followed them and tried to drag Sarah outside. Mother and daughter eventually left the pub and walked around for an hour or so, occasionally confronted by James who would briefly leave the pub to shout abuse at his wife before returning to his drinking. Elizabeth said that she had approached a policeman, PC Lester, and that James eventually promised both her and the policeman that he would not harm his wife if she came home with him. With some trepidation, Elizabeth watched her mother go into the house with her father. Less than an hour later, she was notified that her mother had been murdered.

Elizabeth Clements was succeeded as a witness by the Potters' next-door neighbour, William Edwin Glover, who told the coroner that on the night of the murder he had heard a woman crying 'Murder!' through the party wall. Glover had shouted downstairs to his mother, who went into the yard to investigate, but after the third cry, things went quiet and the Glovers thought no more about it.

The inquest returned a verdict of wilful murder against James Potter, who was committed for trial at the next Derbyshire Assizes in March 1865, where he appeared before Mr Justice Willes. Potter claimed that his wife had run him into debt and stolen his property, accusing John Stone of having killed Sarah.

It was revealed in court that Potter had a maternal aunt in an asylum and also that he had suffered a head injury in an accident around three years prior to the murder, although he never sought medical advice. However, Sergeant Thorpe, who was with Potter when Sarah's body was found, told the court that he had noticed nothing 'crazed' or 'cracked' about Potter.

Henry Francis Gisborne, the surgeon at Derby Gaol, where Potter had been confined since the murder, was acquainted with him, having treated him for dyspepsia three years earlier. Gisborne told the court that, having attended Potter both outside and within prison, he believed that he was sane, adding that the head injury mentioned by Elizabeth Clements appeared nothing more than a minor surface wound. Nevertheless, Gisborne conceded that Potter had a feeble mind, which, coupled with cunning and stubbornness, could be indicative of madness. Potter had answered every single question put to him rationally, with the exception of who had committed Sarah's murder, which he had alternately blamed on John Stone and even on Sarah herself. Potter was quite able to distinguish between right and wrong – he knew what a crime was and he also knew the penalty for committing one.

Unsurprisingly, Potter's defence counsel, Mr Stephen, focused on his client's mental state at the time of his wife's murder. He quoted an old Latin proverb to the jury – 'Anger is but a short madness' – and suggested that Potter was both angry and drunk when he killed his wife and thus may well have not realised what he was doing. If the act was done in a frenzy and Potter did not realise what he was doing, Stephen maintained, then he could not be held accountable for his actions.

'I did not do it,' Potter interrupted.

Stephen continued to question the sanity of a man who had deliberately led a policeman to the scene of his crime. Potter was delusional in believing that his wife was having an intimate affair with their lodger and it was this anger and jealousy that had led him to kill her.

The defence then called several witnesses to testify that Potter's behaviour was often 'strange'. These included neighbour William Glover, who often observed him talking to himself and making strange gestures in the yard, and also noted that Potter tended to spend a long time in the outside lavatory.

Potter's mother told the court that her son had not been 'right' for the past seven years, reiterating the fact that he had several relatives who had spent time in asylums. She had urged her daughter-in-law to leave him, but Sarah had insisted that things would get better in time. The defence also produced a doctor who had treated Potter for severe depression, which he believed might well have been a forerunner of insanity.

In the end, it took only twenty minutes' deliberation for the jury to decide that Potter was not insane and he was pronounced guilty and given the usual death sentence. However, once he was returned to prison to await his execution, he began to exhibit signs of madness. Surgeon Mr Gisborne believed that fear of dying on the public scaffold had turned Potter's mind, suggesting that a month of peace and quiet would restore him to his former state of health. Executioner William Calcraft arrived at the prison but left again the next morning after Potter's execution was postponed for seven days.

Following a visit to the prison by two men especially appointed by Home Secretary Sir George Grey to assess Potter's sanity, the execution was postponed indefinitely and he was taken to Broadmoor. He died there, aged fifty-five, on 9 January 1866 from pleurisy, but a post-mortem examination showed evidence of long-standing disease of the brain.

Peter Whittle: 1811–1885

Peter Whittle was employed as a spinner at a mill in Preston, while his wife, Sarah, worked as a winder at the same company. After their marriage, the couple moved in with Peter's parents in Vicar Street, along with Peter's four sisters, Mary, Margaret, Agnes and Ann, and his two brothers, Andrew and Lawrence. Peter and Sarah went on to have two children and by May 1842 Sarah was about five months pregnant with their third baby.

On 7 May Peter was on short-time working and was not expected to go to his place of employment. He spent part of that morning drinking beer in a public house, although he was not intoxicated. Sarah Whittle was working that day and arrived home for her lunch at just after midday.

Having eaten their lunch together, apparently on the most friendly terms, Peter and Sarah were sitting in the parlour, along with Peter's mother, Ann, who was sewing and had her back to the couple. Hearing a thump, Ann turned round to see her son with one arm wrapped around his wife's neck. Ann thought that Sarah may have been fainting or having a fit. 'Oh, what's to do, Sarah?' she asked, but her daughter-in-law did not reply, so Ann got up from her chair to go to her assistance. She took Sarah's arm and went to lead her out of the room, at which point she noticed blood on her shoulders.

Ann got Sarah as far as the front door before she heard her daughter Mary screaming. Leaving Sarah, Ann rushed back into the house to find Peter in the kitchen, his throat cut. Whittle's father, Thomas, was weaving in the cellar and rushed upstairs to see what the commotion was about. He found his daughter-in-law sitting on a chair at the front door and his son sitting in the kitchen, a blood-stained razor at his feet. Both Sarah and Peter were bleeding profusely from throat wounds.

Thomas snatched up the razor and threw it into a cupboard out of harm's way. By this time, Mary was in the street yelling 'Murder!' at the top of her voice, and the police and a doctor were quick to arrive. Dr Westby Walker examined Sarah's throat, finding two distinct cuts, both gushing blood.

Preston Royal Infirmary, where Whittle was treated. (*Author's collection*)

Both her jugular vein and her lingual artery had been severed and she also had several wounds on her hands, where she had tried to wrest the razor from her husband's grasp. Sarah survived for less than five minutes after the arrival of Dr Walker, who then turned his attention to her husband.

Peter Whittle was well known to Walker, having consulted him just four days previously. At that time, Whittle complained that his head had swelled up so much that he was unable to get his hat on. Noticing that he was actually wearing his hat, the doctor asked him to take it off and put it back on again. 'Your hat goes on easily enough now,' commented Walker, at which Whittle claimed that he now had a bad rash and blisters, and, since developing them, the swelling in his head had subsided. Walker examined him, finding him to have nettle rash on his arm. The doctor prescribed a mild laxative medicine and Whittle left, seeming satisfied.

Whittle's self-inflicted throat wounds were serious, and he was despatched to the 'House of Recovery', as the Preston Royal Infirmary was then known. Initially, it was expected that he would die from his injuries but instead he made a slow recovery. When Walker saw him in the hospital a few days after the murder, he felt it unwise to inform him that Sarah was dead, and when Whittle asked if the doctor was treating her, he replied that he was. 'How is she coming on?' Whittle enquired, and when Walker said that Sarah was not doing very well, her husband burst into tears.

Everyone who knew the Whittles agreed that they were normally a most devoted couple and nobody had ever heard them arguing or exchanging a cross word. At the inquest on Sarah's death, held at Preston Town Hall,

Preston Town Hall, site of the inquest. (*Author's collection*)

Whittle's family were unanimous in stating that he was a sober, steady, church-going man, who had always seemed devoted to his wife and who was looking forward to the birth of his third child. Indeed, shortly before the attack on Sarah, he had been discussing a trip into town to buy a new bonnet for his daughter. However, Whittle's family also felt that he had been 'low' in spirits for the past year or so and often complained about feeling 'poorly'. His father told the inquest that his son had frequently come down to the basement where he was working, saying that he felt 'all wrong' and had a 'maziness' in his head, which affected his eyesight. A few days before the murder, he had appeared in his parents' bedroom in the middle of the night, carrying a candle and saying that he had been poisoned, blaming his condition on some fish he had eaten earlier. When his mother told him to go back to bed, he went without saying anything further, but the following morning he complained that his head had swollen up and went to see Dr Walker.

The inquest jury seemed to agree that any appearance of a rash indicated that the afflicted person was 'overheated', and also that the rash may well have been preceded by a feeling that the head was swelling. Knowing that they were there to investigate Sarah Whittle's death rather than to speculate on her husband's physical and mental condition, they quickly returned a verdict of wilful murder against Whittle.

Eventually, Whittle was deemed sufficiently recovered from his injuries to be transferred from hospital to the prison at Lancaster Castle. By now, he had been informed that his wife had died at his hands, and when coroner

Lancaster Castle. (*Author's collection*)

Interior of Assize Court, Lancaster. (Author's collection)

Lancaster County Asylum. (*Author's collection*)

Mr Palmer visited him before his transfer and read all the evidence from the inquest to him, Whittle said he had no comment whatsoever to make. Throughout his time in the House of Recovery, he had seemed perfectly sane, and when Palmer informed him that he had been committed to the Assizes on the coroner's warrant, he seemed unmoved by the news.

Whittle appeared before Lord Denman at the Lancaster Assizes on 26 July 1842, the contemporary newspapers describing him as 'a rather diminutive looking man of remarkably placid appearance and collected manner.' Although no medical witnesses appeared for Whittle, with the exception of Dr Walker, the jury were quick to find him not guilty due to reasons of insanity.

Whittle was sent to Preston Lunatic Asylum, where there was some argument as to whether he should be classed as a 'pauper lunatic' or a 'criminal pauper lunatic', and, if the former, who should be paying for his stay. He was transferred to Broadmoor Criminal Lunatic Asylum from Lancaster County Asylum on 30 August 1864, remaining there until his death from inflammation of the brain and its membranes on 22 December 1885

James Stevenson: 1812–1879

James Stevenson grew up in a small hamlet in the parish of Lochwinnoch in Renfrewshire, Scotland. Brought up in a strictly Presbyterian home, where the emphasis was on the sovereignty of God and the authority of the Scriptures, Stevenson was indoctrinated with strong religious beliefs throughout his childhood, although he eventually left the Church of Scotland, due to what he described as 'differences'. As an adult, he worked as a homespun weaver and lived a largely unremarkable life until the accession to the throne of Her Majesty Queen Victoria in 1837.

Stevenson was simply unable to accept a woman as a monarch, believing that only a man could be king. He made a vow never to shave as long as Victoria was on the throne and gradually stopped working, instead devoting his time to study of the Scriptures and the Greek New Testament.

In 1843 Stevenson's animosity towards the queen came to a head and he decided to make a pilgrimage to London, with the particular aim of meeting with Prime Minister Sir Robert Peel, in the hope of persuading him to bring about the unification of the Church of Scotland. He was also determined to orchestrate the destruction of Queen Victoria, so that a man might take his rightful place on the throne. He reached Manchester, then walked to Hull, where he took a passage on a steam packet, *Gazelle*, which was captained by a Mr J. Hurst. In conversation with Stevenson, Hurst became ever more concerned by his outrageous claims that both Queen Victoria and Robert Peel must be destroyed. Although he had no idea where Peel lived, Stevenson voiced his determination not to leave London without having

Her Majesty Queen Victoria. (*Author's collection*)

Sir Robert Peel. (*Author's collection*)

met with him, saying that it was every Englishman's duty to help with the prime minister's destruction.

Hurst was so disturbed by Stevenson's extreme views that he brought his passenger to the attention of the authorities on docking in London and Stevenson was arrested while visiting some of London's grander properties in search of Peel's home. He was brought before the lord mayor, charged with using threatening language towards the queen and her prime minister. When searched, he was found to be carrying several letters and poems addressed to both Victoria and Peel.

Madam, in Christ's name I do thee address, because they have put me where by law, I can never stand. Because it would sink any land. Intolerable it must be to make a woman head of me. And if besides me there's a man, I'll speak a word unto the clan, for Scotchmen has all abjured thee, and sworn no prelate shall rule me. And I am no more bound unto her than if I had married my sister.

A letter to Sir Robert Peel, England
Robert, I am a Scotman [sic] born,
And yet this day I sit forlorn.
And though I am near thirty-one,
My minority is scarcely done.
Because a woman is made head,
Which I must neither fear nor dread.
Such oppressors make wise men mad.
That very justly they would stab,
With Chad, though he had few men
Whose success ye may shortly ken;
Of Jehoiada, good and plain,
Who would have had Ethalia slain,
Now God commands as he did then,
Let such as follow her be slain,
When God sets them below woman,
Their lowness tell I never can,
And if in earnest they can pray
That God may lead them long astray
By a curst woman they must be
Low to an awful great degree.

Questioned by the lord mayor, Stevenson backed up his theories by quoting or misquoting the Scriptures. For example, the fact that the Scriptures advised 'Woman, obey your husband in all things' was proof in Stevenson's mind that there should be a king rather than a queen on the British throne. Stevenson admitted that he himself felt qualified to take over as king, adding that since there was nobody in Scotland able to 'expound the Scriptures', he saw it as his personal duty to do so in order to expose the malignity of the human race.

In spite of Stevenson's inclination to ramble on throughout his court appearance, the lord mayor eventually decided to remand him to be confined in prison, pending medical reports on his sanity. When Stevenson was brought back to court, letters were produced from his father, from the minister of his local kirk, and from the postmaster at Lochwinnoch, all of whom expressed the opinion that Stevenson was insane. James Stevenson (senior) told the court that his son has always been seen as 'weak-minded' but that he had worsened when Victoria ascended to the throne, shutting himself away, fasting and praying for days on end.

Drs Sutherland and Bright, two eminent surgeons who had been asked to examine Stevenson, concurred that he was of unsound mind and that it was unsafe for him to be at liberty. They were particularly concerned by Stevenson's insistence that Queen Victoria should either abdicate or be destroyed.

Although Stevenson disagreed with the experts on the matter of his own sanity, he was nevertheless committed to the notorious Bethlem Psychiatric Hospital, better known as Bedlam. His delusions gradually worsened, and in 1864 he was transferred from there to Broadmoor, where he remained until 18 June 1879, when he died, aged sixty-seven, from inflammation of the lungs and bowels. Until the very day of his death, he was still threatening Queen Victoria.

Daniel McNaughten, McNaughton or M'Naghten: 1813–1865

Daniel McNaughten was an illegitimate child, born in Glasgow in 1813. After the death of his mother, Ada, he went to live with his father, also named Daniel McNaughten, working as an apprentice wood turner and later as a journeyman in his father's business. However, after an argument between them, McNaughten senior declined to give his son a partnership. Daniel left the business, spending three years as an actor before returning to Glasgow at his father's behest. After yet another disagreement with his father in 1837, he set up in a wood-turning business on his own

Daniel was an educated, well-read, sober, hard-working man, a regular attendee at the Presbyterian Church, who belonged to a debating society and taught himself French. By living frugally, he managed to save a considerable amount of money, and in 1840 he sold his business and spent the next two years travelling between London and Glasgow, with a brief trip to France. Although he was known to have attended lectures on anatomy, psychology and philosophy in Glasgow, his precise movements during this time are not recorded. However, he did make complaints to his father, the minister of the parish of Gorbals, the Glasgow Commissioner of Police and his local MP, Alexander Johnstone, among others, saying that he was being persecuted by Catholic priests and the Tories and that Tory party spies were following him. He told his father that these spies, who usually wore large, heavy top coats, laughed in his face and shook their fists at him, but claimed that he couldn't point out the men to his father as they only followed him when he was alone. He told his landlady at the time that there were devils in human form who were out to kill him and showed her a pair of pistols that he had bought to use against his perceived tormentors. Nobody took his complaints seriously, believing him to be delusional.

When McNaughten senior died he left his son a number of properties, which he promptly sold, using the proceeds to support himself. In January 1843 McNaughten was seen acting suspiciously in Whitehall, London, prowling around Downing Street, and the offices of the Privy Council and Home Office. Indeed, several police officers and civil servants approached him and asked his business, to which McNaughten usually replied that he was waiting to see a gentleman.

Whitehall, London. (*Author's collection*)

On 20 January civil servant Edward Drummond was walking back to Downing Street, having visited his brother at the family-run Drummond's Bank in Charing Cross. Drummond, who had acted as personal secretary to several prime ministers and was currently fulfilling that role for Sir Robert Peel, was walking along Whitehall when McNaughten approached him from behind and shot him in the back at point-blank range. As he drew his second gun, McNaughten was overpowered and pinioned by a quick-thinking passing policeman, James Silver, and rather than harming its target, the second shot was deflected into the pavement.

Initially, it was believed that fifty-year-old Drummond was not seriously injured. The bullet had entered his body between his eleventh and twelfth ribs, around two inches from his spinal cord, missing all of his vital organs. He managed to walk back home, where surgeons operated through his abdomen to remove the bullet.

Meanwhile McNaughten was taken before magistrates at Bow Street, where he remained taciturn, other than to confirm his name. However, when asked by magistrates if he wanted to make a statement, McNaughten said that he had been driven from his native city by the Tories, who had pursued him from place to place, determined to ruin him. 'My mind is ruined,' he ranted. 'I can get no peace, night or day. They followed me into France and other nations, into all countries and then persecuted me in my own native

Bow Street Police Court. (*Author's collection*)

city. I can get no sleep from the system the Tories have pursued towards me. I am going into a consumption. I once enjoyed good health but I am now in consumption and you will not see this individual again. I have been accused time after time with crimes which I never committed and persecuted as if I were guilty. In fact, they are murdering me. That is all I have to say and it can be supported by evidence. I am quite a different man to what I was, to what I used to be before the annoyance which has for a time been practised towards me.'

While Drummond was treated with leeches and blood-letting, and seemed to be making excellent progress towards recovery, McNaughten was examined in custody by several eminent surgeons to determine whether or not he was sane. The medical men were unanimous in their opinions that he was in his right mind. Meanwhile, McNaughten showed more interest in the food and drink that was served to him at his own expense in prison than he did in the circumstances of his incarceration.

Within a few days of the shooting, Drummond's condition began to unexpectedly deteriorate, and on 25 January 1843 he died. It was reported that he was not in pain and was fully conscious almost until the moment of death. An inquest was held at The Lamb and Goat public house in Grosvenor Square, just a few yards from Drummond's home, presided over by Mr Gell and Mr Higgs, the coroner and deputy coroner for Westminster. The jury found a verdict of wilful murder against McNaughten, who was committed for trial at the next assizes.

He appeared at The Central Criminal Court or Old Bailey on 27 February 1843, by which time McNaughten had been further interviewed by doctors, who listened to his concerns about being persecuted and drew very different conclusions to their contemporaries who had previously examined him. Dr Edward Thomas Monroe told the court that, even without hearing McNaughten's past history, he would have no doubt that he was suffering from paranoia and delusions so severe that they deprived him of all self-control. It was widely believed that McNaughten had intended to shoot Sir Robert Peel and indeed, he told Monroe that he wouldn't have fired had he not believed that Drummond was Peel. Although McNaughten gave every outward appearance of sanity on all subjects other than his paranoia, Monroe observed a particularly wild expression in his eyes and believed that his morbid delusion of persecution acted on his mind to such an extent that it deprived him of his sanity. Monroe's diagnosis was supported by several other doctors, who believed without exception that McNaughten was a dangerous lunatic, and that, at the time of the shooting, he was quite incapable of exercising self-control and of resisting the impulse to shoot.

One after another, the medical witnesses testified, and so powerful was their testimony that McNaughten was found not guilty due to reasons of insanity. Following his acquittal, he was transferred from Newgate Prison to Bethlem Lunatic Asylum. He remained there until 26 March 1864, when he was transferred to the newly opened Broadmoor Criminal Lunatic Asylum. However, by that time he had developed diabetes and heart problems, which were to be the cause of his death, on 3 May 1865.

In the wake of McNaughten's trial, it was suggested that Drummond had died not as a result of being shot but from the incompetence of the medical treatment that he received after the shooting. Following the trial verdict, public outrage led to a review of the legal definition of insanity and a new test was introduced, which became standard in both the United Kingdom and the USA. Under the McNaughten Test, or McNaughten Rules, all defendants are presumed to be sane unless they can prove that, at the time of committing the criminal act, their state of mind caused them to (1) not know what they were doing when they committed said act, or (2) know what they were doing, but not recognising that it was wrong. It was determined by the House of Lords that jurors ought to be told in all cases that every man is to be presumed to be sane, and to possess a sufficient degree of reason to be responsible for his crimes, until the contrary be proved to their satisfaction; and that to establish a defence on the ground of insanity, it must be clearly proved that, at the time of the committing of the act, the party accused was labouring under such a defect of reason, from disease of the mind, as not to know the nature and quality of the act he was doing; or, if he did know it, that he did not know he was doing what was wrong.

Henry Dommett: 1813–1879

Henry Dommett of West Allington, Dorset, stood a fraction over 5ft 2in tall and was described as a quiet, steady, honest and industrious man. Married to Eliza, he was widely thought of as an excellent husband and an affectionate father to the couple's children, John, David, Ellen, Mary, Sarah, Charles and Harry.

On 5 June 1863 Henry rose early, as usual, and went to his job as a hemp sorter for Messrs. J. Gundry and Co, where he had worked for the past forty years. As he always did, Henry came home for his breakfast, which he ate with Eliza and their youngest two children. After finishing their meal, Eliza went to the river to get some water. Six-year-old Charles and three-year-old Henry followed her, but they had barely gone more than a few steps when Henry called the boys back to the house. Eliza assumed that

West Allington, Dorset. (*Author's Collection*)

her husband wanted them to put their caps on and went on towards the river without them. Moments later, Harry caught up with her and announced that his brother's nose was bleeding and that his father had caused it. Knowing that Henry was in the house and would take care of any problems, Eliza paid little attention to her son's chatter and carried on with her errand.

Meanwhile, back at the house, John Dommett lay ill in bed, suffering from a bad leg. At around 8.45am he heard a strange noise and called out to his father. Not getting a reply, he got up and limped downstairs, wearing just his shirt. To his horror, he saw Charles lying bleeding on the floor with his throat cut and his father's work knife on the floor beside him. Henry sat in a nearby chair looking very pale, his head back and his eyes closed as if he were sleeping.

'Oh, father, what have you done?' asked John, to which Henry muttered an unintelligible response.

John called for his mother, who came rushing in from the garden. As soon as she saw the blood, she screamed for her neighbour, Mary Marshalsea, who hurried to fetch a doctor, returning with Dr Samuel Cory, who was also the local coroner. While Eliza cradled the barely-breathing Charles in her arms, Cory began to stitch the four-inch-long wound in his throat. As he did, Charles gave a couple of gasps then died.

Cory then went to Henry, asking him how he was. 'Oh, don't speak to me! It is a dreadful thing that I have done,' moaned Henry. Mrs Marshalsea and another neighbour, Esther Keech, also tried to talk to Henry, only for him to ask several times if Charles was dead yet. Both women were later to say that he seemed very well aware of the crime that he had committed and of the probable consequences for himself and his family. 'My heart is bad', he told Esther Keech, bemoaning the fact that he had brought the knife home from his place of work that morning. Another neighbour, Joseph Ward, found Henry gazing blankly at the pool of blood on the pantry floor. 'Is that a reality?' he asked Ward.

'Yes, my poor man,' replied Ward. 'Whatever made you do it?'

'I don't know,' replied Henry sadly, shaking his head sorrowfully. 'I don't know.'

The police were summoned and Sergeant Lavender of Bridport was the first officer on the scene. He immediately arrested Henry, charging him with wilful murder, to which Henry responded. 'Oh, sergeant, that's a dreadful charge.'

Taken to the Police Station, Henry told officers that he felt like a man lost. He also made several random statements, such as 'Saul forsook the Lord and fled to the witch and fell', and 'I must be aroused – I must not feel like this.'

Coroner Cory held an inquest at The Plymouth Inn. Having heard from John and Eliza Dommett, the next witness was surgeon John Hounsell, the Dommetts' family doctor, who had examined Charles and recorded the cause of his death as being due to a large cut on his neck, which had divided his windpipe and jugular veins.

Once all the witnesses had given their evidence, the coroner addressed Henry Dommett, asking him if he had any questions that he wanted to ask. When Henry replied that he didn't, the coroner turned to the jury. He pointed out that they had heard evidence that Charles Dommett had died from a cut throat and that they must now determine how he came by that injury. Surgeon Hounsell had testified that it would have been impossible for the boy to cut his own throat, suggesting that the wound had been made by 'a sharp instrument, wielded by a vigorous hand'. All the evidence seemed to point to Henry Dommett and the jury had to decide if they believed that he was the killer and, if so, did he commit the act by accident or wilfully. It took the jury only a few minutes to return a verdict of wilful murder against Dommett, who was taken to Dorchester Gaol to await his appearance at the next Dorset Assizes.

It soon became evident that there was a great deal of public sympathy for Dommett, in spite of the horrific nature of his act. Eliza found it almost impossible to understand that her son had died at the hands of the man she described as 'my dear, kind, good husband'. One of Henry's daughters

High West Street, Dorchester, site of the Assize Court. (*Author's collection*)

also found her father's actions difficult to comprehend, telling everyone who would listen, 'My father did not mean to hurt my brother; he is one of the best and kindest of fathers.'

Indeed, the general reaction of those who knew Henry was utter disbelief that he should have committed such a heinous and seemingly motiveless crime. The only reason that anyone could suggest for Charles's murder was that Henry was unduly worried about money, given that his eldest son, John, was lame and was therefore not contributing to the household expenses.

Henry stood before Mr Justice Willes at the Dorset Assizes, where he reportedly looked vacant as he stood in the dock listening to the case against him, often breaking down in tears as the trial unfolded.

For the prosecution, Mr Collier stated that he fully expected the defence to be one of insanity, and if this were indeed the case, then it was up to the jury to determine whether or not the prisoner was in full possession of his senses at the time of the murder. If the jury believed that Henry did not know the nature of the act he was committing, then the jury should acquit him, but if they believed he did, then it would be their painful duty to pronounce him guilty as charged.

The court then heard from those witnesses who had testified at the inquest, with the exception of Eliza Dommett. Most remarked on changes in Henry's personality that they had observed in the two or three months prior to the murder.

John Dommett stated that his father had been very restless at night, often pacing about the house instead of sleeping, complaining of pains in his head and sometimes taking to his bed during the daytime. Having once been a keen gardener, Henry had lost all interest in gardening and had also stopped attending church. He frequently sat alone in the pantry, and although he had always been a rather shy man, who kept himself to himself, he now seemed especially nervous and reclusive, even to the extent of not wishing his neighbours 'good day' in passing. Dommett's work colleagues told the court that he was an extremely moral and steady man, but in the weeks before the murder, he became moody and made numerous uncharacteristic errors in his work.

Witness after witness testified to Dommett's good character, variously describing him as 'a tender husband', 'a devoted and affectionate father', and a 'very religious man'. It was left to prison surgeon John Good to try and throw some light on Dommett's condition.

Good had seen Dommett on several occasions during his incarceration. When Dommett first came to prison on 7 June 1863, he was almost prostrate with grief, looking ill and haggard, with bloodshot eyes, scarcely any discernible pulse and a pronounced nervous tremor. In time, Good noticed that the prisoner had a very unsteady gait and seemed to spend a lot of time closely examining his fingers and hands. Good told the court that insanity usually resulted from some sort of physical ailment, but in Dommett's case, he had been unable to find any such impediment. Good was certain that Dommett knew right from wrong, but at the same time, his conversation was not what would be expected from a man in a sound state of mind. Sometimes he could speak rationally, but equally could be dogged, silent and morose. According to Good, Dommett had some extraordinary religious views and it was highly possible that these had affected his brain.

Finally, Mr Cole addressed the court in defence of Dommett. Here was a man, said Cole, who, previous to this tragic occurrence, had conducted himself in such a way as to secure the approbation, even the admiration, of his neighbours. He was the most kind and affectionate of fathers and husbands and nobody could fathom what motive might possibly have induced this man to have committed such a crime against his child.

The family had breakfasted together in apparent peace and harmony, yet, unusually, the prisoner had brought his work knife home with him. Then, in a moment of frenzy, he had seized this knife and cut the child's throat. Cole maintained that the jury must surely recognize that Dommett had not been in his right mind at the time, and, if they found that this was indeed the case, then Dommett would be taken care of for the rest of his life, carefully watched over and would thus be unable to ever commit a similar crime again.

The jury took only minutes to return a verdict of not guilty on the grounds of insanity and the judge ordered Dommett to be detained until Her Majesty's pleasure was known.

Dommett was sent to the Fisherton Lunatic Asylum in Salisbury, Wiltshire, and transferred to Broadmoor in April 1865. A quiet, inoffensive man, he was admitted to the infirmary on 4 June 1876, remaining there until 31 January 1879, when he died from consumption, aged sixty-six.

John Green: 1815–1876

In 1856 there had been eleven recent fires in the town of Ware, Hertfordshire, and on 25 October a blaze at The Independent Chapel in Bank Street made number twelve. When Abel Field spotted the flames, he ran to get the keys to the chapel, but on his return minutes later, he found that wheelwright Joseph Ansell had already entered the building, having broken a pane of glass and lifted the window catch to get inside. Ansell found that the floor and a pew were on fire and managed to put them out with a pail of water. He then noticed a second fire, a smouldering heap of hymn books and seat cushions, which he also managed to extinguish. On looking round to make sure that there were no more conflagrations, he spotted a piece of cotton handkerchief in a pew, with some lucifer matches, a fragment of newspaper and a wax taper nearby.

As with all of the other fires, thirty-two-year-old former manservant John Green was one of the first on the scene, this time raising the alarm by ringing the bell at the police house occupied by Inspector Beckwith.

Because he was so often seen in the vicinity of fires in the neighbourhood, the police had long suspected that Green was involved in starting them but had been unable to prove it. Now, accused of setting the fire in the chapel, Green denied any knowledge of it, claiming to have been in The French Horn public house all evening. Naturally, Beckwith checked his alibi and was told that Green had left the pub for about twenty minutes at around eleven o'clock that evening, thirty minutes before the fire was first discovered.

Beckwith searched Green and found a torn piece of *Family Herald* newspaper in his pocket, the edges of which exactly corresponded with those of the piece of paper found discarded in the chapel. From marks on the brickwork of the chapel walls, it was obvious that whoever had started the fire had gained entry by scrambling through a window; red brick dust was found on the soles of Green's shoes.

Confronted with the evidence against him, Green eventually confessed to starting the fire in the chapel, explaining in detail how he had done so. 'It was me and no one else that did it,' he stated, telling the Inspector, 'I hope you'll make a good job of this. They say I am mad, but I am no more mad than you are. This is a wretched place; no-one will employ me and I want to be transported.'

As well as a proclivity for arson, Green had a long history of criminality and admission to lunatic asylums. In July 1852 he appeared at the Hertfordshire Assizes, charged with breaking a signal lamp and placing a sleeper on the railway line near Ware. When arrested, Green claimed that he was unable to get work and had no money, therefore had committed the crimes in order to be admitted to prison. He was also accused of climbing a telegraph pole and damaging the wire, and of starting a fire on 11 June 1852.

At his trial in 1852, his defence counsel, Mr Redwell, claimed that Green was 'labouring under mental derangement'. This view was supported by Green's father and also by surgeon Mr McNab, who had known Green for more than twenty years and stated that he was subject to morbid and strange impulses and had previously been an in-patient at St Luke's Hospital for Lunatics in London.

Green was found not guilty by reason of insanity and ordered to be detained until Her Majesty's pleasure be known. He spent only two years in custody before being considered 'cured' and set free, but since then had been admitted to two more lunatic asylums. By 1856 he was at liberty to start setting fires again.

At his trial on 28 March 1857, for maliciously setting fire to a chapel, he was again found not guilty by reason of insanity and was sent to Bethlem

St Luke's Hospital for Lunatics. (*Author's collection*)

Hospital. On 12 March 1864 he was transferred to Broadmoor Criminal Lunatic Asylum, where he was reported to be 'quite incoherent and demented'.

In December 1875 his health began to fail, and he was moved into the infirmary ward and given a special diet. He was permitted visits from his son, but in January 1876 he became completely bedridden. His death, aged sixty-one, in February 1876, was attributed to bronchitis and pneumonia, although at the subsequent inquest held by coroner William Weedon it emerged that, during a post-mortem examination, a piece of clay pipe was found lodged in his windpipe.

Richard Dadd: 1817–1886

On 29 August 1843 butcher Abraham Lyster and his nephew Charles were on their way to the cattle market when they spotted a man lying face down in a field just outside the village of Cobham, Kent. They went to check on him, and when they turned him over, they found that his throat had been cut and he had also been stabbed in his left breast. His face was so caked with coagulated blood that it was impossible to identify him.

The body was taken to a wheelwright's shop in Cobham, and once the face had been washed, he was recognised as Robert Dadd, a former chemist, now a woodcarver and gilder, who had been visiting the area with his son, Richard. Father and son had booked in to The Ship Inn in the village, but, on the previous evening, they had set out together for a walk and hadn't returned.

A post-mortem examination showed that the deceased had extensive bruising to his head, face and hands. The cut to his throat was not severe but the stab wound to his chest was about four inches deep and had fatally punctured both of his lungs. Robert's gold watch was still on his body and he had three sovereigns in his pocket, which seemed to rule out robbery as a motive for his murder.

There was no sign of Robert's twenty-four-year-old son, Richard, who immediately became the prime suspect for his father's murder. Richard was an extremely talented artist, who had exhibited at the Royal Academy. In 1842 he accompanied his patron, Welsh politician, lawyer and businessman Sir Thomas Phillips, on a grand tour through Europe to Greece, Turkey, Southern Syria and, finally, Egypt. However, while travelling by boat up the Nile, Richard underwent a dramatic personality change, becoming delusional and violent and believing himself to be possessed by the Egyptian God Osiris. Phillips eventually grew afraid of Dadd and he was sent back to England alone.

He was initially thought to be suffering from sunstroke, but on his return, in spring 1843, it quickly became obvious that he was not in his right mind. As the year progressed, his condition worsened and Richard decided that he would only eat eggs and ale. The carpet at his lodgings in Oxford Street, London, was entirely covered in eggs and eggshells, and his rooms housed a large quantity of ale and two enormous bowls, each containing in excess of 150 eggs. Only a few days before his father's death, a doctor had advised his family that he was not safe to be at large and should be carefully watched at all times. However, Robert Dadd was somewhat sceptical of the doctor's diagnosis, insisting that all Richard needed was peace, quiet, fresh air, and a change of scene to restore him to full health. With that aim, he took his son to Cobham, but Richard had come to believe that that his father was the Devil personified, and on 29 August 1843, having persuaded Robert to go for a walk, he killed him and fled the area.

The police immediately issued a description of Richard, which was published in the newspapers with an appeal to anyone who might have seen him after 28 August to come forward. 'Every exertion is to be used for the apprehension of the individual in question,' urged the police. Richard was described as, 'Twenty-four years of age, 5'8" high, dark hair, light blue eyes, thick, dark eyebrows, sallow complexion, no whiskers, dressed in a dark blue frock coat, light blue trousers, his linen marked "Richard Dadd" or "R.D."' The description was later updated to say that Richard had been seen in London on 29 August, and asked for particular attention to be paid to railways stations, hotels and lodging houses.

The police were concerned that Richard might flee to France, and indeed, that proved to be the case. Having spent a night at an inn at Dover, where he explained his torn and dishevelled dress by saying that he had fallen from a coach, Richard hired an open boat to take him to Calais. From there, he proceeded to travel to Marseilles and it was on this journey that he began to annoy a French man by repeatedly fiddling with the man's cravat and collar. The man endured the annoyance for around a quarter of an hour before being driven to protest, at which his tormentor withdrew a razor from his pocket and began hacking at the Frenchman's throat. Despite sustaining four wounds, the Frenchman managed to overpower Richard, who was arrested.

Brought before a Justice of Peace, Richard explained that he had recently arrived from England, where he had murdered his father by cutting his throat. He explained that he had attacked his fellow passenger because he had received a message from the stars commanding him to do so, then emptied his pockets of a considerable amount of gold and cash, which he handed to the police so that his French victim might be taken care of. A handwritten list entitled 'People Who Must Die' was found on his person, his father being the number one name on the list.

The British police had to wait until Richard had served time in a French lunatic asylum before two officers from the Metropolitan Police could be sent to collect him and bring him back to England. Hence it was not until 5 August 1844 that he was brought before magistrates in Rochester. As he entered the court, he was said to be very good tempered, nodding at acquaintances and frequently laughing. However, as the proceedings continued, he became more and more deranged, arguing with every piece of evidence presented. The contemporary newspapers reported: 'At one moment he was laughing with almost childish glee, the next he would appear deeply agitated, drawing his breath with a hissing noise and grinding his teeth; then mild and affected almost to tears, with his head bent almost to his knees and afterwards erect, with a fierce, bullying aspect and a loud voice.'

It was believed that Dadd would not survive long enough to be tried for the murder of his father. His brain was said to be wasting away and he spent countless hours standing and staring at the sun. By the opening of the Kent Assizes in November 1844, he had already been declared insane and removed to a Criminal Lunatic Asylum in Surrey, by order of the secretary of state.

On 23 July 1864 Dadd was transferred from Bethlem Asylum to the newly opened Broadmoor Criminal Lunatic Asylum, dying there from consumption on 8 January 1886. Throughout his time in Broadmoor, he continued to paint and was even given his own studio. In 1992 it was reported that his painting 'Contradictions: Oberon and Titania' had sold to an anonymous London bidder for £1.65 million.

Martha Spencer Weaver: 1818–1902

When Martha Spencer Weaver separated from her husband, Henry, she returned to the village of Danbury, near Chelmsford, where she was born. Henry continued to pay her maintenance of 7s 6d a week, allowing her to live independently without having to find employment.

On the morning of 15 April 1861, Martha and her neighbour, Elizabeth Gipson, took Elizabeth's two-and-a-half-year-old illegitimate son, John, into a nearby wood to collect kindling, returning home at around midday. The women stood talking on Elizabeth's door step for about half an hour, watching with interest as a new organ was delivered to the village church. At around half-past one Martha knocked on Elizabeth's door, asking if she could spare a Lucifer match. Elizabeth told her that she didn't have any, at which Martha asked if little John might be sent to the village shop to buy some for her. Martha had always seemed very fond of John and had treated him with great kindness, so Elizabeth was happy to allow her son to run the errand for her neighbour. Martha gave the boy a halfpenny and he toddled off towards the shop.

A little while later, Elizabeth saw John walking back towards Martha's cottage. 'I have got the Lucifers,' he called out to his mother. Elizabeth told him that his dinner was ready and reminded him to hurry home. 'Goodbye mother,' called John, as Elizabeth watched him walk into Martha's cottage, closing the door behind him. It was to be the last time she would see her son alive.

When John didn't return home promptly, Elizabeth went to Martha's cottage looking for him. Martha assured her that the boy had left her home some time ago, saying that he was going to the Green to play. When Elizabeth asked 'What Green?' Martha claimed not to know, before abruptly slamming the door and bolting it behind her, walking upstairs and leaving Elizabeth standing on the doorstep.

Elizabeth ran round the village asking after her son, and when nobody had seen him, she and another neighbour, Mrs Phoebe Nevill, went back to Martha's house and hammered on the door. Martha eventually opened her bedroom window, her hair tousled, rubbing her eyes looking as if she had just woken from a deep sleep.

'Pray, Mrs Weaver, where is my child?' Elizabeth asked her.

Main Road, Danbury. (*Author's collection*)

'I know nothing of your child; he is not here,' replied Martha.

'Pray, come and unlock the door and let me see,' Elizabeth pleaded, but Martha simply ignored her, slamming the window closed again.

In desperation, Elizabeth went to the local curate, Reverend Mr Gervais Thorp, and told him of her fruitless efforts to find John. At Thorp's suggestion, the parish police constable, Alfred Barker, was summoned and together they went back to Martha's cottage, along with Elizabeth's father, Charles, and several other neighbours. Their knocks on the door brought no response and so Charles Gipson fetched a ladder, which was put to the upstairs window. As soon as Charles looked into the window, he saw John lying on his back in the middle of the room, a shawl wound tightly round his neck.

'She has murdered the child. He is lying dead on his back,' Charles called down, before managing to climb through the window and handing the little boy to William Wilson, another neighbour who had followed him up the ladder. Elizabeth fainted on seeing her still-warm child, his face pale and his lips blue, the clothing stripped from his lower body exposing his legs and genitals.

Martha herself lay on the bed in a deep sleep and didn't even wake when Charles Gipson screamed at her 'You harlot! You have murdered my child!' It took Constable Barker several minutes to rouse her, and when she did eventually open her eyes, she began to talk nonsensically. Accused of murdering John, she made no reply, but on being formally arrested, she told the constable, 'I don't mean to live long but I mean to do for some of them before I die.' The policeman then asked her what John had ever done to her to draw her spite against him. 'Never mind who; that's as well out of the world as in it,' she responded.

Martha was in the habit of taking laudanum – a highly addictive tincture of opium containing morphine and codeine – which she told people had the effect of 'quietening her nerves' and helping her to sleep. Several empty bottles were found in her bedroom and it was evident from her rather stupefied state that she had taken a large dose that morning.

A post-mortem examination was conducted by surgeon John Thorp, who found that little John had been a healthy child, whose death was due to manual strangulation. An inquest was held at Griffin Inn, Danbury, before coroner Mr W. Cobb. Martha, who had been detained in prison after her arrest, was brought from Chelmsford to attend the proceedings, but showed no emotion as the evidence unfolded and the jury returned a verdict of wilful murder against her. Offered the chance to ask questions, she made no comment, other than to say that she had no recollection of saying that John was 'as well out of the world as in'.

Martha appeared at the Chelmsford Assizes on 15 July 1861 before Mr Justice Williams. Nobody had ever imagined that Martha could be a threat towards anyone, particularly a child she appeared to love dearly, nor could any motive be determined for John's murder. Defence counsel Mr Pearce argued that the complete absence of motive suggested that John's death may have been a tragic accident; that he could have wrapped the shawl around his own neck and strangled as he tried to extricate himself. Failing that, Pearce asked the jury to consider that the laudanum his client had taken had caused such an aberration of mind that Martha committed the act without any awareness of what she was doing.

In summing up the case for the jury, Mr Justice Williams reminded them that the medical evidence had ruled out any suggestion that John would have had sufficient strength to strangle himself with a shawl. Williams told the court that, in his opinion, he could see no reasonable doubt that the child's death was directly caused by the prisoner. The judge then went on to address the matter of Martha's state of mind at the time. He reiterated the fact that the law presumed everyone to be rational and therefore responsible for their actions, unless the contrary could be proven. In addition, the sort of madness brought on by 'voluntary conduct', such as the abuse of drugs or liquors, was not classed as an exception to this presumption. In Martha's case, there was

Shire Hall, Chelmsford, site of the Assizes. (*Author's collection*)

no evidence of permanent mental malady, so the jury must decide if they believed that she was labouring under a temporary unsoundness of intellect, which prevented her from recognising that she was committing a criminal act. He questioned whether the laudanum had been taken prior to John's murder or after it, reminding the jury that, if they believed that Martha had acted without knowing what she was doing, she could be sentenced to detention during Her Majesty's pleasure rather than facing the death penalty for murder.

After deliberating the case for more than two hours, the jury found Martha Weaver guilty without making any concession to her possible temporary insanity and she was sentenced to death. However, on 25 July, the secretary of state sent a letter commuting her sentence. She showed no emotion when informed of her reprieve.

Her sentence was amended to one of transportation for life, but before Martha could be despatched abroad, she began to show signs of insanity and was sent to Fisherton Asylum in Wiltshire. Martha was admitted to Broadmoor Criminal Lunatic Asylum on 16 June 1863 and remained there until her death, aged eighty-four, on 30 October 1902, from old age and senile decay.

James Senior: 1819–1893

James Senior was well known around his hometown of Sherborne, Dorset. Formerly a farmer, when his farm failed, he set up in business as a seed and corn merchant. He was universally thought of as a steady, hard-working man, who was respected by all who knew him. However, in 1874, Senior began to show symptoms of depression. Suffering from a liver disorder, he believed his business was failing and was so worried about money that, on more than one occasion, he fainted while at the shop.

Over the years, his wife had given birth to six children, all but one of whom had died. The remaining child, a nine-year-old girl, was the apple of her father's eye. A bright, pretty little girl, she could often be seen helping him in his business. However, in early November 1874, Louisa Annie Senior fell ill with scarlet fever, also known as scarlatina. Throughout her illness, her distraught father showed the utmost concern for her well-being, willingly taking his turn to nurse and comfort her and often spending all night at her bedside. 'I could never suffer the last of them all to die,' he told people. 'She is my only joy.'

By 9 November Louisa's condition had worsened and it was feared that she would not survive. When Senior came home for his lunch, he found his wife in the kitchen, preparing a bread poultice to try and reduce the little girl's fever. Senior ate his bread and cheese, then went up to his daughter's room to sit with her. Shortly afterwards, he came downstairs again and his servant, Felicia English, heard him sharpening a knife. Moments later, Mrs Senior heard Louisa shout, 'Papa, what are you doing?' When Mrs Senior went to see what the problem was, she met her husband coming downstairs. 'I have done it,' he told his wife.

'Done what?' asked Mrs Senior.

'I have done for her,' replied her husband.

Mrs Senior went to her daughter's bedroom, where she lay in bed, her face relaxed as if in sleep. Yet she was gasping for breath, her nightdress and bedclothes saturated with blood, and on a nearby dressing table lay a bloody carving knife, with which Senior had inflicted a single stab wound, penetrating the upper right-hand-side of her chest to a depth of more than two inches.

Mrs Senior's screams brought in her neighbour, Harriett Gosney, and when solicitor's clerk George Allen Cook, who happened to be passing the house, looked up to the bedroom window, he noticed Harriett beckoning him to come into the house. 'Oh! He has murdered my child,' Mrs Senior sobbed as Cook ran upstairs.

'What are you making such a bother about? It is nothing,' Senior commented to his wife, before turning to Cook. 'Yes, I have done it,' he told him calmly, pointing to the bloody knife. 'There's the knife I did it with. Poor little thing; she has suffered enough but she will suffer no more.'

Sherborne from the Slopes. (*Author's collection*)

Meanwhile, Felicia English had run outside to fetch the police, when she happened to bump into surgeon Edward Turner. At Felicia's request, Turner went into the house, but Louisa was beyond medical assistance and all Turner could do was to pronounce her life extinct.

Police officers Superintendent Hare and Sergeant Rudyard arrested Senior, who went with them quietly. When asked why he had murdered his daughter, all Senior would say was that it was through poverty. 'She should not lay and suffer through want. I done it and shall be hung for it,' he insisted.

An inquest on Louisa's death was held by coroner Mr J. V. Melmoth, who at times struggled to hold back his tears. Felicia English was the first witness. She told the inquiry that she had sat up with Louisa throughout the whole of the night prior to her death and believed that the child's condition was not improving at all. Felicia insisted that James Senior was a loving and kindly father, who was very fond of his daughter. The servant was aware that her employer had been very low in spirits of late, believing that his despondency had increased since Louisa fell ill. 'If the child dies, it will be the death of me,' he had told Felicia earlier on the morning of the murder.

Passer-by George Cook knew the Senior family well. He described rushing into the little girl's bedroom and hearing the child gasp a couple of times before falling silent. 'No one could be more attached to a child than Mr Senior was to Louisa,' Cook told the coroner, relating how Senior had refused to leave his daughter's bedside to attend church on the Sunday before her death. Cook also testified about Senior's state of mind, describing him as having been in a desponding state for some time.

Surgeon Edward Turner told the coroner about being called to help the child but being able to do no more than pronounce her dead. Turner said that he had asked Senior why he had killed his daughter and Senior had replied that he was afraid of poverty.

Surgeon Horace Nutt had been attending both Louisa and her father in the days prior to her death. He described visiting Louisa two or three times a day, at her father's request. Shortly before her death, he had prescribed wine for her but her father had been horrified at the expense. In the end, Nutt sent wine from his own house, for which Senior seemed very thankful, appearing to be in fear of poverty, 'a fear for which I do not think there were any grounds,' Nutt added. He told the inquest that he had also been treating Louisa's father for 'general derangement of health and liver disorder,' then concluded his testimony by reiterating what others had already said, that James Senior was most affectionate at all times and was very fond of his child. Having known Senior for more than fifteen years, Nutt told the inquest that he was liked by everyone and was never heard to say a bad word against anybody or anything. Police Superintendent Hare also gave Senior a glowing reference saying that, having known him for twenty years, 'he was as good-hearted a fellow as ever breathed.'

Coroner Melmoth then asked the jury whether they thought it necessary for him to request a post-mortem examination, but the jury felt it was not going to further the case, given that the doctors were absolutely sure that Louisa's death had resulted from her being stabbed. The coroner then asked the jury for a show of hands and all but one voted to continue without adjourning for a post-mortem. Melmoth then spent some time explaining the difference between manslaughter and murder to the inquest jury, who, after a ten-minute discussion, returned a verdict of wilful murder against James Senior, making a point of stating that they were well aware that they were prohibited from taking into consideration his state of mind at the time.

At the conclusion of the inquest Senior was taken back to the Police Station by cab, his journey punctuated by boos and hisses of disapproval from the large crowd of people who had gathered to catch a glimpse of him.

Fifty-four-year-old Senior appeared at the Dorset Lent Assizes before Mr Justice Lush on 10 March 1875. While awaiting his trial, he was held in Dorchester Prison, where he apparently went through terrible mental anguish and showed great remorse. As he approached the dock, he trembled and shook so much that he could barely stand and was eventually allowed to sit, slumping down in floods of tears, his face almost always covered by his hands or a handkerchief.

His defence counsel, Mr Collins, told the court that the main question for consideration was whether the defendant was sane on the morning of the murder. 'Had God in his own good purpose inflicted on this man a diseased brain?' he asked. 'How could it be that a sane man, whose kindness of disposition was

Mr Justice Lush. (*Author's collection*)

well known to all, could kill the one person he loved best in all the world? Here was a parent, dotingly fond on his child, hoping against hope that she wouldn't die? How could a sane man have killed her?'

Collins told the court that in 1871 Senior had suffered from a severe concussion after having been thrown from a carriage, and that, according to surgeon Horace Nutt, he had since been a changed man. At this point, Mr Justice Lush interrupted rather testily, saying that it had been abundantly proved that the prisoner was an affectionate husband and father, so any further testimony on that point was superfluous. Collins then brought forward a steady stream of witnesses to testify to Senior's peculiar manner, vacant stare, pains in the head, fits, and practically every other manifestation of lunacy that could be imagined. Once again Lush intervened to halt the further pursuit of this line of enquiry, but Collins defiantly called one more witness, the local vicar, who suggested that Senior's elderly father was affected in his mind, thus indicating a family history of insanity.

Lush summed up for the jury, saying that the defendant's mind seemed to have broken down after his accident and that his daughter's illness had been the crowning calamity of his own mental illness, so that his mind was unhinged to the extent that he didn't know what he was doing when he killed her. It took the jury just three minutes to return a verdict of not guilty on the grounds of insanity and Senior was ordered to be detained during Her Majesty's pleasure.

Senior was sent to Broadmoor Criminal Lunatic Asylum on 9 April 1875, where he was to remain until his death, exactly eight years later, on 9 April 1893. He was aged seventy-four. The cause of his death was given as a combination of old age and anaemia.

Joseph Bones: 1821–1879

The newspapers of 1866 described Joseph Bones as being 'well known' in the village of Billinghay, Lincolnshire, where he lived. The reports were certainly far from complimentary about his physical appearance, since he is described as being of low stature and 'decidedly ugly and of very peculiar physiognomy, the perfect contrariety to ordinary notions of facial regularity, every feature in his face being awry.' The newspapers went on to state that Bones's deformities were all the more repulsive as they were 'congenital and not the result of muscular contraction or distortion,' adding that he had a face 'which appeared to have undergone plastic experiments in ugliness.'

On 16 August 1866 Bones walked into the forge on Billinghay, and without any provocation whatsoever, began to swear at blacksmith Joseph Franklin Benton and his employees. Benton ordered him to leave, at which Bones picked up a piece of wood and threatened to strike a man named Thomas Farnsworth. Somehow, Farnsworth managed to subdue his would-be attacker and frogmarched him out of the premises onto the road outside. Bones promptly walked into a shop opposite, emerging after about fifteen minutes and picking up a handful of stones, which he began to throw at Farnsworth.

Once again, Farnsworth challenged Bones and there was a struggle, which ended with Bones falling to the ground with Farnsworth landing on top of him. As they lay there scuffling, they were approached by a group of young men, who began to cheer Bones on. At this, Eyre Petchell felt compelled to come out of the blacksmith's shop and ask the young men why they were interfering.

The youths immediately ran away, with Bones lying on the floor telling them, 'Come on, he dare not meddle with us.' to try and persuade them to come back and help him. When the young men did not return, Bones picked up more stones, with the obvious intention of throwing them.

Petchell told Bones that if he dropped the stones he would let him get up. Bones let go of the stones and began feeling underneath his own body, as if trying to put his hand in his pocket. When he withdrew his hand, he was holding a double-bladed pocket knife.

Bones tried to stab Petchell in the leg. Farnsworth and Petchell immediately fled, the former running into a house and slamming the door behind him, the latter taking refuge in a yard. Bones followed Petchell to the yard gate and stood there with his knife drawn until Petchell emerged, saying that he would stand and face his attacker. Instantly, Bones lashed out with his knife, slashing Petchell across the abdomen, saying, 'That will cool you down, you bastard.'

Petchell reeled back, the front of his smock red with blood and his intestines hanging from his body in loops. 'He's done me,' he moaned, before walking into the house after Farnsworth and shutting the door behind him. Bones stood in the middle of the road, his knife dripping blood. Benton rushed off to fetch a doctor, and as he ran off, he heard Bones saying that he had sharpened his knife specially and threatening a bystander named Palmer that he would 'serve him the same' if he came any nearer.

Surgeon Ebenezer Thompson hastened to the scene but could do nothing for Petchell, whose intestines had been severed by the knife. As the surgeon tended to him, Bones was disarmed, and his knife handed to

PC William Knowles. Bones did not seem in the slightest bit perturbed by his situation, telling Knowles, 'That's the knife I did it with – the big blade,' adding, 'I know I have done it and I will do someone else if they come near me.' Knowles told Bones that he would have to lock him up. 'Take me and hang me if you like,' responded Bones, seemingly without a care in the world.

In spite of his fearsome injuries, Petchell survived until the following morning. At the inquest on his death, coroner Mr W. Clegg told his jury that there was absolutely no doubt that the victim was deprived of his life by a stab wound caused by Bones, but it was for them to decide whether this was a case of murder or manslaughter.

Every man who killed another was guilty of murder unless he could prove circumstances of excuse or justification, explained the coroner. It was a common misapprehension that if a man was deprived of life during a fight or quarrel, the crime committed was not murder. Indeed, if such were law, no man would be safe, since a person with murderous intent need only to goad his victim into a quarrel to accomplish his intentions and yet escape the full force of the law. There might be a fight, with words and blows exchanged, but if one party used a deadly weapon with thought and design and killed the other, then the appropriate verdict was murder. To return a verdict of manslaughter, the jury must be able to prove an absence of malice and intention or show that the killer received sufficient provocation in the paroxysm of passion and in hot blood to inflict a fatal wound on his adversary.

It was evident that there had been a violent quarrel in Benton's shop and that plenty of inflammatory language was used. All parties were equally culpable, and, had the stabbing been committed at that time, in the height of passion, it would probably have been deemed manslaughter. Yet Bones initially retreated to another shop, where he remained for fifteen minutes. When he came out, he immediately reignited the quarrel, and with considerable deliberation, withdrew his knife, opened it and tried to stab Petchell in the leg. Petchell ran away but Bones pursued him and waited for at least another two minutes until Petchell came out of the yard before stabbing him, while using a verbal expression that clearly indicated malice and intention.

The coroner's jury retired for half an hour before returning to state that they had unanimously agreed on a verdict of wilful murder against Bones. While they recognised that he had been subject to much provocation, they did not believe that it was sufficient to allow for the lesser verdict of manslaughter.

Bones was committed for trial at the Lincoln Assizes. Before the trial began, presiding judge Mr Baron Channell realised that Bones had no one to defend him. When Channell offered him the services of a defence counsel, Bones replied incredulously, 'Defend me! What for?'

Bones's behaviour in court was described as 'stolid'. He gave every appearance of a man who either did not know or did not care what was going on around him. Channell explained that he was charged with a heinous crime and that he was entitled to have someone act on his behalf in court. 'I never done nothing. I can defend myself,' insisted Bones.

When the trial proper opened on 3 December 1866, Channell tried again to persuade Bones to employ the services of a defence counsel and the prisoner eventually agreed. Asked how he pleaded Bones responded 'I never saw a Petchell. I saw one several times when we were at school together.'

Channell addressed James Foster, the governor of Lincoln Prison, asking him how Bones had been in custody. Foster told the judge that he had seen Bones on numerous occasions, as had the prison surgeon. 'It is the most peculiar case I have ever seen,' observed Foster. 'Sometimes the prisoner understands what is said to him as well as I could, while at others he appears to understand nothing. Sometimes he is exceedingly violent and it takes two or three warders to restrain him.'

Surgeon Edward Fox Broadbent was summoned to respond to the judge's concerns about the prisoner's mental state. Broadbent testified that, having seen Bones at least twice a week during his incarceration, he was

The Assize Court, Lincoln Castle. (*Author's collection*)

sure that he was not capable of understanding the charge against him, although the surgeon did believe that he was able to distinguish right from wrong. Broadbent assured Channell that Bones was incapable of following conversations, adding that he was a violent and highly dangerous man, who would think no more of sticking a knife into someone than he would of eating his own dinner. Broadbent concluded by stating that he did not feel that Bones was in a fit mental state to take his trial.

The judge then addressed the jury, telling them that since Bones had refused to plead either guilty or not guilty, they needed to consider whether or not the prisoner was mute of malice. In other words, did Bones understand what was going on and was feigning ignorance or did he not fully comprehend or appreciate the implications of his trial. Although Broadbent had stated that, in his opinion, Bones was able to distinguish right from wrong, which would normally indicate a fitness to stand trial, the surgeon had also given an opinion that the prisoner was incapable of following a trial and would thus not appreciate the finer points differentiating murder and manslaughter. Channell asked the jury to decide whether or not they believed that Bones was in such a state of mind to be able to take his trial, and after a short deliberation, the jury agreed that he was not.

Channell turned to address Bones, telling him that he would be kept in custody until Her Majesty's pleasure be known. Bones was returned to Lincoln County Gaol, from where he was quickly transferred to Broadmoor Criminal Lunatic Asylum. He was to remain there until his death, aged fifty-six, on 23 January 1879, when, suffering from heart disease, he choked on his own vomit.

Mary Crooks (or Crookes): 1825–1874

Former domestic servant Mary Crooks and her husband lived in two rooms on the top floor of a house in John Street, St Sepulchre, London. Sadly, Mary was an alcoholic and spent much of her time inebriated.

On the morning of 13 May 1868, Horatio Philips and his wife, the occupants of the ground floor of the house, were awakened by someone shouting 'Fire!'. Leaving their rooms, they found that the blaze was located at the top of the house in the rooms occupied by forty-three-year-old Mary and her husband. Having roused the other occupants of the building, Horatio helped to form a bucket chain to get water upstairs to douse the flames.

When the fire was eventually extinguished, it was obvious that it had been deliberately started, since there was no fire in the grate, nor any lit candles or lamps in the room that might have started the blaze accidentally. A floorboard in front of the fireplace had been lifted and the hole stuffed with wood shavings, which had been set alight. A table and a bedstead within the rooms had also been burned.

Mary was nowhere to be seen but eventually returned to the house drunk at eleven o'clock that morning. She walked into her rooms, sat down, and without making any comment about the fire, she told neighbour Edmund Lowe, 'That is one of them I wanted.'

The police had been called, and, on the instructions of her landlord, James Hunt, Mary was arrested for arson and taken into custody by PC Alexander Gringburn. The policeman asked Mary if she had heard what the landlord had accused her of and she replied, 'Yes, all right, I have done it,' adding that she had started the fire with a red-hot poker.

Brought before magistrates, Mary claimed to have been suffering from a very bad attack of *delirium tremens* – confusion in someone who is addicted, caused by the sudden withdrawal of alcohol, which can result in severe anxiety, psychosis and paranoia. It would have been her third such bout. 'The devils were all dancing around me and I could see them as well as I can see you now,' she told the magistrate, Mr Cooks, who saw no alternative but to commit her for trial.

She appeared at the Old Bailey on 8 June 1868, charged with 'feloniously setting fire to a dwelling house, persons being therein.' Called to give evidence, Mary's neighbours were all quick to inform the court that they

Interior of the Court at the Old Bailey. (*Author's collection*)

considered her to be completely mad. Horatio Philips stated that Mary had told him that there was a 'galvanic battery', the power from which passed from one house to another and influenced her behaviour. She also believed that a female detective lived in a neighbouring house, along with several people whom she considered to be enemies. According to Philips, Mary was perpetually drunk, although he didn't know where she got the money to buy alcohol from. 'Her husband was very kind to her', he stated, implying that the money for liquor had come from Mr Crooks.

Neighbour Edmund Lowe stated that just a week before the fire, Mary had come to him and claimed that someone was being murdered in her room. Lowe told her, 'You are mad, you had better go indoors', which she obediently did.

It emerged that even before she descended into alcoholism, Mary had spent considerable periods in lunatic asylums at Colney Hatch and Camberwell. Her niece, Mary Ann Dobson, told the court that her aunt had fits, which 'flew to her head', and when she was afflicted, she bought knives with which to stab her family. Only six or seven months earlier, Mary's husband had been forced to have her admitted to the lunatic ward of the local workhouse.

Mary was called to the witness box to explain her actions. 'I fancied I saw my mother,' she told the court. 'I was taken in trouble of mind and fancied the place was full of people and I could not get rid of them; they were coming to tear me to pieces and made all manner of faces and as fast as I went to one end of the room, they came to the other. I was after them

Colney Hatch Lunatic Asylum. (*Author's collection*)

The Asylum, Camberwell. (*Author's collection*)

nine or ten days round the room and I went to my landlord and asked him to come and see them.'

It was blatantly obvious to all in court that Mary Crooks wasn't in her right mind and the court found her not guilty due to insanity. She was ordered to be detained until Her Majesty's pleasure be known. Originally incarcerated in Newgate Prison, she was sent to Broadmoor Criminal Lunatic Asylum on 15 October 1868.

On her admission to Broadmoor, she was said to be 'in a delicate state of health', suffering with problems with her lungs. In 1873 she became completely bedridden, unable to move without assistance, and she died from consumption, aged forty-nine, on 7 June 1874.

Thomas Humphreys (or Humphries): 1828–1879

At four o'clock in the morning of 30 August 1878, Emma Thomas was woken by noises coming from the house next door to hers in Coton Hill, Shrewsbury. The noises, which she described as 'like someone tumbling about', ceased and there was silence for a while, before a final heavy thump.

Emma went back to sleep, and when she awoke at half-past-six, she could hear somebody groaning from next door. Her neighbour, fifty-year-old Thomas Humphreys, was an epileptic and Emma thought that he must have had a fit. However, when the groaning persisted, she eventually went and knocked on Humphreys' door. She called to him but neither he nor his wife, Ann, responded.

Emma went to Richard Tomkins, who was the Humphreys' landlord, at the Bird in Hand public house, and he brought a ladder, which he put up to the open bedroom window. Climbing through, he found forty-five-year-old Ann Humphreys lying dead on the kitchen floor, wearing just her nightdress. Her husband lay close by, naked apart from a nightshirt, badly injured and raving, periodically screaming, 'You murderers, you tyrants, you devils. Fie, for shame!'

A Dr Francis Whitwell was sent for, and, having established that nothing could be done to help Ann, he turned his attention to her husband. Humphreys thrashed and flailed as the doctor tried to examine him and was so violent that it took four men to restrain him so that he could be arrested and taken to Salop Infirmary for treatment.

A post-mortem examination on Ann Humphreys showed that she had a total of thirty wounds on her body and had been stabbed eleven times, mainly on her left side. Her husband had a cut throat and had also been stabbed seventeen times, mainly in the region of his heart.

While in hospital, Humphreys made a statement to Detective Sergeant Francis Lloyd, in which he freely admitted to stabbing his wife. Humphreys stated that he had begun stabbing her while she slept, continuing after she woke up and struggled with him for possession of the knife, which,

Salop Infirmary, where Humphreys was treated. (*Author's collection*)

New Shropshire (Salop) Lunatic Asylum. (*Author's collection*)

having stabbed himself numerous times, he eventually dropped. As they fought, Mr and Mrs Humphreys tumbled downstairs, leaving the knife in the bedroom. Humphreys stated that, had he been able to get the knife, he would have finished himself off but he was too weak from loss of blood to climb the stairs to retrieve it.

Coroner Mr H. C. Clarke held an inquest on Ann's death, at which the verdict was one of wilful murder against her husband, who was soon well enough to leave hospital and move to Shrewsbury Prison, pending his trial at the Assizes in November 1878. There, Humphreys pleaded guilty to causing death, but insisted that the was innocent of any intention of killing his wife.

In his summary for the jury, Lord Justice Bramwell stated that it was quite evident that Humphreys had taken the life of his wife, hence the jury could only acquit him on the grounds of insanity. It took the jury only a few minutes' deliberation to find Humphreys guilty but insane and he was ordered to be detained during Her Majesty's pleasure.

Humphreys' motive for the murder of his wife of twenty years was never satisfactorily explained. A former member of the Birmingham Police Force – although he was variously described in the contemporary newspapers as a gardener and a former spinner – Humphreys' epilepsy made it impossible for him to work and he was supported entirely by his wife from her job as a forewoman at a shirt making factory. It was suggested that Ann Humphreys was growing increasingly frail, and becoming tired of the burden of her husband, was trying to put him in the workhouse or asylum.

Although Humphreys resented being entirely dependent on his wife, the couple were sober, personable people, who apparently lived on good terms with one another. However, according to surgeon Whitwell, Humphreys was suffering from 'epileptic mania', one of the symptoms of which was a propensity for self-injury or injury to friends and family. In the aftermath of his frequent epileptic fits, Humphreys was known to behave strangely and he had apparently tried to commit suicide at least once before. Records suggest that he had also previously spent time in asylums, including a six-month spell in Salop Asylum in 1856.

In court, Humphreys accepted his sentence with the greatest indifference. He was sent to Broadmoor Criminal Lunatic Asylum, where, suffering from pleurisy, he died suddenly, on 7 June 1879, following an epileptic fit.

Christiana Edmunds: 1828–1907

Having reached her forties without ever having married, Christiana Edmunds from Brighton had become a frustrated and bitter old maid. She began to have romantic feelings towards a rather unattainable target – her doctor, Charles Izard Beard – refusing to let the fact that he was a married man stand in her way.

Whereas Beard may have engaged in a little harmless flirting with his female patients, Christiana took this as a sign that he was madly in love with her and began to bombard him with passionate love letters. Embarrassed and unsure what to do about the situation, Beard eventually showed the letters to his wife and they agreed that Christiana's advances were best ignored.

By 1870 Christiana had reached the conclusion that Emily Beard was the only obstacle standing in the way of her happiness with the man of her dreams, and in September of that year she presented her unsuspecting love rival with a gift of chocolate creams. Having eaten them, Mrs Beard fell dreadfully ill, although she fortunately made a full recovery. Her furious husband accused Christiana of trying to poison his wife, but without any proof he did not feel that he could report his suspicions to the police.

Christiana was hurt and devastated by his accusations, believing that she had lost the affections of the man she craved. She decided that if she could prove to him that there was another poisoner at large in Brighton, she might regain his love.

With this goal in mind, on 18 March 1871 Christiana purchased ten grains of strychnine from Isaac Garrett, a chemist and druggist who had a shop on Queens Road, Brighton. She told Garrett that she wanted the poison for killing stray cats, brushing aside his objections that this was cruel.

Garrett warned her of the dangers of the poison she was buying and she reassured him that she was a married woman and that only she and her husband would be handling it. Told that she needed a witness in order to buy the poison, Christiana managed to persuade a local milliner, Mrs Stone, to witness the transaction. Signing the Poisons Register 'Mrs Wood', she made a further purchase on 15 April, and again on 10 May, when she told Garrett that she and her husband were about to leave for Devon and had an elderly, sick dog that could not go with them.

Christiana also bought a regular supply of chocolate creams from G. Maynards, Confectioners, of West Street, Brighton, usually recruiting small boys to make the purchases on her behalf and later returning the chocolates, asking to exchange them for a different kind. Trustingly, the shop's owners would comply, placing the chocolates she returned back in the display case for resale.

Soon, people all over Brighton began to fall ill after eating chocolates bought from Maynards. To divert suspicion from herself, Christiana made a complaint to the shop owner, claiming that a friend had become violently unwell after eating a chocolate cream.

On 12 June 1871 holidaymaker Charles Miller bought some of the chocolates, which he shared with his family throughout the day. While most tasted absolutely fine, his brother Ernest spat his out, claiming it tasted 'coppery', while his four-year-old nephew, Sidney Albert Barker, began to

West Street, Brighton, where Christiana purchased her chocolates. (*Author's collection*)

cry after eating his, saying 'I don't like it. It tastes nasty.' After eating a sweet himself, Mr Miller began to feel dizzy, his limbs strangely stiff and his joints fused. When Sidney's limbs began to stiffen, the family summoned a doctor.

Although Dr Richard Rugg arrived within minutes, he found Sidney convulsing violently. Rugg administered an emetic but Sidney died before it could take effect. The doctor performed a post-mortem examination the following day, finding no reason for the child's death apart from changes to his brain normally associated with convulsions. At the request of coroner David Black, Rugg removed the little boy's stomach and its contents, which were sent to Professor Letheby for analysis.

The Professor found about a quarter of a grain of strychnine in Sidney's stomach – more than a fatal dose for a child of his age. The analyst also tested the remaining chocolates bought by Charles Miller, some of which were also found to contain strychnine.

An inquest was opened at which Christiana Edmunds volunteered to give evidence. She stated that she had twice purchased chocolate creams from Maynards and on both occasions she and a friend had become ill after eating them. She spoke of visiting the shop to complain and telling Mr Maynard that she intended to get the sweets analysed.

The inquest jury found that although Sidney Barker had undoubtedly died from strychnine poisoning, his death could not really be blamed on anybody specific, hence a verdict of accidental death was recorded. The jury did issue a warning to Mr Ware, who made the chocolate creams sold at Maynards, to revise his manufacturing processes. However, Ware was completely baffled by the warning, since he had never before received any complaints about his products and kept no strychnine on his premises.

Soon after the inquest, Sidney's father received three letters, urging him to take legal action against Maynards. All three letters were similar in style and content and Barker handed them straight to the police.

Meanwhile, the anonymous poisoner continued to strike terror into the hearts of Brighton residents. Several more people were taken ill after eating chocolate creams and some people – including Emily Beard – were sent parcels containing fruit or cake, which made them ill when they ate the contents. In some cases, the remains of the supposedly poisoned food were taken to chemists for analysis and all were found to be heavily laced with arsenic. By then, Christiana was making frequent use of her boy messengers, sending them to Isaac Garrett, with a request for arsenic, purporting to come from Glaiyser and Kemp, another chemist's shop in town. She also sent Garrett a message, supposedly on the coroner's behalf, asking to see the Poisons Register. Only when it was returned to Garrett did he notice that several pages had been torn out. When Garrett received a second request for arsenic, he checked with Glaiyser and Kemp and, finding that the request had not come from them, he contacted the police.

The police were busy interviewing everyone who had complained of being poisoned, and when it came to Christiana's turn, they sent her a note, to which she replied immediately. When her handwriting was found to match the notes to Mr Barker, the notes supposedly from Glaisyer and Kemp's and the entries for Mrs Wood in the Poison's Register, she was arrested and charged with indiscriminate poisoning, the attempted murder of Emily Beard and the murder of Sidney Barker.

Because of the depth of bad feeling against her in the Brighton area, Christiana was tried for Sidney's murder on 15 January 1872 at The Old Bailey, where much was made of her family history of insanity. Christiana's father had suffered from homicidal and suicidal mania and had died in an asylum. Her brother also died in an asylum in the throes of an epileptic fit, her sister suffered from nervous hysteria and both of her grandfathers and a first cousin were of unsound mind. Christiana herself had suffered from nervous paralysis and hysteria, and according to those who knew her, about fifteen months earlier had become unusually animated, frequently laughing for no reason, rolling her eyes and complaining that she was going mad.

Several doctors who had examined Christiana while she was incarcerated in Newgate Prison awaiting her trial told the court that they were of the

County Gaol, Lewes, where Christiana was incarcerated. (*Author's collection*)

opinion that she was on the borderline between criminality and insanity. All agreed that she was incapable of comprehending the seriousness of her crime and described her moral sense as deficient. Nevertheless, it took the trial jury less than an hour to decide that Christiana was guilty of the charges against her.

After judge Mr Baron Martin placed the black cap on his head, he asked Christiana if she had anything to say before sentencing. Christiana stated that she wished she had been examined about the improper intimacy said to exist between herself and Dr Beard. 'It is owing to my having been a patient of his and the treatment I received in going to him that I have been brought into this dreadful business,' she complained.

As was customary for female prisoners, Christiana was then asked if there were any reason why her execution should be stayed. Christiana did not understand the question, but when it was explained to her by a warder, she immediately claimed to be pregnant. A jury of matrons was quickly assembled, and with the aid of the prison doctor and another doctor who happened to be a spectator in court, it was quickly established that she was not pregnant and the death sentence was pronounced.

She was returned to Lewes Prison to face the executioner, but ten days after the conclusion of her trial, it was announced that she had been found insane after all and would be committed to Broadmoor Criminal Lunatic Asylum. Reluctantly signing the transfer documents, the medical officer at Lewes Prison stated that he could not agree with the diagnosis of insanity, adding that Christiana was of a delicate constitution and prone to hysteria.

She arrived at Broadmoor on 5 July 1872 and was to remain there until her death in 1907, aged seventy-eight, from 'senile decay' or old age.

John Peacock: 1829–1894

When John Peacock arrived back in England in 1870, after living in California for many years, he had on his person almost US$11,000, gold to the value of £90, two gold watches and almost £100, along with a dagger and a revolver.

Peacock took lodgings with a Mrs Jane Austin in Shepley Street, Manchester, and in the early hours of the morning of Sunday, 11 September 1870, fellow lodger John Plant kicked at the door of Peacock's room before continuing to walk downstairs. Peacock drew his revolver and fired two shots, one of which hit Plant's arm, shattering the bone before ricocheting into his body, lodging in his bowel. Plant was rushed to hospital in a critical condition, and, since he was not expected to survive, magistrates took his deposition. His recollections of the incident were somewhat hazy, given that he was intoxicated at the time. He could not recall whether he was upstairs or downstairs in the house when shot, although he believed it was downstairs. He claimed to clearly recall raising his hands and asking Peacock not to shoot and also stated that he and his fellow lodgers all agreed that Peacock was insane.

In the aftermath of the shooting, Peacock was arrested and told Police Sergeant Gresty that he was awakened in the early hours of the morning by someone trying to open the door to his room. Believing that someone was trying to break in to steal his money, he had called out several warnings before firing two shots. Having heard the commotion, Mrs Austin and her other lodgers rushed to investigate and found Plant sitting on his own bed, bleeding heavily from his arm. Plant, who was the licensee of The Stag Inn at Stafford Street in Derby, had spent the evening drinking with his brother, George, and while George was downstairs fetching him a glass of water, it was assumed that Plant had drunkenly mistaken Peacock's locked door for that of his own bedroom and had been trying to gain entrance.

When Plant died, Peacock was charged with his murder, but the inquest into Plant's death accepted that Peacock had believed that someone was trying to break into his room with the intention of robbing him and the inquest jury recorded a verdict of 'justifiable homicide'.

However, when Peacock appeared before magistrates at Manchester City Police Court, his behaviour and demeanour were judged to be a little strange. Peacock, who claimed to be a former soldier, showed more concern

Manchester Assize Courts. (*Author's collection*)

for the safety of his money and belongings than for his own predicament, protesting his innocence and eventually claiming to be the king of England. In considering the case, the magistrates determined that, while Plant was undoubtedly very drunk, Peacock would have had to have left his room in order to shoot him, suggesting that Plant was already moving away from Peacock's room when he was shot and mortally wounded. The magistrates therefore committed Peacock for trial for manslaughter at the next Manchester Assizes, where he was charged with having feloniously slain Plant.

In the run up to his trial, forty-three-year- old Peacock began to suffer from hallucinations and delusions and was sent to Prestwich Lunatic Asylum. Thus, the first job of the Assize Court was to establish whether or not he was fit to stand trial. Mr Justice Brett was told by Dr Holland, the head of the Prestwich asylum, that, in his opinion, Peacock was capable of recalling that he had killed a man and was able to differentiate between the concepts of guilty and not guilty. However, when Peacock was finally brought into court, he persistently shouted that he was the king of England and that the trial was a usurpation of his rights. Despite the fact that Peacock continued to yell incoherently throughout the proceedings, the jury agreed that he was fit to plead, at which Peacock momentarily recovered his composure to state that he was entirely innocent of the charges against him.

The court then went on to discuss Plant's deposition, which junior house surgeon Dr William Hodgson Carruthers stated was taken from Plant under the premise that he was going to die. According to Carruthers, Peacock, who was present while the deposition was taken, was simply unable to comprehend that he had done anything wrong in shooting Plant. The trial jury returned a verdict that Peacock was not guilty due to reasons of insanity and he was ordered to be detained during her Majesty's pleasure.

Peacock was admitted to Broadmoor Criminal Lunatic Asylum on 23 March 1872, still claiming to be the king of England. He died on 25 January 1894 from inflammation of the lungs.

Mary Ann Parr: 1829–1900

Twenty-three-year-old Mary Ann Parr was an inmate of the Bingham Union Poor House, Nottinghamshire, when she gave birth prematurely to her illegitimate daughter on 24 November 1852. It was evident that Mary Ann was unhappy about her pregnancy, especially as this would not be her first illegitimate child. She made no preparations for the birth and once her daughter arrived, she flatly refused to suckle her. Told that the child would die unless she fed it, Mary Ann's response was 'Let it die', insisting that all the devils out of hell could not force her to suckle her daughter.

The other female inmates were appalled at Mary Ann's coldness towards the baby. Whenever they could, they forced Mary Ann to feed her, and if that proved impossible, some of the women who had recently given birth took it upon themselves to wet nurse the infant. It was noticed that whenever Mary Ann did consent to feed her child, she clutched her so tightly to her breast that there were fears that she would smother her. She was warned by the workhouse surgeon, Charles Rowland, that she might kill her baby if she held it so closely and the workhouse staff were warned never to let her suckle the child alone.

On the morning of 3 December, Agnes Randall, one the female inmates of the workhouse went into Mary Ann's room to help dress the baby. As the child lay in its mother's arms, Agnes heard it give a little gasp then saw its head fall back. Charles Rowland was summoned but found the baby dead. A post-mortem examination later revealed that she had been a perfectly healthy – if rather weak – premature baby and that the cause of her death was suffocation. Because the child was rather frail, Rowland and John Marriott, who performed the post-mortem together, agreed that even a slight, unintentional pressure into the breast might have caused asphyxia and death.

Several inmates accused Mary Ann Parr of smothering her baby, which she vehemently denied. However, a few days after the child's death, she locked herself in the outside lavatory and refused to come out. When one of the other inmates, Sarah Goodson, tried to coax her, Mary Ann confessed to having deliberately killed her baby. She told Sarah that she had not felt easy in her mind since the baby's death and felt the need to unburden herself by confessing.

Coroner Mr Swann held an inquest on the baby's death, at which the main witnesses were other inmates and the workhouse surgeon. Having heard details of Mary Ann's confession, Swann also asked Mary Ann to make a statement, which she obligingly did, saying: 'I did smother the child against my breast. I took the child to my breast at first to suckle it. I then squeezed it against my breast on purpose to take away its life and when I thought it was dead, I was frightened.' Mary Ann revealed that the child's father was a local tailor, and claimed that she had killed her baby because she believed that doing so 'would set my hands at liberty again'. She apparently wanted to be able to go out to work and didn't want to be tied down by an infant who would need regular feeding. Having heard this, the inquest jury were quick to return a verdict of wilful murder against her and she was committed for trial at the Nottinghamshire Lent Assizes of 1853 on the coroner's warrant.

Mary Ann was almost blind and was described in the contemporary newspapers as 'a women of exceedingly low development,' and 'a poor half-witted creature' who 'presented a semi-idiotic appearance'. One newspaper reported: 'Her blindness gives an expression to the countenance of extreme silliness. She unites with her apparent craziness, however, a low cunning and, when she found that the law was likely to execute justice, she made an attempt to scale the Workhouse wall and escape – a design which she failed to consummate.'

When she stood trial at the Nottinghamshire Assizes for the wilful murder of her baby, she pleaded guilty. Warned by the judge of the inevitable dire consequences of her plea, she continued to insist that she was guilty and was taken back to the cells, where her defence counsel eventually persuaded her to retract her plea. Having heard from her fellow workhouse inmates, the court called Dr Rowland, who had by now amended the conclusions that he had drawn at the post-mortem examination, stating that the infant was an eight-month premature baby who could not have lived more than a few days longer, even assuming that her mother had not ill-treated her. Although both doctors had always maintained that the infant's death might have been accidental, the fact that Mary Ann had confessed and her statement to

Broadmoor Asylum. (*Author's collection*)

coroner Swann trumped the medical evidence in the minds of the jury, who found her guilty of wilful murder.

Mary Ann was sentenced to death but her sentence was later commuted to one of transportation for life. However, while confined in Nottingham Gaol, Mary Ann's condition worsened. She complained of terrible pains in her head and claimed that everyone was her enemy and intended to harm her. She constantly dreamed of murders and was believed to be suicidal. After a medical examination, Mary Ann was sent to Bethlem Asylum on 20 March 1854.

When Broadmoor Criminal Lunatic Asylum opened in 1863, Mary Ann became one of its first patients. Descriptions of her on arrival note her 'snagged teeth', which, coupled with the premature birth of her daughter, suggest that she may have been suffering from syphilis. However, she actually died from chronic kidney disease in July 1900.

William Thompson: 1831–1883

There was no love lost between sailor Alexander Ogilvy and ship's cook and steward William Thompson, who were both engaged on the barque *Peru*, sailing between London and Hong Kong under the British flag. In September 1880 the two men quarrelled violently, their argument ending when Ogilvy flung scalding tea at the cook, then threw the empty cup at him, cutting his face.

On 29 September Ogilvy took his coffee pot down to the ship's galley, and as he handed it to the cook to fill, he noticed that Thompson was holding a revolver in his right hand behind his back.

'I will go and ask the Captain if you are allowed to carry a revolver,' said Ogilvy. The ship's Captain was unwell – in fact he died before the ship reached the docks at London – so Ogilvy was told to take his problem to the first mate, William Beaton Ore. Along with the second mate, Robert Bell Stewart, Ore went straight to the galley, with Ogilvy close behind them.

'Cook, where is that revolver?' Ore asked Thompson, who raised his right hand, in which he was holding a knife. 'This is what I had in my hand,' he explained.

'You liar!' exclaimed Ogilvy, at which Thompson drew his revolver and shot at Ore, but the gun misfired. Thomson then fired at Ogilvy, the bullet grazing his back. Rather than running away, the shot sailor turned towards Thompson and tried to grapple with him. At this, Thompson pulled out a second revolver and shot Ogilvy in the neck.

The Barque *Peru*. (*The State Library of Victoria*)

'You cowardly son of a bitch, you have shot me,' yelled Ogilvy, stripping off his shirt to try and see how badly he had been hurt. A fourth shot was fired, luckily without causing further injury to anybody. Then Thompson began running towards the stern of the boat, with the rest of the crew in hot pursuit.

Having cornered Thompson at the boat's stern, Ore demanded that the cook hand over his guns. Thompson refused, saying that there was a plot aboard the ship to kill him and that he needed the guns to defend himself.

'I will warrant there shall be no violence used on you if you give the revolvers up.' Ore promised.

'It will be a very risky business to try and take them from me.' Thompson threatened.

Ore told him that he would soon be forced to try and take the revolvers from him, but would rather do so without further violence if possible.

'I won't give them up while that man is there,' Thompson insisted. But as soon as Ogilvy retired to his cabin, he handed the guns over to Ore without further protest. Both weapons were loaded.

When Thompson had been securely restrained, Ore wrote up the incident in the ship's log before reading the entry out to Thompson, who immediately begged him to erase the report, offering to pay him to do so.

'That is impossible because it is all down in the log,' explained Ore.

'You can easily throw the log book over into the sea,' argued Thompson, but Ore would not be bribed. Thompson then asked to see the captain, but was told that he was too ill to be disturbed.

When *Peru* arrived at London Docks on 10 November, Thames Police Inspector William Robertson was called to the ship and taken to the sail room, where Thompson had been confined since the shooting.

'You are charged with shooting one of the crew,' Robertson told Thompson, who replied simply, 'One tale is good until the other is told.'

Thompson was taken to the police station and searched, and when his shirt was removed, he was found to be wearing body armour that had been crudely fashioned from two flattened biscuit tins. The makeshift protection, bound with a strip of carpet, covered only the front of Thompson's body, and when the police asked him why he had not similarly protected his back, he replied that it didn't matter about that. Asked why he believed that he needed armour, Thompson told the police that he never knew what to expect from the crew.

Magistrates at London Police Courts subsequently found Thompson guilty of feloniously wounding Alexander Ogilvy on the high seas with intent to murder him and he was committed for trial at The Central Criminal Court. When he appeared there on 23 November, the first witnesses were the ship's crew, yet, as far as Thompson was concerned, the most important witness was John Rowland Gipson, who served as the medical officer of Newgate Gaol.

Gipson had seen Thompson every day while he was incarcerated awaiting his trial and believed that the prisoner was suffering from very strong delusions that there was a plot to kill him. Thompson told Gipson that he had taken some papers relating to a property in Carolina, in a biscuit tin on board the ship. Convinced that the ship's crew were out to get him, Thompson threw the papers overboard and used the biscuit tin to fashion his crude body armour.

Thompson told Gipson that he firmly believed that he had been fired at while on board *Peru*, accusing the second mate of being the gunman. Thompson also stated that his food had been poisoned and that the hens and the pig kept on board had also been targeted.

At this, Alexander Ogilvy was recalled and testified that Thompson was particularly fond of Murphy, the ship's pig, and that he was responsible for feeding it with kitchen scraps. The pig apparently returned Thompson's affections and would follow him around like a dog. According to Ogilvy, the pig had been ill several times during the voyage from Hong Kong back

Central Criminal Court or Old Bailey. (*Author's collection*)

to London but had suffered no more than a cold. It had certainly not been poisoned.

Gipson then told the court that Thompson believed he had heard the crew whispering about him and plotting against him, adding that Thompson had frequently extinguished all the lights in the galley or his cabin and sat in the dark so that nobody would know where he was. Convinced that he was about to be attacked at any minute, Thompson felt it necessary to keep his guns on his person at all times in order to defend himself. The prison doctor was confident that Thompson's delusions were genuine and that he was not feigning madness. 'He implicitly believes in these delusions and thoroughly believes in his own sanity,' concluded the Medical Officer.

The trial jury found Thompson not guilty due to reasons of insanity and he was ordered to be detailed during Her Majesty's pleasure. He was sent directly to Broadmoor Criminal Lunatic Asylum, where he died on 13 September 1883 from liver disease and dropsy.

William Brown: 1832–1885

Early on the morning of 17 January 1883, three young children were spotted standing in the upstairs window of a house in Mile Town, Sheerness, Kent. The children were desperately shouting 'Fire!' and 'Murder!'. As passers-by rushed to help them, one of the children – a nine-year-old girl – jumped from the window to the pavement below, fortunately without seriously injuring herself.

A man named Husson got the remaining children to safety, before he and a passing policeman, PC Jacobs, managed to open the front door of the house on Ebenezer Street. Immediately the door was opened, a young man staggered out of the smoke-filled house and collapsed on the pavement, blood gushing from several wounds.

Police and firemen eventually got the blaze under sufficient control for them to be able to enter the premises safely. They found Elizabeth Brown dead inside, and in the attic lay her husband, William Brown, a black man originating from British Guyana, his throat cut and an open razor by his side.

Fifty-year-old Brown was a former seaman in the Royal Navy until his discharge with a certificate of good conduct. He supplemented his naval pension by working for the local Board of Health.

The following day, coroner Mr W. J. Harris opened an inquest on forty-six-year-old Elizabeth. However, her husband was not in a fit state to attend and the principal witness, her son, Alfred Rump, who had collapsed outside the house, was not expected to survive. Twenty-year-old Rump had three stab wounds, one of which had penetrated his left lung close to his heart, a second in the back of his head, and a third in his thigh. Despite the nature of his injuries, Rump was able to give a statement to the police, telling them that he had been woken up by his mother and stepfather quarrelling. When he went downstairs, he found his mother lying in a pool of blood and the room on fire. When he asked his stepfather what had happened, Brown attempted to throw him onto the fire. The two men struggled, then Brown stabbed him. Almost immediately, the front door was broken open and Rump was able to make his escape. It was assumed that William Brown then fled to the attic, where he attempted suicide.

Against all odds, both Rump and William Brown survived. The inquest was adjourned and when it was resumed, it was revealed that Elizabeth's skull had been cleaved by a hatchet, her throat had been cut and she had a further twelve stab wounds. Since Alfred was able to testify and accuse his stepfather of inflicting her injuries, the inquest jury returned a verdict of wilful murder against Brown.

Brown's injuries were such that by the time of his appearances at Lewes Assizes on 18 April 1883, he was forced to use a breathing tube and was unable to speak. It was stated in court that Brown bore an excellent character and was simply seized by a fit of homicidal madness before attacking his wife with a hatchet, knife and razor, stabbing his stepson, setting fire to the house and then attempting to kill himself with a razor.

Brown was sent to Broadmoor Criminal Lunatic Asylum, where he remained, still unable to speak, until his death from congestion of the lungs in July 1885.

William Isaac Robinson: 1833–1893

William Isaac Robinson was a naval pensioner, who received an annual pension of £19 18s. In addition, he also sold wood, coal and potatoes from his home at Stoke, in Plymouth, Devon, as well as being contracted as a cleaner for Stoke Public School. William shared his home with his wife and their three children, two girls and a boy, with a fourth child on the way. William's mother-in-law and sister-in-law lived next door and the Robinson family also had one live-in servant named Emily Albertina Niles, who frequently went to clean the school with her employer.

William was said to be very hard working, a loving husband and a kind and attentive father. However, he had a terrible fondness for drink, and by 1876 he was an habitual drunkard, squandering most of his money on spirits. Although he never raised a hand to his wife and children, he became verbally aggressive when drunk and threatened to kill his entire family, leaving them terrified. On more than one occasion, Mrs Robinson called in the neighbours to help her with his drunken outbursts, and on one occasion she even called the police. She also sent Emily to the local pub with a note, begging the landlord not to sell any more alcohol to her husband

On the morning of 24 April 1876 Emily dressed the children then asked William if he wanted her to go and clean the school. William, who had drunk very little alcohol for the past two days, told her that he would do it, adding that he had promised to take his youngest daughter with him. Emily prepared two-year-old Gertrude Lucy Brenner Robinson to go out with her father, then left her to wait for him by the front door. Moments later, the maid heard the door close as William and Gertrude left the house.

When they didn't return at the expected time, Mrs Robinson sent Emily to the school to look for them, but when she got there the doors were locked. The maid returned home, and fifteen minutes later she was again sent back to the school. Although the doors were still locked, this time she noticed an open window. Peering through it, she noticed Gertrude's cloak lying on a desk. She managed to prize open the window sufficiently to climb through and gain entry. To her horror, she found Gertrude lying on the floor in a pool of blood, her throat cut so deeply that her head was almost severed. She rushed back to the window, and, spotting a newspaper boy, she shouted to him to fetch a policeman.

There was no sign of William Robinson, who had by then locked up the school and left. He went straight to Devonport Police station, where he introduced himself to PC Horn and informed him that a murder had been committed. Horn noticed that Robinson was trembling violently and sweating heavily, and that he reeked of alcohol. Thinking that Robinson may be experiencing a drunken delusion, Horn asked him who had committed the murder. 'I have,' replied Williamson. 'It's my own little girl, Gertrude.'

Horn asked him if he had been drinking and Robinson admitted to having consumed 11d worth of brandy, although he stressed that he had drunk it since killing his daughter. Horn, who was still unsure whether or not to believe what he was hearing, suddenly noticed William's trousers, which were covered in blood and soot. William explained that he had placed Gertrude across his knees before cutting her throat with a dinner knife, which he then left on a desk. He accounted for the soot by explaining that he had stumbled against a coal heap on leaving the school. He told Horn that he had fully intended to kill his older children as well but that Gertrude's death had been so dreadful that he was unable to face killing the others. 'I done it out of pity's sake,' William said, adding that he was constantly being tormented at home by his mother-in-law and sister-in-law, who he strongly suspected were taking goods from his shop without paying, and it was more than he could put up with. With that, William asked to borrow a newspaper that was lying on the police station counter, put on his spectacles and began to read it.

Another policeman was sent to the school to check out Robinson's claims, finding Gertrude exactly where her father had said she would be found. Although a doctor was summoned, Gertrude was beyond any medical help, having bled to death from her throat wound.

Since Robinson had largely abstained from alcohol for the two or three days prior to the murder, it was thought that he could now be suffering from *delirium tremens*. The inquest on Gertrude's death, held by coroner Mr James Vaughan, took no account of William's supposed mental state and he was committed to the next Devon Assizes for wilful murder.

At his trial before Baron Amphlett on 17 July 1876, William Robinson pleaded guilty. However, given that his counsel Mr Carter was intending to offer an insanity defence, it was agreed that a plea of not guilty should be entered so that the defendant could have the benefit of a proper trial. Carter argued that, while drinking was no excuse for murder, if a man's brain was impaired and he had therefore acted under a delusion, then he should be

Exeter Prison, where Robinson was confined. (*Author's collection*)

acquitted. According to Carter, the defendant had no possible motive for the killing and could not possibly have born any malice towards his children, who he frequently referred to as his 'gold leaves'.

Although Carter called several witnesses who stated that William was behaving strangely in the days immediately preceding the murder of his daughter and that he seemed to not be in his right mind, Mr Caird, the surgeon at Exeter Prison, stated that Robinson had shown no signs of *delirium tremens* in the aftermath of the murder. Although the surgeon conceded that, had it been a mild case, Robinson could have recovered quickly rather than becoming agitated and delusional, Robinson had seemed calm and indifferent to his crime and Caird believed him to have been sane.

It took the jury less than thirty minutes of deliberation to find William Robinson not guilty on the grounds of insanity and he was ordered to be detained during Her Majesty's pleasure.

On 21 September 1876 he was admitted to Broadmoor Criminal Lunatic Asylum. He suffered a stroke in 1892, followed by a second six months later, and died on 24 March 1893. The cause of death was given as 'softening of the brain' as a consequence of his strokes.

Robert Edwards: 1834–1879

On 11 December 1875 Dr Bateman, a physician at the Norfolk and Norwich Hospital, admitted a patient named Robert Edwards, who presented with symptoms of indigestion. Edwards, a former weaver, claimed that he had suffered from a diseased stomach for more than six months, which caused him pain after meals and a great deal of flatulence. Consequently, he had to be very particular about his diet and usually needed to take an indigestion remedy after every meal.

Edwards was given a bed on Catherine Ward, where he was seen that evening by house surgeon Dr John Richard Baumgartner. Edwards asked the surgeon to prescribe something to help him to sleep but Baumgartner suggested that he should just take the medicine that Bateman had prescribed earlier. Baumgartner saw Edwards again the following morning and noticed that he seemed rather nervous and irritable, but when the surgeon did his evening round, Edwards was fast asleep in bed.

Early on the morning of 13 December, Angelina Norcliffe, the nurse in charge of Catherine Ward, approached Baumgartner and told him that there was a patient missing. Together with another nurse, Baumgartner and Norcliffe began to search the ward and surrounding corridors, eventually moving up to the next floor of the hospital to continue searching.

Norfolk and Norwich Hospital. (*Author's collection*)

While there they heard a voice calling for help from downstairs, and when they went to investigate, they met fourteen-year-old Henry Frost, who was with Nurse Hannah Denmark. Frost reported that somebody was killing boys, and, acting on what the boy told him, Baumgartner raced to Ward 12 (the Boys' Ward), where he found Edwards wearing only a shirt and a red scarf. Edwards was holding a pair of fire tongs, with which he was belabouring the head of a nine-year-old boy named Edward Lubbock. Baumgartner snatched up the poker from the fireplace, at which Edwards left his assault on Lubbock and ran at the surgeon, the tongs raised as if to strike him. Baumgartner managed to dodge the blows, hitting Edwards on the arm with the poker and knocking him to the floor, where he was able to disarm him and pin him down until help arrived.

As soon as Edwards was secured, Baumgartner ran to check on the other occupants of the room. To his horror, he found that a further four boys had been savagely beaten. Nine-year-old Alfred Clarke was still alive, as was eleven-year-old William Martin, although Martin died from his injuries within the hour and Clarke survived for only a few days. Eleven-year-old Joseph Colman and ten-year-old John Lacy were both dead, their heads beaten to a pulp.

The police were called, and Edwards was removed to the police station. The following day, coroner Edward S. Bignold opened an inquest into the three deaths. It emerged that most of the hospital staff who came into contact with Edwards during his stay believed him to be a little strange, nervous and excitable. Yet none believed him to be insane. Matron Mrs Margaret

Graham claimed to have spoken to Edwards several times and told the coroner that she had entertained some doubts as to whether or not he was actually physically ill. She had made a particular point of telling Nurse Norcliffe to keep a close eye on him but only because she believed he was faking illness.

After the coroner had heard from several witnesses from the hospital, a member of the jury expressed a desire to have Nurse Denmark brought to the inquest. Since it had not been anticipated that she would be called upon to give evidence, she was not present and the coroner adjourned the proceedings while she was summoned.

When the inquest resumed, Nurse Denmark was able to add very little to the accounts already given by her colleagues. Another nurse, Susan Brown, testified that on the night in question, she was sleeping in the staff bedroom on Ward 12. She was awakened by a thumping noise but heard no screaming or shouting. Nevertheless, she got up to investigate, and when she opened the bedroom door, she saw Edwards beating one of the boys with what she first thought was a stick. Edwards turned to confront her, at which Nurse Brown slammed the bedroom door shut and raced to the window to raise the alarm. Being unable to open the window, she smashed two panes of glass with her umbrella, by which time she could hear voices in Ward 12. She opened the door again, to find that Edwards had been subdued by Baumgartner and the porters.

The inquest also heard from Reverend John Gunton, the rector of Marsham, on whose recommendation Edwards had been admitted to the hospital as an in-patient. Gunton stated that he had known Edwards for thirty years and had always found him to be calm and rational. Gunton had received a letter from surgeon Mr Little of Aylsham, informing him that Edwards was 'in a very low physical condition', and would therefore benefit from being in hospital for a month.

The coroner asked Gunton if he had ever been aware of Edwards suffering an outbreak of insanity. Gunton replied that, on occasions, Edwards had been violent, so much so that his family were forced to sit with him until he calmed down, but as far as Gunton was aware, Edwards had never been admitted to an asylum, therefore Gunton had no reason to believe that he was a madman.

'Have you ever been aware of Edwards being restrained as an insane man?' pressed the coroner. When Gunton asked for further explanation of the question, Bignold asked if Gunton was aware of Edwards ever having his arms held or having to wear a straitjacket.

Gunton insisted that he wasn't aware of any such instances, but did concede that on occasion Edwards had been kept in his room by his friends.

'Were you aware that the hospital expressly forbids the admission of those affected by insanity?' probed Bignold.

Gunton confirmed that he was, but did not consider that the rule applied to Edwards when he recommended his admission.

It was pointed out that Edwards' father had accompanied him to the hospital, something that seemed unusual for a man aged over forty. Gunton insisted that Edwards was in a debilitated state due to his physical condition, hence he was not fit to come to the hospital alone. However, Gunton's curate, Reverend R. J. Wright, had visited Edwards and found him to be excitable and strange, and believed him to be insane. Questioned by the coroner, Wright stated that he had not communicated his opinion to Gunton, believing that he would reach his own conclusions as to Edwards' mental state. Edwards's father was also called to give evidence, relating that on numerous occasions his son had begged him to take his razor away from him as he had no control over himself. He also related having to tie his son's hands together at times, since he did not have sufficient physical strength to subdue him and confine him to his bed.

Having heard all of the evidence, the coroner's jury found a verdict of wilful murder against Robert Edwards, leaving the question of his mental state to be dealt with by a higher court. The jury condemned surgeon Mr Little for recommending Edwards to Gunton as a fit person to be admitted to hospital. They also expressed their condemnation of Gunton for giving Edwards an order of admission, contrary to the hospital's strict rules forbidding the admission of lunatics and the insane. Having donated their fees to the hospital's treasurer, the jury also asked the coroner to commend Dr Baumgartner for his courage in tackling the murderer.

Although Edwards was committed to the Assizes for trial for three – and later, after the death of Alfred Clarke, four – counts of wilful murder, he was judged unfit to plead and sent to Broadmoor Criminal Lunatic Asylum, where he died from inflammation of the lungs on 15 July 1879.

Frederick Crawley: 1836–1889

Thirty-five-year-old Frederick Crawley had for many years worked as a porter at the Home for Fallen Women in Everton, Liverpool. Married to Elizabeth Ann, who was known as Betsy, Frederick was said to be a doting husband – a sober, exceedingly religious man, who taught Sunday School.

He was also a very loving father to the couple's twenty-three-month-old son, William Thomas.

Every morning, Frederick would be first out of bed in the house in Rendall Street that he and his family shared with his widowed mother-in-law, Ann Spencer. Having lit the fire in the kitchen, he would usually fetch his son downstairs and give him breakfast. The morning of 22 February 1871 was no different.

From her bedroom, Ann heard William calling out 'Dada, Dada'. She heard her son-in-law coming upstairs to collect the child, then around twenty minutes later, she heard Frederick calling for his wife. When Betsy went downstairs to see what he wanted, she immediately began screaming 'He has cut the child's throat!'

Ann ran downstairs and saw Frederick sitting in the kitchen, his son lying on his back across his knees. Ann took the toddler from his father, and tried to staunch the blood coming from his throat. 'Oh, Fred, how could you do that?' asked Ann, but Fred simply stared into space and gave no response. At Betsy's request, Ann went to fetch a doctor. When she returned, Fred was still sitting exactly where she had left him. According to Betsy, he had neither spoken nor moved.

Dr Thomas J. H. O'Connor arrived at the house within minutes but William had already bled to death. O'Connor tried to question Fred but received no reply. Eventually, the doctor asked him 'Do you know what you have done?' Fred replied quietly and hesitatingly 'Yes'.

'Why did you do it?' persisted O'Connor, but Fred didn't seem to understand him. 'If I take a chair from here and put it there, I do so with some motive,' O'Connor continued.

'I thought I would be hanged,' Fred countered.

O'Connor asked if he had a razor downstairs or if he had gone upstairs to collect it. When he didn't respond, Betsy answered for him, explaining that he had not come upstairs again after collecting his son.

When taken into custody and charged with his son's wilful murder, Crawley offered no resistance and said 'Yes' to indicate his understanding of the charge. He also answered questions about his name and address, but his replies to any questions directed at him were slow and hesitant, almost as if he were unaware of his situation.

Borough coroner Mr C. Aspinall held an inquest on William's death, at which the jury returned a verdict of wilful murder against his father. Taken before magistrates at Dale Street Police Station, Crawley was described as 'quiet-looking' and 'respectably dressed.' He remained very calm as the

St George's Hall, Liverpool, site of the Assizes. (*Author's collection*)

witnesses gave their evidence, until Betsy was called to testify. Seeing her obvious distress, Crawley began to weep piteously.

Crawley was sent to the Liverpool Assizes, where he appeared before Mr Baron Martin on 22 March 1871. Dr O'Connor told the court that Crawley suffered from 'fits of melancholy', describing him as 'a religious monomaniac with melancholic and homicidal tendencies.' Mr Johnson, the surgeon at Kirkdale Gaol, was in complete agreement and both doctors were of the opinion that Crawley could not be held legally responsible for his actions.

The jury found Crawley not guilty through reasons of insanity and he was ordered to be kept in custody until Her Majesty's pleasure be known. He was admitted to Broadmoor Criminal Lunatic Asylum on 11 April 1871, where he remained until his death, at the age of fifty-three, on 28 February 1889. Throughout his entire time in Broadmoor, he was mentally melancholic and in poor physical health, being described by his attendants as 'feeble'. The cause of his death was given as meningitis and cerebral effusion.

William Carew: 1838–1880

Blacksmith William Carew married his wife, Harriet, at Sparkford, Somerset, in 1862. However, the marriage was not a happy one, and by 1873 Mrs Carew had tired of her husband's cruelty towards her and left him, going to stay in a house in the village owned by a Mrs Joy. Magistrates bound Carew over to keep the peace towards his estranged wife, but he ignored them, and in July 1873 went to Mrs Joy's home, where, spotting his wife, he chased her down the garden.

He eventually went away but returned shortly afterwards and, finding the front door locked, began to hack at it with a hatchet. Once again, he was taken to the County Petty Sessions, where he was ordered to pay the sum of 3s in damages and costs.

Less than a week later, thirty-five-year-old Carew was in trouble again. On the evening of 17 July 1873, labourer Robert Brooks arrived in Sparkford at around 10.45 at night. He passed Carew's smithy and saw him inside, before reaching his destination, a house in the village occupied by a widow named Ann Payne. Minutes later, Mrs Payne happened to look out of the window and remarked, 'Oh, dear. There's Mr Carew going to set fire to the house.'

Brooks ran outside and saw Carew behind the neighbouring cottage, which was owned by Carew's mother and tenanted by a man named James Willis. In each hand Carew held an iron rod, the ends of which were glowing red hot. He was thrusting the rods towards the cottage's roof, jumping up so that he could reach the thatch.

Brooks put his hand on Carew's shoulder and asked him what he was playing at. Carew span round and struck Brooks, who was fortunately standing so close to him that the blow on the side of his head had little impact. Carew then tried to run away but Brooks grappled with him, managing to take away one of the rods. At this, Carew threw down the other one and ran off through the village shouting 'Fire!' and 'Murder!'.

Before long, Carew was banging frantically on the door of the house where his mother lived, yelling 'Mother, your house is on fire.' He was eventually overpowered by a group of villagers, who detained him in Ann Payne's house to await the arrival of the police, then handed him over to Acting Sergeant Huish from the nearby village of Queen Camel. When Huish tried to charge him with having attempted to set fire to a house, Carew denied everything. 'It was not I; it was the other one,' he claimed, adding that he had taken the rods out with the intention of trying to scare away two men who he had seen setting fire to the cottage where Willis lived.

Carew was taken to Yeovil police station for questioning. His only comments were to complain bitterly about being 'put upon' and beaten by a crowd of men. He claimed to be completely innocent of the charge against him, attributing the attempted arson to two of his neighbours.

Carew's case was forwarded to the Somerset Assizes at Wells, but by the time he came to trial, it was obvious that he was totally insane and he was acquitted on the grounds of insanity and ordered to be detained during Her Majesty's pleasure. Initially sent to Taunton Prison, he was committed to Broadmoor Criminal Lunatic Asylum in September 1873. By then he was already showing signs of general paralysis of the insane (a condition often associated with syphilis, which could occur anything between ten and thirty years after the sufferer was first infected; initially presenting with headaches, fatigue and insomnia, the sufferer becomes increasingly unhinged as the disease progresses, suffering from delusions, impairment of judgement and exhibiting antisocial behaviours). Carew died, aged forty-two, on 1 December 1880, the cause of his death recorded as 'general paralysis arising from disease of the brain'.

James Edwards: 1840–1894

In the late 1870s James Edwards and his wife ran a greengrocery business from their home in Fore Street, Sale. They also used a pony and trap to take their produce around the streets. The business collapsed after he had an accident and was crushed against a wall by a vehicle while collecting some butter from the railway station. The accident badly damaged his ribs and he was hospitalised for some time, before eventually being awarded £200 in compensation. Frances Edwards was a sober, hard-working woman, who kept her home spotlessly clean. After her husband lost interest in the business, Frances ran it on her own, while he wandered the streets aimlessly. He sold the pony and cart, but in spite of the compensation money, she was forced to take on cleaning jobs to make ends meet.

The couple had two teenage sons, and when a daughter was born in June 1880 Edwards denied being the child's father. He suspected Frances of having an affair and had convinced himself that she planned to leave him and move to Australia with another man, taking all of their money and property with her. The couple rowed endlessly, and on 10 August 1881 Edwards decided to remove most of the furniture from the couple's home into storage, to prevent Frances from taking it.

On 15 August the couple's son, James Henry Edwards, came home at lunchtime from his job, and less than an hour later his father arrived, finding both the front and back doors locked. After hammering on the doors, Edwards left, only to return a short while later with two men, who tried to get into the house by scrambling over a wall at the back. They made so much noise that one of the neighbours came over to remonstrate with them, only to be told by Edwards, 'I know what I am doing. I am Master here. Mind your own business.'

Frances eventually stood on a stepladder and threw a bucket of water over the men, who went away, dripping wet and cursing. However, Edwards was not to be deterred, and at about three o'clock that afternoon he returned with a policeman. Frances opened the door to her husband, asking the policeman to come inside and stop him from taking any furniture. Reluctant to intervene in what he believed was a domestic dispute, PC Moore merely walked away, ignoring France's desperate plea for him to 'Come back and protect me.'

Once the policeman had left, Edwards asked Frances how much money he would need to pay her for her to hand over their bank books, which still showed a healthy balance of £90 remaining from his compensation. 'Let us have a cup of tea together and part friendly,' he suggested.

'You have taken away the furniture; you have no money and then you come and ask for something to eat. You'll not have your tea unless you pay for it,' raged Frances, before calling her son downstairs to help her with some boxes of clothes, which she wanted moved out of her husband's grasp. Edwards offered to help but unsurprisingly Frances brushed him aside angrily.

James junior came down from his bedroom and picked up the first box, which he carried upstairs. His mother brought up a second box before going back downstairs, at which point there was a sudden, piercing scream. James ran downstairs to find his mother collapsed into the arms of their neighbour, Sarah Moores, who had also raced to investigate the source of the noise. As blood pumped from the side of Frances's neck, Sarah bravely wrapped her apron round the wound and half-carried her neighbour into her own house. James turned to his father, who was still clutching a bloody penknife in his hands. Edwards offered no resistance as his son took the knife from him, merely begging him to 'Stab me! Kill me!'

Another neighbour, Mr Duckworth, responded to the commotion and grappled with Edwards. However, all the fight seemed to have left him and he was easily restrained, saying, 'I have done. That will do.' Once handed over to the police, his first question was to ask if Frances were dead. When he was told that she was, Edwards said, 'I am sorry but I should have liked to have done myself at the same time. I don't mind if I hang for it.'

A post-mortem examination carried out by Dr C. J. Renshaw showed that Frances had no fewer than nine stab wounds, five of which were serious. The one that caused her death was just below her left ear and had severed her jugular vein. Edwards had bought the knife he used to inflict the wounds only that morning from a shop just up the road, shortly before enlisting the help of the policeman to gain entry to his marital home.

Hannah Hurst, the shopkeeper who sold it to him, recalled him being in a terrible hurry, chivvying her along impatiently as she got the knife out of the shop window.

Edwards, who is shown on the 1881 census as 'an invalid', believed that his accident had ruined his life. Dr Renshaw had treated his injuries, found him to be morose and taciturn, having to be questioned excessively before he would provide any information. Edwards told the doctor that he had been 'electrified'; that his heart, ribs and liver had been removed and although his liver had been replaced, his heart and his ribs had not. He suffered badly from dyspepsia, was unable to sleep, was depressed and suicidal and could not concentrate on anything. No matter how much the doctor tried to persuade him that his theories were both absurd and totally unfounded, Edwards would not be swayed and Renshaw eventually came to the conclusion that he was a lunatic. The doctor strongly advised Frances to put her husband into an asylum but Frances was unwilling to do so, telling Renshaw that she would 'see how he got on'. Renshaw didn't believe that Edwards presented any threat to anyone but himself and so didn't push for his committal.

Renshaw also attended Frances at the birth of her youngest child, at which time he found her husband particularly low and despondent. Frances explained that her husband did not believe that the baby was his, and when Renshaw asked him why he believed this, he gave what the doctor later described as 'an absurd reason'. Once again, Renshaw urged Frances to put Edwards into the asylum and once again she stalled. Renshaw told her that she was being foolish, but she refused to budge. Meanwhile, Edwards frequently tried to waylay the doctor whenever he met him on the street, stripping off his clothes to show that he had no ribs.

Both the coroner and the magistrates at Sale Petty Sessions committed Edwards for trial at the next Assizes and accordingly he appeared before Mr Justice Kay at the Winter Assizes at Chester, charged with wilful murder. Asked by John Davidson, the medical superintendent at Cheshire Asylum, if he knew why he was facing trial, he responded that he had been told it was for killing his wife but that could not be true because she was not dead. He claimed to be able to still see and hear her, adding that she was in the room with them right now and was smiling at him.

After questioning Edwards at length, Davidson came to the conclusion that he was 'utterly insane', suffering from visual and auditory hallucinations and delusions. According to Davidson, Edwards was unable to concentrate and found it difficult to answer questions, often speaking incoherently. He firmly believed that his wife, doctor and solicitor were conspiring to poison

Chester Castle, site of the Assizes. (*Author's collection*)

him and was convinced that all of his internal organs were upside down, claiming to be unable to walk. However, when Davidson asked him directly if he believed that he was sane, he assured the doctor that his mind was quite sound.

Davidson's evidence was corroborated by Dr McEwen, the prison medical officer, who had observed Edwards throughout his two-month incarceration and also believed he was insane. Thus, it was left to the judge to suggest to the jury that the proper verdict in the case was one of not guilty on the grounds of insanity. When the jury formally gave that verdict, Kay ordered him to be detained during Her Majesty's pleasure.

Edwards was sent straight to Broadmoor, where he was found to be suffering from consumption or tuberculosis. By the time of his death from the disease, aged fifty-four, in January 1894, he had been bedridden for around nine months.

Mary Hirst: 1845–1932

On 9 November 1876 coal miner William Hirst went to work, leaving his thirty-one-year-old wife at home with their children. Soon afterwards, neighbours heard screams coming from the Hirsts' home near Chapeltown, Leeds. Suddenly, a child ran out of the house, shouting 'Mother is killing the baby with a knife'. When they went to investigate, the neighbours found Mary sitting in a chair by the fire. She was attempting to cut her throat with a bread knife, having already cut the throat of her four-month-old son, Wilfred, who lay on the floor at her feet.

Dr Drew was sent for and found baby Wilfred alive but in a critical condition. The doctor stitched the infant's wounds but his windpipe had been severed, his head almost separated from his body. Wilfred was so seriously injured that he was not expected to survive. Mary's attempt on her own life had been thwarted by her neighbours, Samuel Renfern and John Goddard, and so her own wounds were little more than scratches.

Mary was in a frantic state, tearing at her own clothes and hair until she had to be physically restrained. All she would say was 'No one cared for me,' which she repeated over and over again. Dr Drew was convinced from the outset that Mary was not in her right mind and immediately signed a certificate ordering her removal to Wadsley Lunatic Asylum. However, having undergone a medical examination, she was pronounced sane, and sent to the local workhouse instead.

Mary was initially charged with attempted murder and was brought before magistrates at the West Riding Court. In view of the severity of Wilfred's injuries, the police asked for the case against her to be remanded, to see whether or not Wilfred would pull through. Mary then took it upon herself to make a statement. Speaking in a strange, sing-song voice, she claimed to be listening to the voice of her mother, who was in Heaven. 'I have fighted [sic] against Satan for three weeks and done my best to resist him,' she continued. 'But he put a darkness over my eyes and a fire in my head and made me do it.' Mary rambled on about being lonely, claiming to

Wadsley Lunatic Asylum. (*Author's collection*)

have undergone terrible troubles in recent weeks. saying that she loved little Wilfred and had sung to him night and day.

Magistrates asked William Hirst about his wife's condition and William explained that she had been 'queer' and despondent since the baby was born four months earlier. He had taken her to Dr Drew but nothing had been done to help her and she had been especially bad for the last three weeks.

Dr Drew was concerned that Mary would attempt to take her own life again, and this time there would be no neighbour to stop her. He told magistrates that the workhouse was not the right place for her since she needed to be kept under constant observation. The magistrates agreed that neither the workhouse nor a police cell were suitable places for Mary in her current condition and instructed the police to try and get her admitted to the asylum without delay. If that were not possible and she was forced to remain in police custody, Superintendent Kerslaw was told that she was to be treated with every possible kindness.

Little Wilfred died on the morning of 14 November 1876 and coroner Mr Bagshaw held an inquest into his death two days later. Unusually for an inquest, much was made of Mary Hirst's mental state. It emerged that both her mother and her aunt had been confined in lunatic asylums, her mother being certified insane and dying while an asylum patient. According to William Hirst, his wife had not been in her right mind since their son's birth.

Leeds Town Hall, site of the Assizes. (*Author's collection*)

The inquest jury returned a verdict that 'the deceased, Wilfred Hirst, died from wounds received at the hands of his mother', adding that they were unanimous in believing that Mrs Hirst was not in her right mind at the time of the attack and was then – and still was – insane.

Mary was brought before Mr Justice Hawkins at the Leeds Assizes of December 1876. Charged with wilful murder, her response was to say, 'I do not know how I did it. I had nothing to do with it.' Mary's obvious insanity was confirmed by Dr Price, the surgeon at Armley Gaol, who told the court that she was incapable of understanding and defending her rights and was completely unaccountable for her actions.

Hawkins instructed the jury to return a verdict of insanity and ordered her to be kept in strict custody until Her Majesty's pleasure be known.

Mary Hirst was sent to Broadmoor early in 1877, where she was to remain for the next fifty-five years. She died from old age, aged eighty-six, in March 1932.

James Smith: 1846–1890

On 14 February 1885 unemployed factory worker James Smith was walking along Hulme Street in Manchester when a young woman sidled up to him and surreptitiously told him 'The D's are on your track'. At this, Smith abruptly turned round and began walking along Lower Cambridge Street. After about thirty yards, Smith was seen to drop a canvas bag into the gutter by the 'D' – a detective who was tailing him at the time.

As soon as the bag was dropped, the detective caught up with Smith and apprehended him, signalling to a nearby constable to take him into custody. With Smith safely restrained, the detective picked up the bag, finding it to contain sixty-one counterfeit coins, each separately wrapped in a piece of paper. As well as the counterfeit coins – comprising two florins, twenty-one shillings and thirty-eight sixpences – the bag contained 24s 8d in 'good' money, including one florin that bore the same date as the counterfeit coins, which the police believed had been used to create a mould for the forgeries.

Smith was charged with having counterfeit coins in his possession with intent to 'utter' them – i.e., to intentionally defraud by passing them as legitimate coins of the realm, knowing that they were forgeries. He appeared before Mr Justice Wills at the Manchester Spring Assizes in April 1885. Unfortunately, it wasn't Smith's first offence. On 19 April 1869 he had been convicted of uttering false and counterfeit coin, and since he already had two similar convictions, he was then sentenced to twelve months' imprisonment with hard labour. Once released from prison, Smith committed two more similar offences, this time using the alias 'John Walker'. As Walker, Smith was sentenced to twelve months' imprisonment at The Central Criminal Court on 13 January 1879. No sooner had he been released than 'Walker' offended again and was subsequently sentenced to five years' imprisonment at Maidstone Assizes for uttering base coinage.

Mr Justice Wills was obviously in the mood to make an example of Smith. 'You are evidently a determined, resolute and dangerous person,' the judge told him. 'There is no species of crime that brings more petty loss upon people who can least afford it than this in which you have been engaged, for in nine times out of ten, this bad coin

Mr Justice Wills. (*Author's collection*)

passes off. It is a cowardly, mean and cruel occupation and it is one which must be sternly punished because, as a rule, when a man once takes to it, he rarely drops it. The profits are large, the escape from honest industry too easy and it rarely happens that men who have once given themselves up to it turn to anything else. You have already undergone imprisonment for this and I should be wanting in my duty if I were to show you any leniency.'

Smith was distraught. He told the judge that he was 'one of the unfortunates', claiming that he had tried again and again to get legitimate work in Manchester but had failed because he had no 'character' and could not provide references. He claimed that he had barely been in the city for a week before the police got wind of his presence and began to harass him. He explained to the judge that he had only succumbed to the temptation of counterfeiting as a last-ditch attempt to be able to purchase some goods so that he could go straight by working as a hawker, although he added forlornly that he realised that the police would never give him a licence. 'Do, my Lord, give me another chance,' Smith beseeched the judge. 'I promise you that this shall not occur again. I will reform. Do give me another chance – I am old and a cripple.'

Wills took no notice of Smith's promises, sentencing him to ten years' penal servitude with hard labour. At this, Smith burst into noisy tears and begged 'Sentence me to be hung at once, my Lord. I will kill myself if you don't. Sentence me to be hung – I will never do penal servitude, ever!' Smith was then forcibly removed from the court, still sobbing bitterly and repeating 'I won't, I won't.'

In spite of his protests, Smith was sent to Woking Prison to serve his sentence, but was soon showing signs of insanity, and in October 1888 he was transferred to Broadmoor Criminal Lunatic Asylum. In 1890 he fell ill with influenza, from which he developed pleurisy and pneumonia. He died from a combination of these diseases on 1 March 1890, aged forty-four – hardly the old and crippled man he had claimed to be in court just five years earlier.

William Enoch Kirk: 1846–1916

Fifty-five-year-old William Enoch Kirk lived beside the Frith Bank Drain in the marshes of Boston, Lincolnshire, with his wife, Ellen, and those of their six children who were not already in service and living away from home. In the past, William had worked as a platelayer on the Great Northern Railway, but by 1901 he was unemployed and showed no inclination to work, leaving his wife to go out charring to earn enough to keep the family.

Close to the Kirks' home lived farmer Henry 'Harry' William Robinson, whose wife was heavily pregnant. Arrangements had been made some time before the expected birth for Ellen Kirk to move into the Robinsons' home for a week and act as Eliza Robinson's nurse. However, William Kirk was not at all keen on the idea, believing that his wife and Harry Robinson were engaged in an affair. 'You always wear a pleasant look when you are at Mrs Robinson's,' Kirk grumbled jealously.

When she was told on 19 March that the baby's birth was imminent, Ellen went to stay with the Robinsons. William was unable to leave her alone and turned up at the farm every day to speak to his wife, urging her to come and see to her own house and accusing her of being there not to nurse Eliza but to 'see after' Harry. Although he continually forbade his wife from staying at the farm, Ellen was desperate to earn some money, and in spite of her husband's vehement objections, she wasn't about to throw away the chance of a few days' paid employment.

On 21 March the Kirks' son Fred came home for one of his regular twice-weekly visits from his position in service. The previous evening, he had received a note from his mother, telling him that she would be at the Robinsons' farm, so he called there first, finding both of his parents in the kitchen with Harry Robinson and servant Amy Barber. Ellen's note to her son had accused William of 'tormenting her'. It was immediately obvious to Fred that his parents had been arguing, and as he walked home with his father, he tried to persuade him to treat his wife with a little more kindness, pointing out that she was earning money to put food on the table and keep a roof over their heads. Kirk promised that he would do as his son asked and also said that he would see about finding a job.

As Fred walked back to his employment the next morning, he saw his mother standing by the Robinsons' garden gate and went over to talk to her. Almost immediately, his father appeared and demanded angrily 'What's she telling you now?'

Fred left his warring parents to it and returned to his work. Meanwhile, William continued to accuse his wife of 'looking after' Mr Robinson, telling her that he was not going to leave her there to cuckold him. Ellen went back into the house and straight upstairs to tend to Eliza, while her husband confronted Harry Robinson in the kitchen. 'It's you as wants my wife,' William accused him. Harry warned Kirk to be careful of what he was saying, adding that if he were convinced there was something untoward going on, he should prove his words. 'I have witnesses,' Kirk replied enigmatically, and realising that he was never going to convince his accuser of his innocence, Harry left the house to go about his work.

Not long afterwards, Ellen came downstairs, and ignoring her husband, who was sitting on a sofa in the kitchen, she walked straight past him to the outside lavatory. William followed her. On hearing a desperate scream from that direction, sixteen-year-old maid Amy Barber bravely went to see what the matter was. As she neared the toilet, she saw Ellen with her head on a block of wood, William astride her, leaning over and hacking at her neck with a cut-throat razor. Amy called for Harry Robinson, who shouted to William, asking him what he was doing. William immediately ran at Robinson, wielding his razor, leaving the farmer to defend himself with the pitchfork he was carrying.

Kirk eventually ran away. By coincidence, Dr Reginald Tuxford arrived at the farm minutes later to perform a routine check-up on Eliza after her confinement. He rushed to attend to Ellen but sadly she was beyond any medical assistance. At a later post-mortem examination, Tuxford stated that, even if a doctor had been present while she was injured, it would have been impossible to save Ellen's life. The doctor noted a gaping wound across the front of her neck, which had severed her windpipe, gullet and all the blood vessels on the left-hand side of her throat. As well as several more minor gashes on her face and jaw, there was also a wound at the back of her neck, stretching from ear to ear and penetrating her vertebral column. Tuxford

Spilsby Sessions House. (*Author's collection*)

found that Ellen's body was completely bloodless, concluding that she would have bled to death almost instantly from any of her wounds.

As William Kirk fled home, covered in his wife's blood, he met several people on the way. 'I have killed the missus,' he told his friend George Taylor. 'I have cut her head right off,' he told another passer-by, offering to take him and show him the body. Kirk then took out his blood-stained razor again. 'I may as well do it as be hung,' he commented, but George Taylor was able to easily take it from him without any real struggle.

Police were sent to Kirk's home and he was arrested. 'I'm very sorry I've done it,' he told PC Wright. 'It's all through that man Robinson that I've done it but I'm very queer in my head sometimes,' he explained.

William Kirk was known as a sober and very respectable man, although he had not worked since having surgery to drain an abscess some months earlier – an abscess that had since reoccurred and was obviously causing him some pain. The inquest into his wife's death returned a verdict of wilful murder against him, as did magistrates at Spilsby Sessions House, where a large crowd of people flocked to try and catch a glimpse of Kirk as he arrived from Lincoln Prison, where he had been confined since his wife's death. Through talking with his gaolers on the journey, it was apparent that he had resigned himself to being hanged. Throughout the hearing, he gazed steadfastly at the floor, occasionally raising a hand to probe the abscess on the back of his neck. He spoke only once, when asked if he had any statement to offer in his defence. 'It is through Harry Robinson that I did it,' he stated.

Committed for trial at the next Assizes, Kirk appeared at Lincoln Castle before Mr Justice Wright. Charged with his wife's murder, Kirk determinedly pleaded guilty, but at the request of the judge, and on the advice of his counsel, Mr Bonsey, his plea was subsequently withdrawn and replaced by one of not guilty.

Having heard from those witnesses who had already testified at the inquest and before the magistrates, the court heard from prison medical officer Dr Sympson, under whose charge Kirk had been while he was in custody. According to Sympson, Kirk had always talked and behaved perfectly rationally and the doctor had never seen any signs that he was not responsible for his actions. Kirk had, however, complained of being depressed and of having pains in his head and neck. He had also told Sympson that 'something like an oyster' had come out of the abscess on the back of his neck. But though Sympson thought that the

Mr Justice Wright. (*Author's collection*)

Lincoln Prison, where Kirk was confined. (*Author's collection*)

Interior of Lincoln Prison. (*Author's Collection*)

abscess may have affected Kirk's general health, he could not imagine that it could possibly have affected his sanity.

There was no evidence of insanity in Kirk's immediate family, although he had apparently indicated to his defence counsel that he had intended to kill both his wife and Harry Robinson but had lost his nerve. Kirk was not a drinker nor was he a violent man and thus the only possible motive for murdering his wife was that he was labouring under the delusion that she was being unfaithful to him. For defence counsel, Mr Bonsey, this delusion was sufficient to indicate that Kirk was not in his right mind at the time of the killing.

Unfortunately for Bonsey, Mr Justice Wright told the jury that he could see no evidence that the prisoner did not know what he was doing and it took them less than five minutes' deliberation to return their verdict that Kirk was guilty as charged.

Having accepted his death sentence, Kirk left the court calmly and quietly, the contemporary newspapers reporting that, as throughout his trial, he seemed the most unconcerned person in court.

In the aftermath of the trial, Kirk's doctor, Dr Wrinch, wrote to Mr Justice Wright expressing concerns about the verdict, saying that he personally was convinced that Kirk was insane. Wright passed this information to the Home Secretary, who stayed the pending execution and arranged for two doctors to examine Kirk. Drs Nicholson and Brany duly arrived at Lincoln Prison and quickly determined that he was 'of unsound mind'. He was formally reprieved and sent to Broadmoor Criminal Lunatic Asylum, where he remained until his death, aged seventy, in 1916. The cause of his death was not reported.

James Hobbins: 1848–1875

In May 1873, twenty-five-year-old soldier James Hobbins was a patient at Netley Military Hospital in Hampshire. On 16 May army surgeon Sidney Keyworth Ray came to do his ward rounds and was standing sorting out diet sheets when Private Hobbins walked behind him, placed his left arm across the surgeon's forehead, pulled back his head and cut his throat with a razor that he had concealed in his right hand. Ray tried to pull the razor away from his throat, badly cutting three of his fingers in the process.

'Oh, my poor wife,' he moaned, as blood gushed from his wounds.

Other patients and staff rushed to Ray's aid and Hobbins was quickly disarmed and subdued, leaving Ray with a four-and-a-half-inch-long cut on his throat. Although Ray lost a lot of blood, surgeon Mr William Alexander

Military Hospital, Netley. (*Author's collection*)

McKinnon was on hand to stitch up his wounds and he fortunately survived the unprovoked attack.

Hobbins was indicted for attempted murder, appearing at the Hampshire Assizes in July 1873, charged with 'feloniously, by cutting, attempting to kill Sidney Keyworth Ray'. The court was told that Hobbins had been a member of the 1st Battalion of the 21st Regiment, serving in India, but had been shipped home suffering from consumption and an irregular heartbeat and admitted to Netley for treatment.

Sergeant Henry Gilmour of the Army Hospital Corps testified to having approached Hobbins after the incident and asked him to hand over the razor. 'Yes, Sergeant, I'll give it you,' responded Hobbins, adding, 'I have done for him as the ******* has done for me.' Gilmour had noticed nothing unusual about Hobbins prior to the attack apart from the fact that he was suspicious and especially morose, although this was his normal demeanour.

Surgeon Major Thomas Blatherwick, who was in charge of the hospital's lunatic ward, had spoken to Hobbins after the attack and told the court that it was his opinion that he was insane. Hobbins had been given medical treatment at a hospital in India, and also on the voyage home. He was delusional, convinced that doctors in India and at Netley were causing him harm, in particular Sidney Ray, whose hands he believed did him harm every time they came near him. Hobbins believed that Ray had ordered his discharge from hospital, something he didn't want to happen. He told Blatherwick that he had killed Ray to rid himself of adverse influence

The Asylum, Netley Hospital. (*Author's collection*)

or harm. Asked if he was sorry for what he had done, Hobbins wept and insisted that he was.

It was suggested that Hobbins had suffered from sunstroke while in India, and that this had somehow turned his brain. Asked if he had anything to say, the defendant replied, 'I am ignorant that I was to be discharged. I did not want it.'

In his summary of the case, judge Mr Fitzjames Stephen told the jury that there was no question about the fact that Hobbins had attacked Ray, since several eyewitnesses had seen him doing so. The crux of the case was whether or not he was sane at the time. According to Stephen, the law of insanity was that if a man knew that what he was doing was wrong but could abstain from doing it, he was not insane. However, if he could not abstain, knowing it was wrong, he was considered to be insane.

The jury determined that Hobbins was insane, finding him not guilty due to insanity, and he was ordered to be detained during her Majesty's pleasure. Initially sent to the Hampshire County Prison, he was admitted to Broadmoor Criminal Lunatic Asylum on 12 August 1873.

In April 1875 Assistant Medical Officer David M. Cassidy was called to the toilets, where Hobbins had hanged himself with a rope made from a torn and twisted bed sheet. At the inquest on Hobbins's death, Cassidy told coroner Mr W. Weedon that Hobbins was a very dangerous patient with strong suicidal tendencies. When his body was discovered, Hobbins was already heavily bruised, having previously knocked his head against a wall until his eyes swelled almost shut in an effort to kill himself. He should have been on constant suicide watch and should not have been allowed to go to the toilet on his own but had somehow eluded his attendants. The inquest jury returned a verdict of suicide by hanging while in an unsound state of mind.

Sarah Ann Bull: 1848–1884

On the morning of 19 July 1880 George Bull of Shepherd's Bush, London, went to his work as a school board visitor as normal. When he returned home later that day for lunch, it was to find his nineteen-month-old daughter, Florence Kate, lying dead in a bath of water in the kitchen. George's wife, Sarah Ann, was in her children's bedroom with the door locked. When George finally managed to get into the room, he found his wife unconscious, a thick, silk handkerchief tied tightly around her neck.

Doctor Edward Ryan Jennison (or Tennison) was summoned, finding Sarah lying on her back in bed. The heavy handkerchief was wrapped tightly around her neck twice and knotted at the front, leaving the doctor in no doubt that Sarah had intended to kill herself. When the handkerchief was loosened, Sarah began to breathe again, at which point Jennison went downstairs to look at Florence.

The little girl was lying naked on her side in a zinc footbath, which was half filled with water, her legs drawn up and her face underwater. Jennison estimated that she had been dead for an hour or more and a post-mortem examination revealed marks on her left arm, as if the toddler had been held down. There was a bar of soap in the bath, as if Sarah had been washing her daughter, and Florence's lunch had been prepared and was waiting for her on the table.

At the inquest on the child's death, Jennison was asked whether Florence could have fallen into the water accidentally. Jennison admitted that this was possible but insisted that it was not probable; if she had fallen in, Florence should have been able to climb out of the bath unaided.

Thirty-two-year-old Sarah had two other children and was always thought of as an excellent wife and mother, spending all her spare time making clothes for her daughter and doing everything possible for her husband and children. However, in recent months, she had been severely depressed, complaining of constant pains in her head and drowsiness.

Dr Jennison had attended her in November and December of 1879, at which time he believed that she was not in her right state of mind. Jennison told George that Sarah should be looked after, suggesting that he hire a cheerful companion to be with her constantly, to take charge of her. Even so, at that time Jennison had no concerns about the safety of Sarah's children

– he was later to state that she was most kind and attentive towards them, particularly towards little Florence.

Sarah was also attended by another doctor named William Stephen Knockhold, who had actually called to see her at home on the morning of the murder but had received no reply when he knocked on the door. Knockhold had been treating Sarah for depression since February 1880 and both he and Jennison concurred that she was not accountable for her actions at the time of her daughter's killing.

Committed for trial on the coroner's warrant at the Old Bailey on 13 September 1880, Sarah's mental state was endorsed by surgeon John Rowland Gipson, the surgeon at Newgate Prison, where Sarah had been incarcerated since the murder. Like Knockhold and Jennison, Gipson believed that Sarah was not of sound mind, and she was consequently found not guilty on the grounds of insanity and ordered to be detained during Her Majesty's pleasure.

Sarah was admitted to Broadmoor Criminal Lunatic Asylum in October 1881. She and George had been very happily married and she described him as 'one of the best and kindest men'. George continued to write to her and visit her during her time in Broadmoor. Over the years, her mental and physical health improved, and though she had previously shown suicidal tendencies, she was taken off suicide watch, at her own request.

Activities at Broadmoor Criminal Lunatic Asylum. (*Author's collection*)

On 7 June 1884 she was found sitting upright in her bed, a piece of tape wrapped tightly around her neck and fastened to a shutter. On a letter from her husband, she had written a brief note, saying, 'I have felt dreadful strange for some days. I fear I shall never get out of this living tomb. What anxiety for my husband! It is far better to be relieved as such a burden.'

George Bull had visited Sarah only a few days before her death and had no idea that she had planned to kill herself. Her cause of death was recorded as 'suicide while of unsound mind'.

Eliza Whorlow: 1848–1893

At around eight o'clock on the morning of 1 January 1890, there was a knock at the door of 1 Granville Terrace, Wood Green. It was answered by Mary Whorlow, the sister of the head of the household, bicycle salesman Henry Thomas Whorlow. Mary found a policeman standing on the doorstep and what PC Thomas Matcham told her had her running upstairs to wake her brother. According to Matcham, Henry's wife, Eliza, had just arrived at Wood Green Police Station, where she had confessed to having murdered her youngest son.

Henry rushed to the attic bedroom that his wife shared with three of their children and found eight-year-old Harold Ernest Whorlow lying dead in bed, his throat cut with a razor. His sisters were still fast asleep in the bed beside him.

An inquest on Harold's death held by assistant coroner Mr Hodgkinson revealed several peculiarities in the Whorlows' family life. Apparently, Eliza was not an affectionate wife or mother. She often threatened to kill her husband and children, threats which nobody took very seriously, believing them to be just 'idle words'. According to Henry, Eliza imagined all sorts of domestic troubles, and often accused her husband of leading an immoral life and having women in the house.

Henry and Eliza no longer shared a bedroom as Henry described her as dirty in her habits, usually sleeping with her clothes on. She talked in her sleep and often had delusions or particularly vivid dreams and insisted on waking her husband in the middle of the night to discuss them. She rarely left the house, and, on occasion, she ripped up her bedsheets, tablecloths and other household linen for no apparent reason. She frequently sat alone in the dark, and on Christmas Day had refused to come downstairs to join her family until forced to do so by her brother and brother-in-law.

On the evening prior to Harold's death, there had been a party at the house and everyone had stayed up until the early hours of the morning. Eliza

Holloway Castle Prison. (*Author's collection*)

had declined to join the celebrations and when Henry tried to persuade her, she became angry and threatening. Henry last saw her at about midnight. He went to bed at around half-past three in the morning.

'And, knowing that she had threatened the children, you left her alone with them?' asked the coroner.

'I did not think she meant it or I should certainly have taken precautions,' replied Henry.

The inquest jury returned a verdict of wilful murder against Eliza, asking the coroner to officially reprimand her husband for allowing her to sleep with the children when he was fully aware of her homicidal tendencies.

Eliza's trial took place at The Old Bailey on 13 January 1890, where it emerged that, while everyone seemed to be aware that Eliza was not in her right mind, nobody had done anything to protect the children from her. Mary Whorlow stated that she had moved into her brother's house twelve years earlier to look after Eliza and the children because of Eliza's eccentricity and 'strangeness of manner'. Eliza had not consulted a doctor for more than ten years, and at that time Dr Fouracre believed that she was not sufficiently deranged to merit being placed in an asylum.

Frederick Cook, a friend of the family, stated in court that he had always viewed Eliza as 'insane, but seemingly harmless and silly'. Whereas Cook believed that Eliza belonged in an asylum, it was more because of her slovenliness than due to any fear that she might be violent and harm her family.

Eliza had been confined in Holloway Prison between the murder and her trial, and the medical officer, Philip Francis Gilbert, was able to offer the court more of an insight into her mental state. He described her as 'very strange', spending much of her time simply staring at the floor, smiling vacantly. Gilbert asked her why she had killed Harold, who was allegedly her favourite child. Eliza explained that she had done it for love, after voices in her head told her 'Don't leave it at home to be beaten.' She told Gilbert that she had suffered a stroke nine years earlier, which had left her weakened. She insisted that she loved Harold, adding that it had first occurred to her to kill him a year ago, but she could not pluck up enough courage to do so. Finally, Gilbert told the court that Eliza was in poor physical health, suffering from heart disease and consumption, and that, in his opinion, she was a chronic lunatic. 'I do not think at the time she did this she was responsible for her actions,' he concluded.

Eliza's only comment was ,'I have nothing to say. I wish to die.'

The court found that Eliza Whorlow was guilty of the act of murder but insane and she was ordered to be detained during Her Majesty's pleasure. She was admitted to Broadmoor Criminal Lunatic Asylum on 20 January 1880 and died there from heart disease on 27 March 1893.

Sarah Ann Binstead: 1849–1919

Between the years of 1914 and 1919, Wittering (or Wittring) Court in Daws Heath, Essex, was used as a private asylum for 'imbeciles and epileptics'. It was run by Sarah Ann Binstead, and though she had worked as a mental nurse for more than twenty years, she had no formal qualifications. Initially described in the cotemporary newspapers as 'a strong, capable, energetic woman', on 28 August 1915 Mrs Binstead suffered a debilitating stroke that left her paralysed down one side and incapable of speech. Her condition meant that she was unable to continue running Wittering Court, so her niece, Florence Newman, took over the day-to-day management of the premises.

Florence had previously worked as a housekeeper at Wittering Court, but the added responsibility of management proved too much for her and she left her aunt's employ in 1916. The running of the home now passed to Freda Binstead, Sarah's nineteen-year-old adopted daughter. Nurse Mary Lee was engaged to help her in 1917, but lasted only two weeks at Wittering Court before handing in her notice, not liking how the home was run. Shortly afterwards, Freda also left, leaving the home with nobody in charge.

Wittering Court. Daws Heath reproduced by kind permission of Peter Lewsey and Hadleigh and Thundersley Community Archive

Harry Hall was an estate agent and auctioneer, who had arranged the purchase of several properties for Sarah Binstead, including Wittering Court in 1913. Sarah obviously trusted Hall, who had occasionally lent her money, and shortly after her stroke, she arranged for him to have power of attorney over her affairs in the event of her having a second stroke. With conditions at Wittering Court growing ever worse, Emily Firman, another of Sarah's nieces, spoke to her aunt and Mr Hall, suggesting that the patients should be moved to another institution, where they might receive proper care. However, Emily's concerns were ignored and conditions at the home continued to deteriorate.

By 1918 all of the staff had left and the only person working at Wittering Court was one of the patients, who was then in the advanced stages of tuberculosis. After attending to treat another patient, Jessie Charlotte Spurling, for a bad attack of diarrhoea, local physician Dr W. F. Adams discussed his concerns about the state of the place with Hall and later notified both the medical inspector and the sanitary inspector at the rural district council. Unfortunately, no official investigation was instigated as a result of the doctor's report.

On 5 January 1919 forty-five-year-old Jessie Spurling was found dead in her bed. Jessie was said to be 'a complete imbecile', who was practically bedridden and incapable of feeding herself or of communicating beyond grunts. If left with food, she either stuffed it into her mouth until she choked or refused to eat at all. She was first admitted to an asylum in Peckham in 1900 when she was twenty-seven years old, but was released three years later and sent to Mrs Binstead, who was paid £1 a week to care for her. A post-mortem examination on Miss Spurling found that she was extremely emaciated and very dirty. Although there was no specific disease found, it was agreed that she had died from wastage of the muscles of her heart, exacerbated by starvation and neglect, and her death was therefore reported to the local coroner, Mr C. E. Lewis. It was suggested that, had a doctor been called to attend to her only a few days before her death, she may have been saved.

In the wake of Miss Spurling's death Wittering Court was inspected by Dr Finlay MacDonald, the medical officer of health, who described conditions there as 'deplorable'. According to MacDonald, the bedclothes were filthy, the furniture in all twenty-three rooms was thick with dust, and the entire premises reeked of faeces and rotting food. At the inquest into Miss Spurling's death, MacDonald was asked if he had noticed whether there was any food in the larder, but MacDonald claimed that the smell in the home was so appalling that he had been anxious to leave and had therefore taken very little notice. (An inquest juror, forced to inspect the premises, commented that the smell was 'enough to choke one'.)

MacDonald was accompanied on his visit by a sanitary inspector, who told the inquest about the containers of putrefying food that were heaped on the kitchen table. It was noted that all the home's bed linen had since been burned and the remaining patients removed to the safety of a nearby hospital.

Dr John Turner, the medical superintendent of the Essex County Asylum, had also visited the premises in the wake of Miss Spurling's death and told the inquest that in the course of his experience, he had never seen 'such an abode of dirt and disorder'. Having examined Mrs Binstead and the four patients remaining at the home, Turner stated that he believed Mrs Binstead had organic brain damage, adding that she was certainly not in a fit state to be in charge of Wittering Court. Regarding the remaining patients, Turner told the inquest that while two required extensive daily supervision, the other two were easily certifiable as insane.

Dr Adams was questioned by the coroner about his responsibility to act on the conditions he had observed at Wittering Court. The coroner pointed out that between 1913 and 1919 there had been nine deaths in the home and that Adams had certified eight of those. Adams told the coroner that, with the exception of Miss Spurling, all the deaths had occurred when there were nursing staff employed at Wittering Court, hence conditions there had seemed acceptable. Four of the deaths had occurred since Mrs Binstead suffered her stroke in 1915, and Adams stated that he had approached Mr Hall in 1917 with concerns about the running of the home. Adams said that he had tried to instigate the hiring of an experienced nurse to act as matron but she had been unable to agree terms with Hall.

Florence Newman told the inquest that Wittering Court had been perfectly clean and comfortable when she left in 1916, but when she visited at Christmas 1918, seventy-year-old Sarah Binstead was 'as bad as any of the patients', and incapable of running the home. Asked if there had been any food on the premises when she visited, Mrs Newman told the inquest that there had been a Christmas turkey but there was barely enough coal to cook it. She claimed to have spoken to Harry Hall at the time, warning him that there would be a scandal if nothing was done. Hall, meanwhile, complained to the coroner that Mrs Newman had said that Sarah Binstead was as 'more trouble than all the patients put together', describing her aunt as 'an ungrateful woman, who deserves whatever befalls her'.

Sarah Anne Binstead was sufficiently mentally capable of giving evidence at the inquest, although her answers were confined to simple 'Yes' or 'No'.

The inquest was adjourned and resumed several times before the jury found a verdict of manslaughter against both Harry Hall and Sarah Ann Binstead. They were committed on the coroner's warrant for trial at the next Essex Assizes in Chelmsford. Both were indicted for manslaughter and Hall was additionally charged with 'aiding, abetting, procuring and counselling Sarah Ann Binstead to commit said offence.'

Appearing before Mr Justice Horridge on 4 June 1919, Sarah Ann Binstead was carried into court on a chair. Prosecuting Counsel Mr Travers Humphreys immediately stated that he wished to ask a medical witness about Mrs Binstead's fitness to plead. Dr Macnamara, a physician for mental diseases at Charing Cross Hospital, told the court that he had examined Mrs Binstead on 23 May, at which time she was in a very decrepit condition, both physically and mentally, following an epileptic seizure. It was Macnamara's opinion that Mrs Binstead was incapable of understanding her trial and the judge therefore ordered that she should be detained during His Majesty's pleasure.

Hall pleaded 'Not Guilty' and claimed to have had nothing to do with the day-to-day running of Wittering Court beyond arranging a mortgage for Mrs Binstead to purchase the property. However, having heard the evidence against him, the jury found him guilty of manslaughter and he was sentenced to three months' imprisonment with hard labour.

Law Courts, London, home of the Court of Criminal Appeal. (*Author's collection*)

In the aftermath of the guilty verdict against him, Hall appealed his conviction at the Court of Criminal Appeal. His counsel, Sir E. Marshall Hall K.C. (no relation) argued that Mrs Binstead had been capable of giving evidence at the inquest, but by the time of the trial her fitness to plead had been called into question and she had consequently not testified. Hall had been granted power of attorney over her affairs only in the event of her having a second stroke and there was nothing to suggest that this had ever occurred, thus there was no evidence to suggest that Hall had ever acted under the power of attorney. It was therefore contended that Hall had no obligation or legal duty to provide care for Miss Spurling and that his obligations were confined solely to financial matters should Mrs Binstead have had a further stroke.

Hall's appeal was upheld by the Court of Criminal Appeal and his conviction was quashed. Meanwhile, Mrs Binstead was taken to Broadmoor Criminal Lunatic Asylum, where she died on 26 December 1919. At the time of her death, arrangements were being made for her release, and, had she survived just one more week, she would have been freed.

Elizabeth Hammond: 1849–1933

Farm labourer Isaac Hammond lived in Newton-on-Ouse, near Easingwold in Yorkshire, with his wife, Elizabeth, and their six children. Although Elizabeth was generally a good mother, she seemed totally indifferent to her youngest child, John, who was born in 1878. To the consternation of her neighbours, she frequently left him either alone and unattended, or in the care of one of his young siblings, while she went out to work. She often told people that she wanted him 'out of the road' and frequently claimed that John wasn't Isaac's child but that the boy had been fathered by a man named Mr Smallwood.

In 1879 one-year-old John was badly burned on his legs, and although he was taken to Dr Lantour for treatment, the doctor could never get a satisfactory explanation as to what had caused the boy's burns as his mother gave several conflicting accounts. Nevertheless, John made a good recovery and was soon able to toddle around like any other child of his age.

Yet while John's health was quickly returning to normal, Dr Lantour harboured grave concerns about the boy's mother. He first saw her on 16 December 1877, before John was born, when she was suffering from delusions. Lantour suggested that Elizabeth should spend some time recovering in the workhouse infirmary at Easingwold, but she returned home after a week or so, declaring herself to be perfectly all right. However, once John was born, her behaviour towards him worried her neighbours, and believing that the baby was being deliberately starved, they eventually contacted Lantour.

Lantour called on Elizabeth and challenged her with the neighbours' suspicions, which she immediately confirmed. 'It wants to be with the angels,' she told Lantour, who strongly rebuked her, saying that she would get into trouble if she didn't take proper care of her child. Elizabeth appears to have taken note of the doctor's warnings as John's condition improved. Lantour continued to keep a close eye on her and although he believed that she was 'in a very peculiar state of mind', the doctor had no immediate concerns for her youngest son's safety.

On 4 May 1879 John developed a cough and began vomiting. When Isaac got home from work and saw that the child had thrown up what looked like milky tea, he went for a doctor and was given a bottle of medicine and told that Lantour would visit the following day. Acting on the doctor's instructions, Isaac gave his son a teaspoonful of medicine on his return home, but the following day was a Sunday and so Lantour decided to postpone his visit until Monday morning.

Isaac left for work early on Monday 6 May, leaving his wife in bed, with John lying awake at her side. By lunch time, a message had been sent asking him to return home immediately, and when he did, he found John dead.

Throughout the day there was a constant procession of neighbours in and out of the Hammond's house, all of whom would later give evidence at the inquest on John's death, held by coroner Mr J. P. Wood at The Dawnay Arms, Newton-on-Ouse.

Mary Hume stated that Elizabeth had come to her house at about eight o'clock on the morning of 6 May. 'I am glad to come and tell you that Johnny's dead,' Elizabeth told her, asking if she would mind fetching Isaac from work. Mary asked if there was anyone else in the house, to which Elizabeth replied, 'Nobody but myself and boy [sic]. We wanted nobody else.'

Mary Nelson told the inquest that she had gone into the house and seen John lying on a pillow on the bed. Elizabeth had picked the boy up by one arm and insisted that he wasn't dead, but Mary knew better. 'It is dead. It will not stir any more unless you stir it,' she argued.

Elizabeth Hammond then sent one of her children to fetch Mary Ann Tuckman so that she might lay John out. Mrs Tuckman did as she was asked, noticing nothing unusual about the boy except for the fact that his back was very dark in colour.

Margaret 'Polly' Nelson was next to visit and found Elizabeth on her knees in the bedroom by her dead child. Polly touched John, noticing that his legs and feet were cold but his chest seemed unusually warm. 'Poor little thing. You have often wanted him out of the way and he's gone now'. Polly said she had often passed by the Hammonds' cottage and had heard John repeatedly calling 'Mamma, drink'. She told the inquest that she had not gone to him as Elizabeth had claimed that people were going into her home and stealing from her. However, Polly had quarrelled with Elizabeth on a regular basis about her neglect of John and had been instrumental in reporting her to Dr Lantour.

Jane Dawson was taken upstairs by Mrs Hammond to see the dead child. 'Poor thing. Have you hurt it?' she asked Elizabeth.

'Yes, I don't doubt I have,' replied the boy's mother, explaining that John had asked for a drink and she had wet his lips before sitting on his chest until he was dead.

'How long was it before he died?' Jane asked, horrified.

'Oh, not long,' Elizabeth replied casually.

When Dr Lantour arrived for his promised visit, John was already dead. As the doctor was examining John, Elizabeth suddenly asked 'Do you think I hung the child?'

'What made you ask that?' asked Lantour.

'I may ask, I suppose,' Elizabeth said nonchalantly.

Lantour asked if there was anyone in the house with her when John died. 'Yes, Polly Nelson,' replied Elizabeth, telling the doctor that Polly was next door. Lantour went off to speak to her before returning and telling Elizabeth that he did not feel able to issue a death certificate.

The doctor reported his concerns to the police and Elizabeth was visited by PC William Ambler, who found the newly bereaved mother sitting by the fire, calmly sewing.

'I hear you have a child dead?' Ambler challenged her.

Elizabeth agreed that this was true. She took Ambler upstairs to see the boy's body, telling him that she had sat on her child until he was dead, pointing out bruises on John's head, face and neck. 'I did that with sitting upon it,' she claimed, telling the policeman that she had given her son laudanum a few days earlier but that the boy had vomited up the poison without coming to any harm.

Elizabeth was taken to Shipton Police Station and kept in custody until returned to the village for the inquest. Isaac Hammond struggled to control his grief as he gave evidence before the coroner, leading his wife to admonish him sternly. 'Don't cry. I have shed plenty of tears without shedding any more.'

Having heard Elizabeth's claim that she had given laudanum to her son, the coroner adjourned the inquest to allow for the contents of the child's stomach to be analysed. When the proceedings resumed, Lantour stated that no poison had been found in John's body at all, concluding that the cause of death was asphyxiation either through the child being sat upon or by being accidentally overlain. With that, the inquest jury returned a verdict

Assize Courts, York. (*Author's collection*)

of wilful murder against Elizabeth Hammond and she was committed for trial at the next assizes.

When the case came to court at York before Mr Justice Baron Bramwell, it was evident that Elizabeth Hammond was quite insane, and having heard from medical experts that she was unfit to plead, the judge ordered her to be detained during Her Majesty's pleasure. She was sent to Broadmoor Criminal Lunatic Asylum on 14 August 1879, remaining there until her death from senile decay on 29 May 1933. At that time, she was Broadmoor's oldest and longest serving patient, having been confined there for fifty-four years.

Mr Justice Baron Bramwell. (*Author's collection*)

Joseph Shill: 1852–1885

Tailor Joseph Shill and his wife Maria were married in October 1878 and quickly had three daughters but theirs was not a happy union. Maria claimed that Joseph ill-used her, often beating her and telling her he was going to kill her. In October 1884, he was brought before magistrates, charged with threatening Maria and, unable to pay his fine, he was sentenced to two months' imprisonment with hard labour. Left alone with three children aged five and under, Maria took a job as a charwoman for a butcher, paying a girl to watch them.

Shill returned to his wife and family on 1 December 1884 and, while Maria continued to work, her husband worked from home and so rarely left their room. The house in Victoria Gardens, Windsor, in which the Shills lived, was owned by labourer George Henry Grimsdale, and his mother, Jane Holt, also had a room there. On 19 December, Maria told Jane that her husband had taken his shirt from the washing line, along with three pawn tickets and had gone 'on the tramp' looking for work.

When Jane returned from work at about five o'clock that evening, the two older Shill girls, Emily and Eleanor, were playing with her grandchildren. Jane decided to take them out for a walk to see the shops that had been decorated for Christmas and sent them to their room to get their outdoor clothes. She brought the girls back at about a quarter to nine that evening but

High Street, Windsor. (*Author's collection*)

when she knocked on their door, she found it locked and, peering through the keyhole, she could see a key in the lock inside the room. Jane could hear sixteen-month-old Edith Shill crying and was aware that there was a lamp burning on a table. Frightened that Edith might knock it over and set the house alight and unable to get a response to her knocks and shouts at the door, Jane went in search of a policeman.

P. C. Thomas Laney managed to insert his knife under a window latch and forced it open. He and Jane could see Shill lying on the bed but no matter how much the constable shouted, even poking Shill on the hip with his staff, he couldn't rouse him. Being too big to get through the window himself, Lang suggested lifting Emily through, so that she could pass him the baby. Once Edith was safely in her hands, Jane took the three children to her room and kept them overnight. When she took them back to their room the following morning, Shill was there alone and, having given her some bread and dripping for his daughters and told her that he didn't know where his wife was, he closed the door.

Over the next couple of days, the three little girls were either in the room with their father or in the care of Jane Holt. Shill maintained that he had no idea of Maria's whereabouts, although he did not seem unduly concerned by her absence. On 21 December, Maria's two brothers visited the house in search of her, popping into her room for a few minutes and giving the children some sweets, before going off in search of Shill, who had by then reported his wife missing and was supposedly out looking for her.

On 22 December, Jane's nine-year-old granddaughter Annie Grimsdale, went to the Shills' room to sweep it, as she did every week. After a few minutes, she went to find her grandmother and told her that Mrs Shill's shawl was under the bed and there was also something hard under there. Jane sent for her son, who looked under the bed and found Maria Shill's body.

Meanwhile, on the previous afternoon, Maria's brothers had ended up at the police station, reporting their sister missing, saying that they believed that she may well have committed suicide. Accordingly, Superintendent Hayes notified his colleagues to look out for her, as well as informing the local lock keepers that she might have thrown herself into the river Thames. Hearing about the discovery of the body at Victoria Gardens, Hayes initiated a search for Joseph Shill, who was apprehended later that day in Egham, his clothes heavily splattered with blood. Told that he was being arrested for the murder of his wife, Shill was incredulous. 'Me? Murder my wife?' he queried.

'Yes, that is the charge against you' confirmed Inspector Collins of the Surrey Police. 'You reported your wife missing and do you know she is dead? She was found in the room where you have been sleeping at Windsor'.

'I know nothing at all about it' insisted Shill.

A post-mortem was carried out by Dr Edmund Stacey Norris, who concluded that Maria had died from being hit repeatedly on the head with a blunt object. She had numerous head wounds and had been hit so heavily that her skull was smashed in like an eggshell. Norris believed that the blows had been dealt with considerable force and could not possibly have been self-inflicted, no matter how suicidal Maria was believed to be, nor could they be the result of a fall onto an object such as the fender in the room, which was slightly bent and spotted with blood. A large flat iron, which Norris believed was the murder weapon, was found in a cupboard in the Shills' room, still besmirched with clots of dried blood and hair that was similar in colour and character to that of Maria Shill.

Shill was held in custody in a cell which was only a few yards from the public mortuary, where his dead wife lay awaiting the inquest on her death, which was held by coroner Henry A. Marlin. The jury returned a verdict of wilful murder against Shill, who steadfastly maintained throughout that he knew nothing about his wife's fate. When he was brought before magistrates, he insisted that he had last seen his wife on 19 December and that he had spent the rest of the weekend looking for her, visiting her employers in Eton and some friends at Chertsey to see if she was there.

The magistrates joined the coroner in committing Shill for trial at the next Reading Assizes and on 13 January 1885, he appeared before Mr Justice Hawkins.

Joseph Shill, who was described as a very small man with a distinct humped back, pleaded not guilty. The court heard from all the witnesses who had appeared at the inquest and also from a woman named Sarah Morris, who had heard someone screaming 'Murder' at a quarter to nine that evening but dismissed it as children playing.

It emerged that Shill had written to his mother-in-law on 20 December. *'Dear Mother, Come at once if you have not seen Maria, or one of you tonight. I cannot make it out at all, so one had better come. I feel so worried about her I do not know what will be done.'*

Mr Justice Hawkins. (*Author's collection*)

It was this letter that had prompted Maria's brothers to go and look for her. Thomas William Prior told the court that he and his brother went to their sister's room and saw the three children, who did not know where their mother was. The brothers then went to the police station to report her missing, then continued on to Egham, where they suspected they might find Joseph. They found him sitting in a pub, with a tankard of beer and berated him for writing to them asking them to come and then going out. Shill offered William his hand to shake but William refused to take it, saying that he would not shake hands with a murderer. At this point, the pub landlord intervened, saying that he would not tolerate any arguments on his premises, so Shill and the Priors went outside. William accused Shill of driving his sister to suicide, eventually slapping his face. Shill was most indignant, claiming that he knew nothing about Maria's whereabouts.

Shill's counsel, Mr Darling, who had only taken on his defence at the last moment, claimed that there was absolutely no motive for Shill to have murdered his wife. He reasoned that, while numerous ear witnesses had testified to hearing baby Edith crying, not one person had heard any quarrel or scuffle between the Shills on the night in question. If indeed Shill had murdered his wife, why had he not fled the scene? And why was he lying on the bed seemingly insensible when the police or neighbours could easily have come into the room and discovered that his wife's body was concealed under the very bed on which he lay? Why would Shill invite a search for his wife, both by writing to her family and by reporting her missing to the police? 'Was this the conduct of a sober, or sane man?' asked Darling.

In summing up the case for the jury, Mr Justice Hawkins told them that, since both suicide and accidental death seemed impossible, the only reasonable conclusion must be that Maria Shill was murdered. The only question for the jury was to ascertain by whom the violence was occasioned. Hawkins asked the jury to imagine that the assassin was not Shill. Putting aside the fact that a charwoman living in one room was an unlikely target for a robber, Hawkins asked how the killer could have locked the door from inside the room and made his escape. Even accepting Darling's argument that Shill had no reason to kill his wife, surely any man finding his wife dead would have raised a hue and cry?

After debating the matter for just forty-five minutes, the jury found Shill guilty and he was sentenced to death. However, as he waited for his execution, he began to exhibit signs of insanity and on 24 January 1885, he was certified insane. Five days later, he was transferred from Reading Prison to Broadmoor Criminal Lunatic Asylum.

Shill's confinement in Broadmoor proved to be a relatively short one. He was said to be in 'indifferent health' on his admission and on 30 November 1885, he died, aged thirty-three. In the days prior to his demise, he had

Reading Prison, where Shill was confined. (*Author's collection*)

complained of having a piece of meat stuck in his throat and, although the doctors at the Asylum examined him, they could find no trace of any obstruction. When a post-mortem examination was carried out, a piece of bone was indeed found lodged in the passage leading to Shill's stomach, although this was not believed to have contributed to his death, which was officially recorded as being due to inflammation of the lungs.

Walter Deavin: 1852–1934

On 21 July 1916 widow Florence Elizabeth Chapman was disturbed by a loud argument coming from the house next door to hers in Bridge Road, Woolston, Hampshire. By putting her ear to the party wall, the was able to distinguish a woman's voice saying indignantly, 'How dare you!' followed shortly afterwards by, 'You dare! You dare! Put that down at once!'

Mrs Chapman recognised the voice as that of Miss Louisa Fryer, who acted as a housekeeper to her neighbour, sixty-four-year-old former house agent and rent collector Walter Deavin. Louisa was known to be afraid of her employer and had made arrangements with Mrs Chapman for her to be on the alert for any signs of trouble.

As Mrs Chapman listened for any further words, she suddenly heard a terrified scream, followed by her own name being called twice. Immediately afterwards, there was a series of loud bangs. Mrs Chapman froze in fear for a few moments, before bravely picking up a walking stick from her hall stand and rushing next door. She expected Louisa to answer her knocks on Deavin's door but instead it was Deavin himself who responded. Once again, Mrs Chapman found herself frozen with fear, but she eventually managed to say that she thought she had heard Miss Fryer calling her.

'Yes, she did call for you,' Deavin confirmed, adding 'I shot her.'

Only now did Mrs Chapman notice the revolver in her neighbour's hand. 'Oh, no, you couldn't have done any such thing,' she stammered.

'Oh, yes, I have. Come and see for yourself,' Deavin replied.

Mrs Chapman suggested that a doctor should be sent for, but Deavin dismissed the idea, saying that his housekeeper was quite dead, so sending for a doctor would be pointless. Nevertheless, Mrs Chapman went back to her own home and asked her maid to run for medical assistance and the police. She then bravely went back to her neighbour's house and asked if he was sure that Miss Fryer was dead.

'Yes, come and see for yourself,' Deavin repeated, but when Mrs Chapman tried to go into the house, he raised his gun and threatened to shoot her if she went any further. He then went inside and stood at the front room window as if on guard.

Looking through the window, Mrs Chapman could see a woman's body lying on the floor, although she couldn't see the head or face. Mrs Chapman asked Deavin to move away from the window and let her into the house, but Deavin merely threatened to shoot her if she didn't go away.

A man approached Mrs Chapman in Deavin's garden and asked if everything was all right. Mrs Chapman pointed to Deavin and explained that she believed that a woman had been shot in the house and asked the man to go indoors with her to check. The man remarked that it was perhaps rather foolhardy to attempt to go into the house of an armed man against his will. Nevertheless, he did tap on the window and ask Deavin to go away and let them enter. At this Deavin again threatened to shoot, so the man led Mrs Chapman to wait for the police round the corner of the house, out of harm's way.

When Police Superintendent Littlewood arrived, having been telephoned by Mrs Chapman's maid, Deavin was prowling up and down his garden mumbling and threatening to shoot anyone who approached him. Littlewood sent for reinforcements, but while he waited for them to arrive he saw Deavin putting the revolver into a leather bag that he was carrying. Littlewood seized his chance and managed to overpower Deavin before he could take his gun out again.

As Deavin was taken by car to the police station, a doctor was finally able to enter the house and pronounce Louisa Fryer dead. Dr Arthur Anderson Rogers noted a bullet wound in the palm of her right hand, around which the skin was blackened and scorched. The cause of Miss Fryer's death seemed to be a bullet wound in the left side of her chest, and when Rogers later carried out a post-mortem examination, he discovered that her heart had been hit by a bullet and one side of her chest was filled with blood. In addition, Miss Fryer had two shattered ribs and a further gunshot wound on the outside of her right thigh.

At the police station, Deavin was charged with killing and slaying Louisa Fryer with malice aforethought. 'She made me do it,' he responded. 'She annoyed me by setting the chimney on fire.'

County coroner Mr P. B. Ingoldby held an inquest on Louisa Fryer's death, at which he commended the bravery of Mrs Chapman, Dr Rogers and Superintendent Littlewood in tackling an armed man, adding that it was very fortunate that none of them had met with harm. The coroner's jury also asked Ingoldby to commend the witnesses on their behalf, with particular recognition given to Littlewood. (The policeman was later to say

Winchester County Hospital and Prison, where Deavin was incarcerated. (*Author's collection*)

that, although he had only engaged with Deavin for fifty-five minutes, the gruelling ordeal felt more like fifty-five hours.)

The inquest recorded a verdict of wilful murder against Deavin, who was sent to Hampshire Assizes, appearing before Mr Justice Rowlatt on 10 November 1916 and pleading not guilty, adding that, at the time of the incident, he was completely unaware of what he was doing.

The jury was told that Deavin sometimes had delusions that people were persecuting him, although these were interspersed with periods of lucidity. It emerged that Deavin's brother had committed suicide and his father had died while in an asylum. Several other of the accused's relatives had also spent time in asylums, and prison medical officer Dr D. T. Richards told the court that having observed Deavin while he was in prison awaiting his trial, he was convinced of his insanity, which took the form of melancholia and delusions of persecution.

Having heard the medical evidence, Mr Justice Rowlatt asked the jury if they believed that there was any point in continuing with the trial. The jury immediately returned a verdict of guilty but of unsound mind, leaving the judge to order Deavin to be detained during His Majesty's pleasure. He was taken first to Winchester Prison, then to Broadmoor Criminal Lunatic Asylum where he died, aged eighty-two, on Christmas Eve 1934 from bronchial pneumonia.

Eliza Blanche Bastable: 1853–1880

Eliza 'Blanche' Bastable was the daughter of a prosperous dairy farmer from the village of East Orchard in Dorset. Her parents were very keen on educating their eight children and Eliza was sent to a private boarding school, after which she became a teacher.

The Bastables were a warm, loving family, but Blanche was particularly close to her sister Mary Jane. Sadly, Mary Jane died from tuberculosis, aged nineteen, in 1871 and Blanche was very much affected by the loss of her best friend and confidante. She began to suffer from religious mania, and so serious was her condition that in August 1875 her family were obliged to place her in the Brislington Asylum near Bristol. She remained there until the following June, when she was said to be 'harmless' and was released into the care of her family.

Although willing to allow Blanche to live at home, the Bastables engaged a farm labourer, William Lodge, whose main duties were to supervise her at all times. Yet while Lodge was able to control Blanche and didn't believe that she was a danger either to herself or others, her family believed that her mental state was deteriorating. She seemed very depressed, and her demeanour would swing wildly from morose to manically excited and back. Blanche appeared so unbalanced that her mother, Elizabeth, no longer felt safe in the house with her daughter there. The family doctor, Decimus Curme, was consulted and advised her parents to confine her again for her own protection, impressing upon them the need to watch her at all times. It was eventually decided to have her admitted to Fisherton Asylum in Wiltshire, and to this end Blanche's mother intended to visit the asylum with her son on 6 August 1877 to make the necessary arrangements, although Blanche herself was told nothing of her family's plans to commit her.

On the afternoon of 5 August Blanche was sitting in the parlour at home sewing, under the watchful eye of William Lodge, when he was called away to attend to some farm work. Left unsupervised, Blanche picked up a gun that her uncle John had earlier been using to shoot rooks and had left loaded in the gun rack above the fireplace. Walking into the garden, she aimed the rifle at her mother and pulled the trigger. Fifty-five-year-old Elizabeth was shot in the back of the head and immediately dropped to the ground. Although Dr Curme arrived quickly, he told the family that she had most probably died instantly. Curme spoke to Blanche, asking her why she had shot her mother. 'Well, the law must be fulfilled. All the wicked shall be abolished off the earth,' replied Blanche, calmly, before assuring the doctor 'She will live again in Jesus'.

Blanche seemed to have no concept of what had happened. Retiring to her bedroom, she repeatedly quoted the Gospel of Luke, saying 'Let me lift her up – she is not dead, she only sleepeth. She will rise again.'

Police Superintendent John Pitfield arrived at the house that night to find that Elizabeth had been moved indoors and was laid out on the sofa. She had a single wound on the back of her head, exposing her brain beneath. Having retrieved the gun from the garden, Pitfield was taken upstairs to interview Blanche. 'I shall take you into custody on a charge of killing your mother this day,' he told her.

'You are evil in my eyes and so are you, William,' she responded, referring to Lodge, who had been charged by her father with guarding her while waiting for the arrival of the police.

An inquest was held on Elizabeth's death by coroner Mr J. C Leach. There, the jury heard from William Lodge that he had once attended a funfair with Blanche, her mother and two of her sisters. While there, Blanche had expressed a desire to shoot at a couple of the rifle ranges and had proved herself to be an excellent shot. From this, the inquest jury inferred that she had deliberately aimed the gun at the back of her mother's head – in other words, the shooting had been no accident.

The jury returned a verdict of wilful murder against Blanche, who was not present to hear her fate. However, she did appear before magistrates, appearing to pay little attention to the proceedings unless a name was mentioned that was known to her. When this happened, she would visibly

Broadmoor Asylum. (*Author's collection*)

start, staring around her with wild eyes. At all times, she clutched a well-worn Bible, and when asked by the magistrates if she wanted to speak, she replied, 'I have nothing to say.' Both the coroner and the magistrates committed her for trial at the next Dorset Assizes.

She was remanded to prison to await her trial but was so obviously insane that after an investigation initiated by the secretary of state, she was transferred to Charminster Lunatic Asylum on 28 November 1877. On 17 April 1878 she was moved from Charminster to Broadmoor Criminal Lunatic Asylum, still believing that she was under direct instructions from God to rid the world of sinners. By 1879 it became evident that she had contracted tuberculosis, from which she died, aged twenty-seven, on 14 January 1880.

Frederick Marshall: 1854–1887

On the night of 21/22 December 1884 seventeen-year-old servant Laura Wilson was asleep in her bedroom at Beresford Street, Woolwich, when somebody climbed through the window and stabbed her. Laura managed to stagger to the bedroom occupied by her employer, tobacconist Sarah Hewitt, and cried out, 'I am stabbed, stabbed to the heart', before collapsing. Laura's father was a carver and gilder, who occupied the shop adjoining Mrs Hewitt's premises. He had a large family and had welcomed his neighbour taking on Laura as a servant and giving her a room in her house. Now, alerted by Mrs Hewitt's frantic hammering on their party wall, Wilson rushed next door to find his daughter lying mortally wounded. Although a doctor, Dr Ingleden, was summoned urgently, by the time he arrived Laura was already dead from the single stab wound in her left breast that had penetrated her heart.

Suspicion immediately fell on twenty-one-year-old Frederick Marshall. He had been courting Laura until she broke off their engagement because of his jealousy of her relationship with a family friend named Charles 'Charlie' Merritt, who was the son of Laura's mother's second cousin. As well as visiting the shop daily for tobacco since Laura ended the relationship, Marshall had been seen hanging round Mrs Hewitt's house and scaling a garden wall so that he could look in on his former fiancée. On one occasion Mrs Hewitt even found him hiding in her coal cellar.

Laura had been so keen to avoid Marshall that she had decided to leave her employment with Mrs Hewitt – on the day of her death – to take up a new position. Marshall had also written a number of vitriolic letters to Laura, in which he referred to her as 'a deceitful to-faced young woman' (sic). It was evident from the content of the letters that Laura and Frederick had enjoyed a sexual relationship, which Laura eventually admitted to her employer had occurred under Mrs Hewitt's roof. Marshall threatened to reveal this to both Charlie and Laura's father unless she wrote back to him. He wrote: 'I feel nearly mad to think all our days and hours are all spent for nothing. I made up my mind to have you … from your ever true lover Fred xxx'. In another letter, Fred wrote: 'I am not very well. I feel nearly mad when I think of you.'

Marshall also wrote letters to Laura's father, William Wilson, who had initially approved of his daughter's engagement, believing Marshall – who was a Sunday School teacher – to be a respectable young man from a good family. However, he gradually changed his opinion of his daughter's fiancé, finding him to be lazy and a liar, and ordered Laura to break off the engagement. When Marshall was found in Mrs Hewitt's coal cellar, William confronted him, suggesting that his intentions had either been to burgle Mrs Hewitt or to seduce his daughter. Although Marshall claimed that his trespass was 'just a lark', William warned his daughter to steer well clear of him, refusing to allow him into his home.

Marshall immediately penned another long, rambling letter to Laura's father:

Dear Wilson,
Hoping these few lines will find you quite well, as they leave me half dead. I write hoping that you will forgive me for the past. If you knew what I was there for, you would not keep me outside. I meant no harm to Laura. It was only to have a lark with her and get my supper – as you know, she gave me food over the fence. If I had meant any harm to her, I could have done it without going in there to get copped. I did not think Mrs Hewitt would have taken it like she did or I would not have gone there. Didn't I do the same in your place one night? If I meant any harm, the Lord strike me dead before you get this letter […] You will be punished for it someday […] I mean to have her, dear Wilson – I know no-one else will. She'd have me back but for Charlie – I will swing for it if I see her with him.

A post-mortem examination on Laura's body, carried out by Dr Ingleden, showed a single stab wound just above her left nipple, which had penetrated her chest to a depth of five inches and entered her heart.

An inquest on Laura's death was opened by coroner Mr Carter, who heard that Frederick had approached Laura's sister Mary Ann several times in the weeks before the murder, trying to get her to persuade her sister to take him back. Mary Ann stated that she had indeed spoken to Laura on Marshall's behalf, but that Laura had refused to have anything further to do with him. Mary Ann had relayed this message to Marshall, who had told her that he intended to 'swing for' Charlie. According to Mary Ann, Charlie seemed very fond of her sister, but his feelings were not reciprocated.

Sarah Hewitt told the inquest that on the night of the murder, she was feeding her baby when she heard scuffling noises coming from Laura's bedroom. Mrs Hewitt shouted to ask if everything was all right, at which Laura burst into her bedroom, bleeding heavily. As she was lifting Laura from the floor, Mrs Hewitt had heard more scuffling, as though someone was escaping from the girl's room.

An examination of the front of Mrs Hewitt's house showed a chunk of plaster missing from the outside wall, which had fallen onto the pavement below. Laura's window was about sixteen feet from the ground, and it was evident that whoever climbed through it had first mounted a set of railings beneath the window, before scrambling onto a narrow ledge and hauling himself into the room.

In the aftermath of the murder, police went to interview Marshall, who was described as 'a young man of powerful frame and mild countenance'. 'Nobody saw me do it,' Marshall insisted, adding that he was only under suspicion because he was known to carry a dagger, but he had recently lost it and had no idea what had become of it. Police searched Marshall but did not find any weapons or any signs of blood about his person or clothing, although he did have a fresh graze on one wrist.

It emerged that Marshall had been in love with another woman prior to meeting Laura, and when that relationship ended, he had tried to commit suicide by taking poison. He had also tried to purchase a revolver, telling Elizabeth Youlton – a friend of Laura's – that if he found her with Charlie he would put two bullets in both of them and two in himself. When he was unable to obtain a gun, he made do with buying a dagger, telling Elizabeth it was 'for Charlie'.

The inquest found a verdict of wilful murder against Frederick Marshall and he was scheduled for trial at The Old Bailey. However, while incarcerated in Clerkenwell Gaol, the medical officer there noted that Marshall suffered from constant pains in his head and believed that he failed to understand the gravity of the accusations against him. 'He has no comprehension of moral obligation,' stated the prison doctor's report, which was forwarded to the Home Secretary, who immediately asked two doctors to examine Marshall and give their opinion on his sanity.

Broadmoor Asylum. (*Author's collection*)

When Marshall was found to be insane, his trial was cancelled, and on 3 February 1885 he was controversially sent directly to Broadmoor Criminal Lunatic Asylum, thus forfeiting his right to a fair trial. Questions about this decision were raised in Parliament, since the fundamental ethos of the British Justice System was that prisoners were assumed to be innocent until found otherwise by trial. Thus, by depriving Marshall of a trial, it could be said that an innocent man had been sent to an institution for the criminally insane. Although it was argued that Marshall should have stood trial before being declared insane, the Home Secretary's decision remained unchanged.

While at Broadmoor, Marshall proved himself very useful, helping on the wards, and occupying himself with music in the evenings. In November 1888 he made a brief escape from the asylum but was very quickly recaptured. He remained at Broadmoor until his death, aged thirty-three, from an abscess of the brain on 22 February 1897.

Roderick Edward McClean (or Maclean): 1854–1921

On 2 March 1882 Her Majesty Queen Victoria left Buckingham Palace accompanied by her daughter, Princess Beatrice, and their entourage. The royal party proceeded to Paddington Station, where they caught a train to Windsor.

On arriving at Windsor, the queen climbed into the royal carriage for the conclusion of her journey to the castle. A small crowd of people had gathered to cheer the royal party, including a number of boys from Eton College, one of whom noticed a man pushing to the front of the crowd and raising his arms. Realising that the man had a gun, which he was pointing at the queen, the boy gave a loud yell of warning.

When the man fired towards the royal carriage, he was pounced on by three Eton pupils, who attacked him with their umbrellas and knocked him to the ground, sending the shots intended for the queen into the cobbles, close to the hooves of the horses pulling her carriage. There are various descriptions of the gun (or guns) used in the attempted regicide, with some contemporary newspapers referring to it as German pinfire revolver, some as an American Colt revolver, some as a cheap Belgian replica and others as a 'toy gun.' Some reports suggest that two different pistols were used; some state that the gunman fired one shot, while others state that he fired twice.

Whatever weapon or weapons were used, the shooter fortunately missed his intended target and the royal carriage drove off without any injury to its occupants or the horses. Meanwhile, the would-be assassin was hauled to his feet and handed over to Police Superintendent Hayes and PC Alexander, who happened to be standing nearby. Twenty-eight-year-old Roderick Edward McClean offered no resistance, asking the police 'Please, don't hurt me', but he was in mortal danger of being lynched by the patriotic crowd. He was eventually placed in a cab and conveyed to the nearest police station, where he was searched. Twelve bullets were found on his person, while his gun still had two loaded chambers.

While being questioned, he was said to show no signs of madness and police later said that he talked like a sane man. The only explanation he could offer for his actions was that he did it because he was starving. He told the police that his intention had been only to frighten the queen and alarm the public, to draw attention to his financial problems. A letter found in his pocket read: 'I should not have done this crime had you, as you should have done, allowed the 10s per week instead of offering the insultingly small sum of 6s per week and expecting me to live on it. So, you perceive the great good a little money might have done, had you not treated me as a fool and set me more than ever against those bloated aristocrats ruled by the old lady, Mrs. Vic., who is a licensed robber in all senses.'

Although the police initially believed McClean to be sane and had even commented on his astuteness at questioning witnesses at his first appearance before magistrates, by his second appearance at Windsor Police Court, some facts had begun to emerge about his past. Having come from the workhouse at Brighton, McClean had been living in Portsmouth for a few weeks when he decided to walk to London, leaving his lodgings to do so on 23 February.

His landlord, Mr Hucker, believed him to be quite insane. McClean represented himself as a writer and a poet, although he spent most of his time playing a concertina and talking about politics. He was filthy in his personal habits, and on the rare occasions when he could be persuaded to wash himself, would merely dip a corner of a towel in water and wipe his face with it. He didn't eat properly, and out of pity his landlord had occasionally given him meals. He would sit still for long periods, punctuated only by bursts of maniacal laughter.

The contemporary newspapers made much of McClean's physical appearance, describing him as 'having the features of a man not in his right mind'. 'The forehead is low, but broad,' reported journalists attending the magistrate's court, 'with dark hair closely cropped along the top and the contour of the face slopes quickly down to an exceedingly narrow chin, while the development of the skull at the back of the head seems abnormally high. The eyes are large, without expression and with a peculiar nervous tremor about their corners, which gave an appearance of unnatural feebleness to that part of the face. The nose is straight but afflicted with the same feeble twitchings that characterise the eyes and sometimes, when an attempt to speak is made, the lips are unable to form the words.'

McClean's own father was afraid of him, and in 1874 had made a formal complaint to Henry Essex, the relieving officer for the parish of Kensington. Hector McClean apparently went in fear of his life, while his son secreted knives about his person and hid in corners, muttering threats that he would kill his father. Roderick refused to work, but when visited at home by a doctor at Essex's behest, it was decided that his condition was not quite severe enough to admit him to an asylum. However, in June 1880 he was certified insane and spent time in the Somerset and Bath Lunatic Asylum in Wells, only being released in July 1881. The reason for his admittance to the asylum was given as homicidal mania and paranoia; he believed that everyone in England was conspiring to hurt him. 'They only pretend to be friendly to annoy and to cause untold misery,' he wrote to his

Lord Chief Justice Coleridge. (*Author's collection*)

sister Caroline. He had apparently told doctors that he could not control his impulses and that he would certainly commit murder, and the more difficulties that were placed in his way, the more victims there would be. During his time in Wells, McClean constantly complained of pains in his head and told Caroline that he would probably have to murder someone for 'wearing blue'.

After his appearance before magistrates, McClean's case was forwarded to the Reading Assizes, where he appeared before Baron Huddleston and Lord Coleridge on the rare charge of High Treason, for intending to shoot and murder the queen. If found guilty, McClean could face the death penalty, but after hearing evidence from several doctors, Huddleston directed the jury to find McClean not guilty due to insanity, which, after a few minutes' deliberation, they duly did. He was sentenced to be kept in strict custody until Her Majesty's pleasure be known. He was admitted to Broadmoor Criminal Lunatic Asylum on 8 May 1882, where he remained until his death from apoplexy, aged sixty-seven, on 3 June 1921.

It was said that Queen Victoria was annoyed at what she saw as McClean's 'acquittal' and pressed Parliament to introduce verdict of guilty but insane, believing that this would act as a deterrent to attacks by mentally ill individuals. This resulted in the 'Trial of Lunatics Act' of 1883.

Frederick Ernest Page: 1856–1886

Twenty-four-year-old Fanny 'Ann' Pleasant Clarke worked as a domestic servant on a farm at Brantham, near Ipswich. She was said to be a very pretty brunette and also to be rather better educated than most girls in service, so it was hardly surprising that she attracted the attentions of nineteen-year-old Frederick Ernest Page, a respectable farmer's son. Although Page worked as a clerk for a wine merchant in Colchester and no longer lived with his parents at Brantham Hall, he returned there most Saturday evenings after work, then on Sundays he would go out walking with Ann. Whenever he was away from home, the two would write to each other.

Their courtship continued for a year or so, yet while Frederick was living and working away from home, his older brother, Robert Everett Page, was not and Ann found herself falling for him. Eventually, she wrote to Frederick, admitting that she preferred his brother and ending their romance.

Frederick was outraged, and on his next visit home, on 8 August 1875, he confronted Ann and Robert as they were out walking together, demanding that she return all the letters he had written to her. In a fit of anger, he accused Ann of having sexual relations not only with him, but also with another young man and with her employer, William Green. This accusation greatly distressed her, so much so that she returned to her employment in floods of tears, eventually fainting in distress. She debated whether to send Frederick's letters to his father, but eventually bundled them up and sent them to his lodgings in Colchester. On receiving them, Frederick wrote back, apologising for insulting her and hoping that they could part as friends. He asked to meet her one last time, and Robert, who had already proposed to Ann, gave his consent, although he urged her to keep the meeting as brief as possible.

On the evening of 15 August, Ann and Frederick went out for a walk. Just before nine o'clock, William Green, and his yard man, Samuel Smith, were standing in Green's farmyard when they heard a noise that sounded like someone hitting a haystack several times. A few minutes later, after Green went indoors, Smith saw Ann staggering across the yard. He assisted her into the house, calling for Green, who found Ann slumped in a chair in the kitchen, apparently unconscious, her dress covered with dust. Her face was swollen and misshapen and she was bleeding copiously from several head wounds. Green tried without success to get her to drink some brandy and also questioned her about what had happened to her, but she was incapable of answering. Green then searched her pockets and found the letter from Frederick Page arranging to meet her, which he later handed to the police.

A doctor was summoned but surgeon Frederick Manning was entertaining visitors at home and so sent his assistant, Mr Holman, who reported back that there seemed to have been a lover's tiff and a girl had been hit over the head. Since Ann's injuries weren't believed to be life threatening, Green decided to delay sending for the police, believing that Ann would most probably wake up in the morning and be able to tell them what had happened to her.

Manning himself didn't see Ann until the next afternoon, and at his behest the police were finally notified. She lay in bed, apparently sleeping peacefully. 'I attempted to rouse her by bawling into her ear, but I could produce no effect,' Manning later told the coroner. However, when he pinched her, Manning believed that Ann mumbled 'Don't do that'. Initially, the surgeon believed that Ann's wounds were caused by her being hit with a sharp instrument such as a bradawl, but she never regained consciousness and died on 18 August. On conducting a post-mortem examination, Manning found that she had been shot. Two bullets remained lodged in her brain and a third had passed clean through her head, leaving an entry and an exit wound. Manning also noticed extensive bruising on Ann's face, arms, elbows, and the inside of her knees, which he surmised were the result of her either being hit or having fallen over

Police officers managed to follow a trail of blood leading from Mr Green's farm to a spot about 400 yards away, where a large pool of blood marked the scene of the shooting, and everyone was astonished that Ann could have made it back from there to the farm after having been shot multiple times in the head. Given the letter that Mr Green had handed over, and the fact that numerous witnesses had seen him out walking with Ann on the night in question, Frederick immediately became the number one suspect. The police went to speak to him, and a search of his house revealed a coat and shirt that were spotted with blood, along with two blood-soaked handkerchiefs. Frederick was arrested and charged with attempted murder, refusing to answer any questions put to him by the police.

Reading between the lines of the reports in the contemporary newspapers suggests that Frederick confessed to shooting Ann; first to his brother, then to his parents. After Ann was shot, Frederick returned home at just after nine o'clock and retired to bed. Noticing that he had a rather wild look in his eyes, Robert feared for Ann's safety and began to urge his brother to tell him what had happened. 'For God's sake, tell me,' he pleaded. 'It will be much better for you.' Whatever was said that night, it prompted Frederick's father to visit the murder scene, after which he took possession of a revolver in a case from Frederick, which was still loaded with one bullet. However, at both the inquest held by coroner Mr H. B. Ross and at the magistrates' hearing, Frederick's statement was supressed, as it was thought that it may have been made under pressure. What was revealed was that a man matching Frederick's description had purchased a gun in Colchester on 10 August and Frederick had later shown a revolver to a colleague at work, claiming to need it for protection when he walked home from the station late on Saturday nights.

Although Frederick's counsel, Mr Philbrick, made vigorous attempts to quash any evidence that might implicate his client in Ann Clarke's death, the inquest jury found that Ann had been wilfully murdered by Frederick Page and he was committed for trial on the coroner's warrant. Holman was chastised by the coroner for not notifying the police about the attack on the young servant, but claimed he didn't know that he had the authority to do so. Soon after the termination of the proceedings, Ann was buried at the churchyard in Earl Stonham. Her funeral was made all the more poignant because it followed that of her sister, who died two years earlier from typhoid fever.

Confined in the county gaol at Ipswich awaiting his trial, Frederick began to show signs of insanity. He had a major speech impediment, which, prior to his arrest, had led to him becoming very depressed, believing that he would never make anything of himself. On at least one occasion, his depression had

Church at Earl Stonham, where Ann Clarke was buried. (*Author's collection*)

led him to attempt suicide by putting his head on a railway line, although he was pulled clear by a porter. On the orders of prison doctors, he was removed to Broadmoor Criminal Lunatic Asylum on 11 January 1876, and, unable to obtain a progress report on his condition, his solicitor had no option but to prepare for trial in the usual way.

When the Suffolk Lent Assizes opened in April 1876, Lord Chief Justice Coleridge told the jury that he had been informed that Page was in no fit state to stand trial. Although the grand jury returned a true bill against him, Coleridge postponed the proceedings until such time as Page was capable of pleading to the indictment, and he was ordered to be detained as a criminal lunatic during Her Majesty's pleasure.

Frederick Page never became capable of pleading. He died in Broadmoor on 28 August 1886 from chronic inflammation of the stomach and bowels. He was thirty years old.

Emma Jackson: (approximately) 1859–1888

On 18 May 1880 a woman went into the bakery in Nelson Street, Greenwich, and bought two buns. Owner Matthew Crawford watched her hand over half a crown to his son to pay for her purchases. However, when the boy passed him the coin, Crawford instantly recognised it as a forgery. He told the woman that the coin was 'bad', at which she told him 'Break it.' Crawford immediately broke it into three pieces, which he handed back to the woman, who remarked that it was a cruel and wicked thing to pass such things on to innocent people, as it might get them into trouble.

Crawford sought out a policeman and spoke to him about the counterfeit coin, giving a detailed description of the young woman who had tried to pay for her buns with it. PC Steven Sheath set off to look for her, and as he was doing so, he was approached by Thomas Maloney, the barman at The Cricketers' Arms pub, which was about four doors from Crawford's bakery. Maloney told Sheath that a young woman had ordered half a pint of mild and bitter, which she paid for with a fake florin. Maloney returned the coin to the woman, who then paid with good money.

Meanwhile, George Stephenson, a park keeper at Greenwich Park, had approached another policeman to show him a suspicious parcel, which he had just watched a youth and a young woman burying in the park. PC George Wilson unwrapped the package, finding it to contain counterfeit coins – twelve two-shilling pieces and seven half-crowns – each individually wrapped in tissue paper then rolled up in brown paper. Wilson asked Stephenson to take the package back to the park and rebury it, keeping a close eye on the spot in case it was reclaimed.

By now, PC Sheath had located his suspect coming out of Greenwich Park. He followed her as she walked past Mr Crawford's shop to Greenwich Pier, where she waited for about half an hour, before moving on to Church Street. Having looked into three different pubs as she passed them, she returned to the park. Sheath had met up with Wilson, who had shown him the spot where the coins had been buried, and the woman took a seat about sixty yards away. When she left the park, Sheath tailed her down Silver Street, where she was joined by a man and another woman. The three went into a pub, at which point Sheath sent for George Stephenson to identify them. When he confirmed that the man and one of the women were the same people he had seen burying the parcel of coins, Sheath stepped forward and arrested Emma Jackson for uttering a counterfeit half-crown coin and also for being involved in burying a quantity of coins in Greenwich Park.

Twenty-two-year-old Emma swore she knew nothing about any bad coins. She claimed to have come to Greenwich for a holiday and met the youth, whose name was James Edgar Thompson. Magistrates committed Emma and sixteen-year-old Thompson for trial at the Assizes.

They appeared at the Central Criminal Court on consecutive days. Thompson, who was tried first, pleaded guilty to having counterfeit coin in his possession with intent to utter it and was sentenced to six months' imprisonment. However, Emma was recognised as someone who had committed the same offence before in both 1873 and 1876, when she was tried under the alias Ellen Blown. In 1876 she had been sentenced to five years' imprisonment and had not long gained her freedom when she reoffended.

At her trial for feloniously uttering counterfeit coin, Emma stuck to her story of meeting Thompson while she was on holiday. Mr Crawford and Mr Maloney both testified for the prosecution, as did park keeper Stephenson, who told the court that he had hidden behind a tree and watched as Thompson kicked up a divot of turf in the park, hid the package beneath it, then stamped it down again, before urinating up against the wall nearby as if marking the spot. Told by PC Wilson to rebury the parcel, Stephenson described hiding behind the tree as the man returned, looked at the place where it was buried then walked away. He also saw Emma Jackson sitting near to where the coins were concealed, then shortly afterwards he was sent for to identify her to the two policemen.

Emma was found guilty and sentenced to seven years' imprisonment, which she initially served in Fulham Prison. However, on 25 February 1884 it was decided that she was insane and an application was made to transfer her to Broadmoor Criminal Lunatic Asylum.

Emma's sentence expired while she was an inmate at Broadmoor, but by then she was judged to be too unwell to be moved. At the time of her death from general paralysis on 1 February 1888, she was no longer a criminal lunatic.

The Terrace, Broadmoor. (*Author's collection*)

Richard Millar Archer: 1859–1937

Richard Millar Archer of Dundee had aspirations to become an actor, and when his parents moved to London in 1875, Richard followed them. Adopting the stage name Richard Arthur Prince, he began appearing in small roles in the London theatres.

One of the leading actors of the time was William Charles James Lewin, who worked under the name William Terriss, and he soon befriended Prince, putting his name forward for roles in various productions. However, contrary to his own view of his skills, Prince was not a particularly good actor and often had to rely on the Actors' Benevolent Fund to survive, or return to Dundee, where he would work as a labourer. Despondent at his lack of roles, Prince increasingly abused alcohol and gradually became ever more mentally unstable.

On 23 October 1897 Prince replied to an advertisement for a theatre company in Newcastle and was engaged to play small parts for a weekly wage of 25s. However, the company manager, Ralph Croydon, quickly became disillusioned with the newly hired Prince, who had obviously exaggerated his experience in order to get the job. Croydon found Prince incapable of playing any part – he found it impossible to learn his lines and was over dramatic in his acting style. Prince told Croydon that his brain 'had gone wrong'.

Finding it impossible to work with Prince, Croydon fired him, only to have Prince turn up at his lodgings the following day demanding to be paid. Croydon refused to give him any money, at which Prince flew into a temper, saying that he should never have left the Adelphi Theatre and would still have been there had it not been for that 'dirty dog William Terriss'.

Croydon told Prince that he must be mad to talk like that. 'The world will ring with my madness before long,' Prince assured him.

Prince returned to London and made further claims for financial assistance from the Actors' Benevolent Fund. On 13 December he and Terriss argued in Terriss's dressing room at the Adelphi, with Prince convinced that the more experienced actor was somehow conspiring to prevent him from getting parts.

On 16 December Prince was told that he was not entitled to any more pay-outs from the Benevolent Fund. That evening, Terriss and his lifelong friend Henry Graves were approaching a side door of the Adelphi Theatre. As Terriss fumbled in his pocket for his keys, Prince rushed across the street towards him and struck him twice on the back. Terriss turned round and Prince struck a third blow on his chest.

The Adelphi Theatre. (*Author's Collection*)

Victim Mr Terriss. (*Author's collection*)

Terriss moaned, 'My God, I am stabbed. Arrest that man!' before falling to the floor. His attacker fled, with Graves in pursuit. When Graves spotted a policeman, he called to him, 'I charge this man with stabbing Mr Terriss.' PC John Bragg took hold of Prince's arm and began to walk him to the police station, accompanied by Mr Graves.

As they walked along, Graves asked, 'What made you do such a dreadful thing?'

'In revenge. He blackmailed me for ten years,' replied Prince. 'I have given him due warnings plenty of times. I should either have to die in the street or have my revenge.'

On arrival at Bow Street Police Station, Prince was asked what had happened to the knife he had used to stab Terriss, and he produced it from his coat pocket, still wet with blood. When news reached the police that Terriss was dead, Prince was charged with murdering him. Prince listened to the charge quietly and calmly, asking only that somebody should notify his sister of his situation. When a message came back to him that his sister wanted nothing to do with him, he commented that it was obvious that she was in league with Terriss in blackmailing him. He told the police that he had asked his sister for money about an hour before the murder and she had told him that she would rather see him dead in the gutter than give him a farthing. 'Had she given me ten shillings, this would never have happened,' mused Prince.

A post-mortem examination on Terriss revealed three stab wounds, along with a superficial cut on his wrist. One wound was near the spine, a second in the left shoulder and the third – the fatal wound – penetrated his heart. All the injuries had been inflicted with a thin knife, using great force.

Prince was sent for trial at The Old Bailey before Mr Justice Channell, where he initially pleaded 'Guilty but with the greatest provocation' but was ultimately persuaded by his counsel to plead not guilty. In his defence, his mother claimed that he had suffered sun stroke as a young baby, which had permanently affected his mind. Mrs Archer claimed that her son was always angry, passionate, jealous, and bad tempered and that he accused her of tampering with and poisoning his food. At one time, he told his mother that she was the Virgin Mary and that he was therefore Lord Jesus Christ. Describing her son as vain and having very high self-esteem, Mrs Archer revealed that Richard had a half-brother who was 'never right in the head' and a brother, James who had been admitted to Fisherton Asylum after falling out of a coach and landing on his head. The chief medical officer at Fisherton was called and told the court that James had a tendency towards insanity before the accident.

Prince's brother, Harry, confirmed his mother's evidence, adding that his brother frequently accused different people of blackmailing him and had attacked him several times – once with a poker and a knife – for no particular reason.

Theatrical manager Mr Alliston had also employed Prince and had been peppered with accusatory letters and postcards in which Prince referred to him as a 'hell hound' and a 'Judas'. Some of the cards were read out in court. In one, Prince wrote: 'What am I to understand by your silence? I demand my reference. No more blackmailing for me. If you do not send it at once, I will fight again for it in London'. A second read: 'Another thing I will tell you, you cannot fight an actor with money or he would have horsewhipped you for blackmailing him for seven years. I am not a woman: a Highlander is Richard A. Prince.'

Dr Henry Charles Bastian had visited Prince twice in Holloway Prison and had also read letters he had sent. He believed that Prince was of unsound mind and would consequently be safer in an asylum. Bastian described Prince as excitable and often incoherent, suffering from delusions of persecution. Although Prince believed that numerous people were conspiring against him, he believed that Terriss was the main culprit, sending instructions and directions all around the country, and therefore Terriss's murder was an act of justice. The doctor described the killing as 'the climax of Prince's mental disease', saying, 'A man with that amount of mental aberration under trying circumstances … would have very little control over his body.'

Doctor, lecturer and 'demonstrator of psychology' Theophilus Bulkeley Hyslop concurred with Bastian's conclusions that Prince was suffering from delusional insanity, adding that Prince had told him that in killing Terriss he was carrying out God's will. There was some question in court as to whether or not Prince might be feigning mental illness, but the doctor at Holloway Prison, James Scott, was adamant that this was not the case. After a short deliberation, the jury concluded that while Prince was well aware of what he was doing and to whom he was doing it, according to the medical evidence he was insane and thus could not be held responsible for his actions. Prince was therefore ordered to be detained until Her Majesty's pleasure be known.

He was sent to Broadmoor Criminal Lunatic Asylum, where he soon became involved in organising the inmates' entertainment and conducting the asylum's orchestra. He remained there for the rest of his life, dying, aged seventy-seven, from natural causes on 25 January 1937.

James Kelly: 1860–1927

James Kelly was an illegitimate child, born to fifteen-year-old Sarah Kelly, who quickly abandoned him to the care of her own mother, Teresa. In 1870 Sarah married John Allen, a master mariner. However, the marriage was short-lived, as John died less than four years later, leaving his widow a house and a share of a ship. Sadly, Sarah died only two months after her husband, leaving James more than £25,000, to be held in trust until his twenty-fifth birthday – the equivalent of almost £3,000,000 today.

After leaving school, Kelly began an apprenticeship as an upholsterer, and shortly afterwards, his grandmother – who he had always believed to be his mother – told him the truth about his parentage and about the legacy in trust for him. Kelly immediately withdrew from his apprenticeship, choosing instead to study bookkeeping and clerical skills at Dr Robert Hurworth's Commercial Academy in New Brighton.

Once qualified, Kelly began working for a Liverpool pawnbroker, Isaac H. Jones. At around this time, he began to experience mood swings and to act irrationally. He decided to return to upholstering and moved to London to seek a job, but fell prey to the temptations of city life, spending his time drinking heavily and visiting prostitutes, picking up casual work wherever he could find it.

In 1881 Kelly met and fell in love with Sarah Brider, and in March of the following year he moved in with the Brider family at their home 21 Cottage Street, City Road, St Luke's, sharing a room with another lodger. His new-found romance led him to cut down on his drinking and eventually he and Sarah became intimate. However, it is reported that the couple's attempts at intercourse were a failure, with Kelly, who had only previously slept with prostitutes, believing Sarah to be in some way deformed.

Kelly became ever more depressed at his inability to deflower Sarah and his mood swings grew ever wilder. Sarah began to withdraw her affections, and sensing her becoming distant, Kelly proposed marriage. After a considerable delay, she agreed to become his wife. However, while waiting for Sarah to make her mind up, Kelly discovered that he had caught venereal disease. Afraid to admit this to Sarah and her family, he determined to treat it himself, refusing to seek medical advice and telling the Briders that he was suffering from a condition called 'upholsterers' itch' to explain the medication in his room.

In April 1883 Kelly found a permanent job as an upholsterer but was sacked after just two months as his employer felt that he was 'obviously not right in the head'. Pushed into setting a date for the wedding, Kelly managed to get some money from his trust fund and he and Sarah were married on 4 June 1883. On the same day, Kelly started a new job. Although the newlyweds moved in with Mr and Mrs Brider, they did not share a bedroom. Kelly continued to sleep with the other lodger, and it is believed that the marriage was never consummated. Still convinced that his wife had a deformity, Kelly demanded that she consult a doctor. Sarah asked her parents' advice, and when her father, John, spoke to his son-in-law about the matter, Kelly revealed that Sarah had told him that she had previously been molested by her uncle.

Kelly continued to brood about his lack of a sexual relationship with his wife and eventually decided that he and Sarah needed to move out of the Briders' home and set up on their own. To that end he withdrew some more money from his trust fund. However, while he was away in Liverpool arranging this, Mrs Brider found the syringe and drugs with which he was treating himself for venereal disease. On his return to London, she and Sarah confronted Kelly, who flew into a rage and accused Sarah of being a prostitute and infecting him, suggesting that she and her mother tricked him into marriage to get their hands on his inheritance.

It was Sarah's birthday on 18 June 1883 and a remorseful Kelly decided to take her out to celebrate. However, Sarah was almost an hour late returning from her job at De La Rue Stationers. She ignored Kelly and told her mother that she was feeling unwell. Kelly instantly lost his temper, screaming at Sarah, dragging her into the kitchen and threatening to stab her with the carving knife unless she told him where she had been. When a terrified Sarah told him that she had been to purchase some quinine for him, Kelly immediately calmed down.

The couple had another row on 21 June, with Sarah locking herself in her room to escape her husband's ranting. Kelly broke down the door, all the while screaming at his wife, calling her a whore. Sarah told him that she never wanted to see him again. 'You will have something to answer for before your God!' Kelly yelled at her.

'And so will you,' Sarah retorted. 'You have called me a whore.'

Kelly immediately denied having said any such thing, telling her that he was going to make sure that she gave up her job so that he could keep an eye on her at all times.

'Go away from me. I never want to see you anymore,' Sarah sobbed, at which Kelly suddenly became contrite and begged her to forgive him.

'You won't leave me. I'll stop you from going,' he insisted.

'I can never forgive you,' Sarah told him. Hearing this, Kelly sprang at his wife, knocking her to the floor, and appeared to dig something into her neck, just below her ear. 'He is murdering me, mother. He is murdering me,' Sarah cried, at which her mother grabbed Kelly by the hair and tried to pull him away from her daughter.

'You villain! What are you at? What are you doing?' Mrs Brider challenged him, but Kelly brushed her aside without speaking, hurting her arm before running out of the room and locking himself in his bedroom.

St Bartholomew's Hospital, where Sarah was treated. (*Author's collection*)

'Mother, I am dying,' Sarah groaned. Mrs Brider rushed out of the house, shouting for help. Kelly was arrested by PC Forbes James and charged with stabbing his wife with intent to murder. 'I don't know what I am about. I must be mad,' he insisted.

Sarah was sent by cab to St Bartholomew's Hospital, where, with her husband present under police guard, she was able to give a deposition to magistrates before dying on 24 June. Sarah stated that she and Kelly had begun arguing in the street about some boots. Sarah told him that she didn't want to be married to him anymore, to which he replied, 'When we get home, we'll see.' Then, within minutes of arriving home, he pulled a knife from his pocket and stabbed her without warning.

A post-mortem examination carried out by house surgeon Hugh Rayner revealed a single three-inch-deep stab wound about two inches below Sarah's left ear, which had partially divided her spinal cord. The wound had been made by a blade, and, according to Rayner, considerable force had been used to inflict it.

Not knowing that his wife had died, Kelly wrote letters from Clerkenwell Prison to both Sarah and her mother. To Sarah he wrote professing his undying love for her: 'I feel so wretched and have such pains in my head that I have no power to think.' The letter continued to express Kelly's sorrow and remorse for stabbing her, stating that he had meant only to frighten her, but something had come over him and he went mad. 'I loved you too much and you drove me mad,' Kelly concluded.

On Sarah's death, coroner Mr S. F. Langham held an inquest at St Bartholomew's Hospital at which the jury returned a verdict of wilful murder against Kelly, who was sent for trial at the Old Bailey. Prior to his trial he appeared before magistrates and made a statement: 'I can say that I did it in my madness. I did not know what I was doing. I was led to do it by certain things that was said and done. I loved my wife and I love her still; she had many faults, which I was not going to mention for my wife's sake and, as I had caused great trouble in the family, I did not want to cause more. I shall tell all now, as I can see a great many lies have been told and false witnesses brought up. That is all I have to say.'

At Kelly's trial the main witnesses were the Brider family, the policemen involved in Kelly's arrest, a coachman who had witnessed the couple arguing in the street, and surgeon Hugh Rayner. It was suggested that Kelly had suffered from an abscess in his head that had burst and discharged through his ears, but according to Oliver Treadwell, the assistant surgeon at Clerkenwell Prison, this was the first he had heard of it. Having seen him numerous times during his incarceration, Kelly had always conducted himself as a rational and sane man and Treadwell had never noticed any symptoms of insanity.

The jury deliberated for forty-five minutes before returning to pronounce James Kelly guilty of murder, although they recommended mercy. Sentence of death was duly pronounced but a petition was quickly raised appealing for clemency, which was reputedly signed by both Mr and Mrs Brider. Although the Home Secretary initially refused to consider postponing the execution, which was set for 20 August 1883, it was arranged for Kelly to be examined by the superintendent of Broadmoor Criminal Lunatic Asylum, Dr William Orange, who declared him to be insane. His sentence was therefore commuted to one of detention during Her Majesty's pleasure and he was sent to Broadmoor.

Kelly apparently made the most of his time in Broadmoor, playing violin in the asylum band and working in the gardens, although he made no secret of his intentions to escape when he got the chance. In 1888 he fashioned a duplicate key from scrap metal, and on 23 January he used the key to access the gardens at night, scaled a wall and escaped.

Kelly managed to evade recapture for many years, during which time he travelled the world, either picking up casual work as an upholsterer or working as a seaman to pay his passage. In 1896 he went to the British Consulate in New Orleans and gave himself up to the authorities. He was placed on a ship bound for Liverpool, where he was supposed to be met by staff from Broadmoor. However, the SS *Capella* arrived in Liverpool a day earlier than scheduled and having waited around for some time to be arrested, Kelly left. After three years working as a coach trimmer in Guildford, Kelly boarded the SS *Beechdale* for Vancouver. Once there, he again handed himself in to the British Consulate, but this time nobody from Broadmoor seemed interested.

He spent the next few years either working as a coach trimmer or an upholsterer in England or travelling to and from America, and in 1907 he was officially discharged from Broadmoor in his absence. Yet, on 11 February 1927, Kelly presented himself at the asylum asking to be readmitted. By that time, he was deaf and unwell, and although staff at Broadmoor doubted him when he told them his name, his identity was checked and he was allowed back through the gates.

'I have no friends and am all alone in the world,' he told warders.' I have wandered all these years feeling that I am a fugitive who might be pounced upon by any policeman I passed. I am getting feeble now through constant fear and I dread the idea of dying alone. I am very tired and want to die with my friends.'

Indeed, Kelly did not die alone. On 17 September 1929, aged sixty-nine, he succumbed to double pneumonia. During his period of freedom, he was strongly suspected of being Jack the Ripper, since he had a long-held grudge against the prostitutes who had infected him with venereal disease. At the height of the Ripper murders in 1888, when Kelly was allegedly in London, his former home in Cottage Lane was visited by the Metropolitan Police, who questioned Mrs Brider about his whereabouts. However, in spite of the fact that there were several prostitutes murdered in a similar fashion in New York while Kelly was known to be in the area, there is no real evidence to support his involvement in the Ripper murders.

George James Bland: 1860–1934

George James Bland and his wife, Mary Ann, spent the evening of 19 April 1883 socialising with a neighbour, George Pratt, who was Bland's boss on the Clifden Estate in Naseby, Northamptonshire. Having readily helped his host in the yard with a horse, Bland and his wife ate supper with Pratt and his family before Mary Ann announced at ten o'clock that it was time for them to leave.

The couple left together to head for their tied cottage on the estate, which was detached and had no near neighbours. The following morning Bland didn't turn up for his work as a cowman and after an hour and a half, Pratt went to the Blands' cottage to see why. Having knocked and shouted and received no answer, Pratt tried the door, finding it locked. Becoming ever more concerned, Pratt took a ladder from a nearby hay rick and put it up to the Blands' bedroom window. Looking in, he saw a woman dressed in her nightclothes, lying on the floor.

Pratt managed to enter the cottage through the window, finding twenty-two-year-old Mary Ann Bland lying dead on the floor, her throat bisected by an eight-inch-long wound, stretching from ear to ear, which was deep enough to have almost decapitated her. Pratt was followed into the bedroom by labourer Odessa Ringrose and together the two men searched the cottage, finding a blood-caked knife and a bowl of bloody water on the kitchen table but no sign of Bland.

Ringrose went for the police, and on arriving, PC Davies sent out a flurry of telegrams to police officers in the immediate area, advising them to be on the look-out for Bland, who was described as 5ft 9in tall, of slim build with 'dark features'. Assisted by Pratt, Davies searched all the farm buildings on the estate before news reached him that Bland had been seen at 6.30 that morning in the village of Kelmarsh, where he was walking at a rapid pace, swinging his arms so high as he walked that they were almost over his head. He later visited Kelmarsh Station, where his cousin Samuel Jarman was working, and after trying unsuccessfully to borrow some money, he suddenly picked up a shovel and hit him with it twice, once on the back of the head and once on the arm. Bland then threw himself across the railway lines, but fortunately the engine driver saw him and was able to stop the train before hitting him, leaving Bland to flee unharmed.

From Kelmarsh, Bland went to Oxenden, where he met another cousin, Charles Henry Bland, with whom he went for a drink in a pub. Bland told his cousin that he had done something and it was all through 'that b******, Sam'. Although Bland didn't explain exactly what he had done, his cousin assumed that he was referring to hitting Jarman, since there was a history of disagreements between them. Bland said that he was heading for Market Harborough, where he was going to pay a debt and then drown himself.

However, having left Oxenden, Bland got only as far as Tur Langton, where he got himself a job as a herdsman. On the evening of 20 April, PC Joseph Collyer spotted him in the street, carrying a pail of milk, his hands and clothes still heavily stained with blood. Collyer tapped Bland on the shoulder and asked his name, repeating the question when Bland did not reply. Bland eventually gave his name as Chester, at which Collyer arrested him on the charge of murdering his wife. Bland insisted that he was innocent and that the policeman had the wrong man. However, as he was being taken to Bowden Police Station, he repeatedly muttered to himself,

Tur Langton, where Bland was apprehended. (*Author's collection*)

'Temporary insanity. That will be it'. On arrival at the police station, Bland was formally charged and claimed to have lost his memory and to know nothing about any murder. Yet, while locked up in the cells, he spoke to the wife of Inspector Wallace, saying, 'Oh, dear, Missus! What shall I do? I cannot think what made me do it. I am sorry I have done it. There is an angel in Heaven now. I did not think it would come to this.'

There seemed to have been no motive for Mary Ann's murder, although it was suggested that Bland was a particularly jealous husband and that he may have suspected Samuel Jarman of being enamoured of her. Bland had been working at Clifden since December 1882, prior to which he had worked as a porter in a drapery and as an assistant in a wine merchant. He and Mary Ann married in July 1882, after which Bland left his work and moved from farm to farm before apparently settling at Clifden. However, on 3 April 1883 Bland told his foreman that he was leaving his job, having accepted another some distance away. He roamed aimlessly around the countryside for a few days, at which Mary Ann left their home and returned to her parents. Bland followed her and managed to persuade her to come back to him, promising to be a better husband. When she agreed to return, he went back to Clifden and begged for his old job back. Since he had always been a good worker, he was rehired on 13 April.

Yet, although Bland's work was satisfactory, his state of mind didn't seem to be quite right, and on the day before his wife's murder he complained to his foreman that he was 'lost'. 'Three years ago, I was happy. I was right for Heaven, but I ceased to watch, and I knew from that time I was a lost man and will go to Hell, die when I would. I know Hell's my portion.' When Pratt tried to reassure him that God was merciful and would not forsake him, Bland thanked him for his advice but insisted, 'God has given me up and that is all which is the matter with me, I assure you.'

An inquest on Mary Ann's death, held by coroner Mr W. Terry, was told that Bland was a sober man, who was thought of as a good worker and who apparently had a friendly and loving relationship with his wife. In the room where her body was found, a noose was discovered dangling from a beam, as though someone had intended to hang him or herself but had lost their nerve. It also emerged that Bland had frightened his wife on a previous occasion, having deliberately locked the cottage doors and sharpened the knife as she watched, forcing her to escape out of the window, afraid for her life.

The inquest jury returned a verdict of wilful murder against George Bland, who was committed for trial at the next Assizes on the coroner's warrant. He appeared before Baron Huddleston on 10 July 1883, where it was revealed that Mary Ann had been pregnant at the time of her death.

Letters between them showed that they seem to have shared a loving and affectionate relationship, although Mary Ann was obviously worried because her husband was depressed and had shown suicidal tendencies in the past. Such was her concern that she had once asked a friend, David Wilford, to stay with him overnight as she was afraid that he intended to kill himself. Wilford told the court that he and Bland went for a walk together, during which Bland pointed out a pond, saying, 'That's my dwelling place'. As Wilford tried to lead him away from the water, Bland told him, 'I am a lost man and shall be ruined for ever and ever.'

Other witnesses testified to Bland's gloomy demeanour in the weeks prior to the murder, claiming that he had often refused to eat and had to be persuaded to go to work. Yet all agreed that his wife was not afraid of him, even after being advised by relatives that she should not be alone with him in his current condition.

The medical superintendent of the county lunatic asylum had interviewed Bland at length while he was awaiting his trial and was convinced that he was not of sound mind. Dr Greene told the court that he had personally seen around 6,000 cases of insanity and was certain that Bland was not malingering. According to Greene, he wore a dull and dazed expression throughout their interview and vacillated between declaring that he had sinned against the Holy Ghost and should never be forgiven and then insisting that God would save him. A second doctor, Joseph Bayley, had seen Bland only two days before the start of his trial and had at first been unable to get him to answer any questions at all. Bayley described Bland as being in 'a great state of nervous depression', and though the doctor believed that Bland was capable of understanding his trial, he thought that he was suffering from homicidal mania, accompanied by suicidal tendencies and extreme depression. Whereas Bland would have known what he was doing when he murdered his wife, Bayley believed that he would have found himself unable to resist the impulse to do so.

While the defence produced several witnesses to testify to Bland's mental state, the prosecution called an equal number who quickly refuted any idea that he might be of unsound mind. The surgeon at Northampton County Gaol, the prison schoolmaster and two warders all stated that, although they agreed that Bland was a little low, they had noticed no signs of insanity during his incarceration.

Bland's mother, Mary, told the court that her son had been a very slow learner at school and that prior to the murder she had been so concerned about his mental state that she had made arrangements for him to see a doctor. Sadly, Mary Ann's death took place before the planned consultation.

Bland's defence counsel, Mr Lloyd, told the jury that he wasn't expecting them to restore his client to a life of freedom and happiness but asked them to agree that he was not responsible for his actions at the time of the murder, thus enabling him to be safely confined in an asylum during Her Majesty's pleasure. Lloyd explained that there were several instances of insanity in Bland's family and that Bland himself had received a head injury around three years earlier and was still complaining about the effects of that.

The prosecution counsel, Mr Sills, argued that while Bland may have been melancholic and of low intellectual powers, there was absolutely nothing to suggest that he was insane. Indeed, his actions after his wife's murder in locking up the cottage, fleeing the scene and almost immediately finding a new job under a false name suggested precisely the opposite.

In summing up the case, Baron Huddleston told the jury that there was very little doubt as to who killed Mary Ann Bland, hence the task for the jury was to decide on the killer's mental state at the time of the murder. If they believed that Bland was responsible for his actions, they must find him guilty. If they thought he was not responsible, they must find him not guilty due to reasons of insanity. Huddleston reminded the jury that the law of the land decreed that every man was assumed to be sane unless proven otherwise. Thus, the question for the jury to consider was had the defence done enough to prove Bland's insanity? It took the jury just twenty minutes to decide that they had.

Found not guilty due to insanity, Bland was to spend more than fifty years in Broadmoor Criminal Lunatic Asylum before dying from cancer in July 1934 at the age of seventy-four.

John Henry Lush: 1860–1936

On 11 September 1886 Londoner Walter White was visiting his sister in Bournemouth and decided to take an afternoon stroll on the common between Bournemouth and Westbourne. He was observed by a servant, Miss Penton, who happened to be looking out of the window of her place of employment and saw him pass by a man with a limp, later identified as John Henry Lush, who was walking in the opposite direction. Almost immediately, Lush turned and twice fired a gun at White, before dragging him onto the heather, then firing a third shot.

Miss Penton ran to find her mistress, and after a reviving shot of brandy, they ran to assist the fallen man. When they arrived on the scene, they found that Lush had already been detained and disarmed by two passers-by and an off-duty policeman, coincidentally also named Lush, who just happened to have been sitting nearby reading a newspaper. White, meanwhile, lay bleeding on the ground, shot twice in the back, the third shot having grazed his ear. One of the bullets had lodged close to his spine, leaving him paralysed in both legs.

Twenty-six-year-old Lush was charged with wounding with intent to murder, but so precarious was White's condition that it was decided to postpone his trial, since it was fully expected that White would die. White passed away on 5 January 1887 as a result of his injuries and the charge against Lush was elevated to one of wilful murder.

Mr Justice Denman. (*Author's collection*)

Lush appeared at the Hampshire Assizes at Winchester on 4 February 1887 before Mr Justice Denman. As he was particularly nervous, he was allowed to sit on a chair throughout the proceedings. Defence counsel Mr Greenwood was quick to inform the court that he would be relying on an insanity defence, stating that when Lush killed White, he was in fact so insane as to be legally and morally irresponsible for the act.

The Judge and Escort, Winchester Assizes. (*Author's collection*)

The Great Hall, Winchester Castle, site of the Assizes. (*Authors collection*)

The defendant had a long history of physical illness and one of the first witnesses called was his mother, Jemima Potter, who stated that he was the son of her first husband, who died in 1862, when his son was just two years old. According to Mrs Potter, John was a particularly delicate child, who seemed to have no power in his left arm and leg. He spent a considerable period of time in Exeter Hospital, being treated for paralysis, and from the age of six onwards, he suffered from frequent epileptic fits, especially in hot weather.

Mrs Potter married her second husband in 1875. Unfortunately, he and John didn't get on and eventually his stepfather turned John out of the house. The youth found it difficult to find work because of his partial paralysis. At the time of the shooting, he had been out of work for eight months and was living on his wife's earnings. However, his wife, Jane, was about to give birth to their first child and Lush knew that she couldn't continue to support him.

About a month before the murder, Jemima Potter visited her son and his wife, finding John to be rather dull and low in spirits, which she put down to him being out of work. Mrs Potter told the court that John had suffered from depression in the past and had a tendency to withdraw from company and read the Bible alone. Everyone who knew John found him to be devoted to his wife and invariably good tempered, adding that he tried everything in his power to get a job.

From May to July of 1886 John was hospitalised with scarlet fever and a fellow patient on the same ward happened to be a surgeon. Mr Ernest Solly told the court that the defendant was paralysed on the left-hand side, which Solly believed to be caused by a clot in one of the arteries of the brain.

This meant that Lush suffered from an incurable brain disease, which would probably get worse as he got older. Solly believed that this apoplexy, coupled with epilepsy, could predispose Lush to insanity, resulting in uncontrollable homicidal tendencies.

Prosecution counsel Mr Bullen, who firmly believed that the motive for White's killing was simply robbery, argued that a person could be paralysed and epileptic and yet still be perfectly sane, adding that he personally had never seen any signs that Lush was suffering from any weakness of mind.

Dr T. Worthington, who was the superintendent of the Hampshire County Asylum, had been asked to examine Lush on two occasions and considered him to be insane. Worthington found Lush to be experiencing a loss of sensation, feeling and motion on his left side, coupled with muscle wastage and an uncontrollable spasm. He also claimed to suffer frequent headaches.

Bullen called Dr W. A. Richards, the surgeon at Winchester Prison, where Lush had awaited his trial. Richards gave his opinion that Lush was above average intelligence, adding that he had never seen any reason to doubt the prisoner's sanity. Prison Governor Captain Hill concurred with the surgeon's views.

Whereas it was universally agreed that Lush was suffering from a disease of the brain, there was considerable disagreement as to whether or not this affected his sanity. Mr Justice Denman suggested that the shooting of White was the act of a madman and that, as a consequence of his diseased brain, Lush had no control over his actions. The jury agreed and found that Lush acted while in an unsound state of mind, finding him not guilty on the grounds of insanity.

Ordered to be detained during Her Majesty's pleasure, Lush was transferred from Winchester Prison to Broadmoor Criminal Lunatic Asylum at the conclusion of his trial. After nineteen years there, he made an unsuccessful attempt to escape by cutting through the floor of his cell with a four-inch-long steel cutter. He died from pneumonia in 1936, having spent forty-nine years as a patient.

John White: 1861–1933

Thirty-eight-year-old John White was the landlord of the Victoria Vaults public house in Coventry, and on 29 April 1899 he started a petty argument with his wife, Annie. John accused her of ordering a bicycle without his knowledge, something that Annie strongly denied. John told her that he would smash the bicycle – and her – to pieces the minute it appeared in the house. When she asked who had told him that she had ordered a bicycle, John refused to tell her, at which Annie lost her temper and stormed out of their bedroom, saying that she would sleep with Alice, the couple's adopted daughter. John leapt out of bed and told her that he would blow her brains out, and those of the child. 'We three will die together,' he promised.

Knowing that John had a revolver, which was kept on top of the wardrobe, Annie ran from the bedroom, holding the door closed from the outside. She was no match for her husband's strength, and when she felt the door being pulled open, she bolted for the sitting room. John tried to force that door, but Annie hung on for her life. She braced herself against the mantlepiece and, as she did, she heard a loud bang and felt a bullet whizz over her head.

'Now for Alice,' John said. Annie pleaded with her husband to spare the child but heard him running upstairs to her bedroom. When Alice screamed in terror, Annie made a desperate run for the street and shouted for help.

Fortunately, Alice was able to escape and alerted a passer-by to the situation within the pub. Alfred W. Payne bravely went inside, and after escorting Annie and Alice to a neighbour's house, he arrived back just in time to see John White being arrested by PC Johnson. The police discovered that a revolver had been fired through the closed door of the sitting room at a height of 4ft 11in, travelling in a slightly downwards direction. Annie White was 5ft 1in tall, and had she not ducked down to put her weight behind keeping the door closed, she would have been shot in the head.

John White appeared at the Coventry Police Court charged with feloniously shooting at his wife with intent to kill and murder her. The case was forwarded to the Warwick Assizes, but the jury found that rather than trying to kill his wife, John had fired his gun simply intending to frighten her. The case was dismissed, and John White walked from court a free man.

Unsurprisingly, his marriage didn't survive, and John moved out of the pub to live with his mother, Mary Ann. As the years passed, he moved in with a young woman and is reported to have sired at least two children.

Apart from a bad cough, Mary Ann enjoyed good health, but by November 1909 John began telling people that she was unwell, saying that she had made a will in his favour and was using the promise of his sizeable inheritance to borrow money. He obtained two gold rings under false pretences and also wrongly represented himself as a detective.

By December of 1909 John was telling people that his mother was near to death, even though she was still very active and was regularly seen out and about. Mary Ann told neighbour Mary Lathbury that she was convinced that John was up to something, adding that she was afraid he might either poison her, or hit her over the head. 'I feel in terror of my life', Mary Ann told everyone.

When people asked John about his mother's health, he told them that she was slightly better as he had given her some laudanum. However, on 9 January 1910, seventy-five-year-old Mrs White was found dead by a neighbour. On a table at her side were a bottle of lemonade, a packet of tartaric acid and a wine glass full of liquid, which by its distinctive smell was easily recognisable as the poison cyanide of potassium. The police and a doctor were called, along with John White, who, when told of his mother's death, cried 'What? Mother dead?' and dropped dramatically to the floor in a pretend faint.

Asked by the police about the contents of the wine glass at his mother's side, John sniffed it and immediately identified it as cyanide of potassium, adding that he had bought some for hardening tools and put it in a cupboard at his mother's house. He could not explain how it had come to be dissolved in a glass at his mother's side. As it was no longer where he had left it, he theorised that she may have mistaken the poison for the sugar that she was accustomed to adding to her nightly tot of rum or whisky.

Coroner Dr C.W. Iliffe held an inquest on Mary Ann's death, where it was revealed that John had told people that he could treat his mother's illness as well as any doctor. Mary Lathbury told the coroner that on a previous occasion Mary Ann had become dreadfully ill after taking some 'medicine' given to her by her son. As a consequence, she had banned him from visiting, although he persisted in coming. According to Mrs Lathbury, Mary Ann was frightened of what John might do to her and had even considered calling the police to make an official complaint about him.

Mary Ann's doctor had last treated her on 24 December 1909, when she had a bad bout of bronchitis. He had next seen her when he was called to the scene of her death. Although Dr Lowman immediately identified the liquid by her side as cyanide of potassium, he had been unable to smell it on her mouth. On 12 January 1910 Lowman and Dr Phillips conducted a post-mortem examination on Mary Ann but found nothing to suggest what might have killed her. The contents of the wine glass were also analysed and found to contain only two grains of cyanide of potassium, whereas a fatal dose would be a minimum of five grains. Most tellingly, no trace of cyanide of potassium was found in the stomach contents, and the chemists who performed the analysis quite categorically stated that the presence of poison was precluded.

Both Lowman and Phillips admitted that though it was highly unlikely, it was just possible that traces of the poison might have disappeared in the sixty hours between her death and the analysis of her stomach contents. Neither of the doctors could swear that Mary Ann White died from cyanide poisoning, but at the same time neither could be certain that she didn't.

Having heard all the evidence, the coroner summed up the case for the inquest jury, suggesting that an open verdict was appropriate, simply finding that the deceased was found dead, without expressing an opinion as to the cause of death. However, the inquest jury had other ideas, telling the coroner that they unanimously believed that Mary Ann White died from cyanide poisoning and that the poison was administered by her son.

Mr Justice Darling. (*Author's collection*)

'You therefore want me to commit him on a charge of wilful murder?' asked the coroner.

'That is our verdict,' confirmed the foreman of the jury.

White was promptly arrested and committed for trial at the next Warwickshire Assizes, where he appeared before Mr Justice Darling on 15 March 1910. By the time of the trial, the doctors had concluded that Mary Ann White had simply died of fright.

Mr Justice Darling asked the analytical chemist to leave the court and mix up a solution of cyanide of potassium of the same strength of that found next to Mary Ann's body. Having sniffed the liquid, Darling cautiously tasted it, before passing it to the jury and suggesting that they should taste it too.

'The consequences would be terrible, my lord, if all the jury died of fright,' protested defence counsel Mr Maddocks, amid nervous laughter in the court. However, he too was eventually persuaded to taste the solution of poison, as was the prosecuting counsel, Mr Ryland Adkins.

When Adkins was about to begin presenting his case, he was stopped from doing so by the judge, who told him, 'I shall tell the jury that they ought not, on the evidence, and having regard especially to the medical evidence, must not find the defendant guilty of murder. However, I will leave the jury to decide whether or not he is guilty of attempted murder.'

John White: 1861–1933 151

Parkhurst and Portland Prisons, where White served his sentence. (*Author's collection*)

Adkins then proceeded to tell the jury that the defendant, who was indisputably the last person to see his mother alive, was, at the time of her death, in dire financial straits. Unemployed and in arrears with his rent, he had borrowed heavily from his friends and more than thirty pawn tickets were found on his person. Knowing that her son had given her 'medicine' which had made her terribly ill, the prosecution contended that being given a glass of strange-smelling liquid by her son was enough to cause her to die of fright.

A witness came forward to say that White had shown him the cyanide of potassium and told him that it was a deadly poison and that even a small amount could be fatal. The prosecution took this to mean that White did not know how much poison constituted a lethal dose for his mother and was therefore unaware that he had not mixed enough to kill her.

No witnesses were called for the defence and the jury were quick to find White guilty of the attempted murder of his mother. Mr Justice Darling told him that he would not be doing his duty if he didn't award White the longest possible sentence for his crime, which was one of life imprisonment.

White appealed his conviction, with his solicitors pointing out that he had never actually been charged with attempted murder but only with murder, hence it was not constitutional to find him guilty of something with which he was never charged. Indeed, Mr Maddocks contended that there was absolutely nothing to indicate that Mary Ann White had not died from natural causes such as an epileptic fit, heart failure or a stroke. Although White had shown numerous people his mother's will in order to borrow money, the document was dated 1903, so he had not forced his mother to make a will in his favour and then killed her.

Finally, Maddocks argued that there could not have been an attempted murder without intent and the prosecution had failed to prove that White had intended to murder his mother. Maddocks insisted that there

Interior, Portland Prison. (*Author's collection*)

was no evidence whatsoever of attempted murder, and even if there was, Mr Justice Darling had no power to sentence White to more than two years' imprisonment with hard labour.

In the event, the appeal court ruled against White, saying that it was their opinion that this was a case of 'slow' poisoning – it may only have been the beginning of an attempt to murder Mrs White, but there had still been an attempt. White's life sentence was therefore ruled to be just and his appeal was denied.

After serving nineteen years of his life sentence at Portland and Parkhurst prisons, White was judged to be insane and was transferred to Broadmoor Criminal Lunatic Asylum in 1929. While there, he became increasingly violent and deranged, eventually refusing to eat or sleep. He died in 1933, aged seventy-three, the cause of his death given as 'exhaustion'.

Samuel Bentall Collis: 1862–1899

By 1896 the Collis family had worked Brompton's Farm in Pebmarsh, Essex, for many generations, and when John Collis died, his son-in-law, Thomas Turpin, was appointed executor to his will. Thomas and his wife, Ellen, lived at the farm with John's widow, Susannah. In due course, a farm bailiff was appointed to assist with the daily running, but this did not sit well with John's youngest son, Samuel Bentall Collis, who obviously believed that he should have taken over the farm or at very least been appointed as bailiff. Samuel was well known among his neighbours for what was described as 'his queer state of mind'. His late father was supposedly terrified of him, particularly when he began to try and maim himself by firing a gun at his own feet. Now, he harboured a grudge against both his brother-in-law and the bailiff, Robert John Cockrill, and as the years passed, it seemed as though the strength of his feelings was slowly driving him insane.

In around 1887 Collis was sent to a lunatic asylum, where he remained for eleven months before being discharged as 'cured'. Once released, he took on a farm at Pebmarsh, which he worked for two years before going to live in a cottage on his mother's estate. Twelve months later, he took on another farm, but by the end August 1896 Collis was scheduled to appear at Colchester Bankruptcy Court, although he failed to show up on the day.

On 2 September 1896 Ellen Turpin looked out of her bedroom window and saw her brother Samuel walking around the farm on stilts. As always, Ellen rose at just before 6am and went into the farmyard to feed the chickens. Samuel was now standing at the garden gate and began throwing sticks at the hens. Ellen ignored him, but as soon as her back was turned, and without any warning, her brother rushed at her and knocked her to the ground, saying that he meant to 'do for the whole lot of them'. Ellen screamed to the farm labourer Walter Warren to fetch a policeman. Susannah Collis heard the commotion from her bedroom window and shouted down, 'You shan't touch my daughter.' Samuel merely shook his fist at her, so Susannah ran out into the yard, grabbed Ellen's arm and dragged her into the house, barricading the doors behind them.

Meanwhile, Samuel had crossed the yard and was deep in conversation with bailiff Cockrill. Walter Warren saw Samuel raise his hand and hit Cockrill hard on the side of his head. Immediately afterwards he heard gunshots and fled in terror to summon police assistance.

PC Harry C. Cook accompanied Walter back to Brompton's Farm, where they met Samuel on the roadside. He was carrying two dead chickens in one hand and a gun in the other and had a large bowl tucked underneath one arm. 'What have you been up to, Sam?' the policeman asked him.

'I have killed a sheep and here's its head,' replied Collis, proffering the bowl. Cook took a swift glance and saw that it contained not a sheep's head but the head of a man, who Cook clearly recognised as Cockrill. At that moment Collis leaned towards the policeman and told him, 'Forgive me. I want to kiss you.' As he did so, his coat fell open, revealing a long knife in his inside pocket.

Cook took both the knife and gun away from Collis, who immediately protested, 'I'm going to have that knife.'

'No, you are not. You have killed poor Cockrill, so now you must come with me,' Cook told him. The policeman led him to the back door of the farmhouse and knocked loudly but the occupants were all hiding from Collis and refused to open the door. Eventually, Mrs Turpin put her head out of the bedroom window and was persuaded to come downstairs, where Cook handed her the knife and the gun for safekeeping. As he did, Collis eluded him and leapt a fence, before racing away across fields behind the farm with Cook in pursuit.

The policeman passed the headless body of the bailiff as he followed Collis across the fields, finally catching him as he was about to enter a wood. Only then did Cook notice that his quarry had a revolver in his right hand.

'Sam, stop,' Cook begged him. 'It's no good. You won't get away.'

'You bastard. I'll shoot you,' Collis replied.

Cook drew his truncheon and told Collis that he would split his head open.

'Don't do that, for God's sake,' responded Collis, finally lowering the revolver and putting it in his pocket. Cook rushed him and managed to knock him over. 'I want my razor and I'll do for you,' Collis vowed. He struggled violently until Cook managed to pin him to the ground, assisted by Walter Warren, who had followed the pursuit from the farm.

In due course, Mark Rust, Samuel Rayment and John Whiting arrived with some rope and Collis was securely trussed up and taken to the lock-up at Halstead. As they travelled, Collis made a series of nonsensical statements, claiming to be 'Prince Napoleon' and 'Pitt', adding that he had killed a girl and an angel about a week ago and that he had been to Hell but refused to stay there as there was nobody to keep him company.

When Collis's home was searched after his arrest, it was found to be very well-kept, thanks to the efforts of a local woman whom Collis had hired to do the housework, but there were putrefying heads of a sheep, a rabbit and a hen, which hung from beams in the kitchen. In the living room an apple on a piece of string was suspended from the ceiling, bullet holes in the wall opposite indicating that it had been used for target practice.

Collis appeared before magistrates charged with wilful murder. The court heard from everyone who had been at the farm on the day of Cockrill's death, and as was usual in such cases, Collis was offered the opportunity to question the witnesses. However, he denied knowing any of them, including his sister and Walter Warren. When asked if he had any questions for PC Cook, Collis remarked, 'I have swallowed an egg. That's all I know.'

Although committed to trial at the Essex Assizes by the magistrates and on the coroner's warrant, it became evident during his incarceration

Chelmsford Prison, where Collis was held awaiting his trial. (*Author's collection*)

Chelmsford Prison. (*Author's collection*)

at Chelmsford Prison that Collis was insane and he was certified on 8 September 1896, after which he was immediately transferred to Broadmoor Criminal Lunatic Asylum. Although he was considered dangerous, he was largely contented and jovial, until he lapsed into a uraemic coma on 23 May 1899 and died within hours.

In the aftermath of Cockrill's brutal murder, PC Cook was commended for his bravery and was promoted to acting sergeant. While Cook claimed to have suffered from insomnia since the day he confronted Collis, his twenty-seven-year-old wife went almost insane with terror at the thought of what might have happened to her husband. She was eventually sent to her mother's home by the seaside for a change of air. Meanwhile, the local vicar organised a collection for Cockrill, who left a wife and eight children. It was paid out to his widow in the form of a pension.

James Shaw: 1862–1947

James Shaw was an army reserve man who had served in the Coldstream Guards for seven years. On 10 July 1897, having left the army only the previous week, he made a visit to his home village of Sulgrave, Northamptonshire, calling in to see his nephew and niece, the children of his late sister, Elizabeth, and her husband, Francis Smith. Although Shaw didn't spend long visiting, he took the opportunity to take thirteen-year-old Albert upstairs alone, where it was believed that he indecently assaulted him.

Sulgrave Village. (*Author's collection*)

A few days later, Shaw went back to visit Albert and his eight-year-old sister, Alice Sarah Smith. When he arrived, the children's father was at his work as an agricultural labourer, and the children were at home alone. Delighted to see their uncle, they wandered about the village for a little while, with Shaw handing over money for them to buy sweets at Mr Godfrey's shop. He then told the children that he was planning to walk to the station at Helmdon and invited them to walk with him.

When they reached the halfway point between Sulgrave and Helmdon, Albert was walking a little way ahead. Out of her brother's sight, Shaw bundled Alice across a stile into a corn field, lifted her clothes and sexually assaulted her, before telling her to go home. Alice, who was absolutely devoted to her brother, was reluctant to leave him, but was eventually persuaded to go by the promise of more sweets.

When Francis Smith arrived home from work, he found his daughter alone in the house. He asked where Albert was and Alice said that he had gone for a walk with their Uncle Jim. Not knowing what Shaw had been doing with his children in his absence, Smith thought no more about it, trusting that the boy was safe with his uncle. However, as it grew late, Smith began to worry that Albert had not yet come home. He, Alice and her older brother, George, walked the road towards Helmdon, calling Albert's name as they went. They continued to search until almost two o'clock in the morning, before returning home exhausted and worried, hoping that Shaw may have taken Albert into Banbury to stay overnight at his sister, Sarah Ann Hobbs's house.

Sulgrave. (*Author's collection*)

The following morning, Smith reported his son missing to village policeman PC Coles. Meanwhile, George set off to walk to Banbury, where he found Shaw at his sister's. Albert was not with him, but Shaw assured George that he had left him by the blacksmith's shop to walk home, having given him 5d for more sweets for himself and his sister.

When the search for Albert that day proved fruitless, it was agreed that Alice would lead them to the exact spot where she had left her brother and uncle. The little girl took her father and Coles to the corn field where she had last seen them and a search of the area was begun.

It had grown dark by the time Coles found Albert's body in a ditch at the side of a field of oats. It lay under an ash tree and had been partly covered with grass. When Coles moved the covering vegetation from the body and lit a match, he was horrified to see that Albert's head had been completely severed from his body. 'Here he is. His head is cut off,' Coles shouted, shock no doubt causing him to forget that the dead boy's sister and father were there helping with the search.

When day broke it revealed a bloody razor just two feet from Albert's body, which Smith identified as an old one that he kept upstairs at home and used only for trimming his corns. Since the razor had been removed from Smith's home, it was immediately obvious that whoever had killed Albert had been in the boy's house at some time and taken it. As the search expanded, the police found a flattened area in the oats, as if someone had laid down there. And close to where Albert's body was found was an area of flattened and broken grass, where it was evident that a frantic struggle had taken place. The search also revealed a picture of Cleopatra's Needle, a cap, a button, a piece of knotted string and a few scattered sweets. Smith recognised the picture as one that Albert and Alice had been looking at when he left for work on the morning that his son disappeared. He identified the cap as belonging to Albert and the button as having come from his son's jacket. As for the knotted string, it was identical to one that Albert used to set his spinning top in motion, and the sweets were later identified by shopkeeper Mr Godfrey as being the same as those he had sold to the Smith children a couple of days earlier. Finally, it was noted that Albert's trousers had been 'disturbed'.

Once the body had been removed from the field, PC Coles and Inspector White went to Banbury to speak to Shaw, finding him at the home of his sister. (Coles had actually seen Shaw walking with Albert on the Saturday afternoon but that was obviously before he was informed that the boy was missing.) Told that he was being arrested for the murder of his nephew, Shaw seemed neither surprised nor unduly concerned to learn that the boy was dead. Taken to Brackley Police Station, Shaw told the arresting officers that Albert had been alive and perfectly well when he left him to walk home from the blacksmith's shop. Another policeman, Sergeant J. Cottingham, had also seen Shaw out and about in the vicinity of the murder on the Sunday morning, although he was of course unaware that a murder had taken place.

An inquest on Albert's death was convened by coroner Mr F. M. Percival, and Shaw, who was handcuffed and closely guarded by two police officers, watched the proceedings with interest. Given the opportunity to question witnesses, Shaw continued to insist that Albert had been alive and well when he left him.

In summarising the case for the jury, Percival stated that a foul murder had been committed and that Albert had last been seen alive in the company of his uncle, James Shaw. The blue serge suit that Shaw was wearing when he visited his nephew and niece had been seized by the police and bore spots of what appeared to be blood. The fact that the boy's killer had a razor in his possession that had previously belonged to the victim's father suggested that the murder had been premeditated and committed by someone with access to the Smiths' family home. Although there was no obvious motive for the murder, the victim's clothing had been disarranged and there was evidence of a tremendous struggle.

The inquest jury took just ten minutes to find a verdict of wilful murder against James Shaw, who was committed for trial at the next Assizes on the coroner's warrant. Shaw's departure was greeted by a cacophony of boos and hisses from the large crowd of people who had assembled outside the inquest, hoping to catch a glimpse of him. In the wake of the proceedings, the inquest jury donated their fees to Francis Smith to go towards the costs of Albert's funeral, the coroner adding half a crown from his own pocket.

By the time Shaw appeared before magistrates at Brackley, the spots on his clothing had been verified as mammalian blood by a scientific analyst from the Home Office. When magistrates followed the coroner in committing Shaw to the Assizes, he was taken to the station to be transported to Northampton County Gaol. Waiting for the train, Shaw suddenly made a desperate break for freedom, evading his two escorts and vaulting a fence. As he ran from the station, a passer-by spotted his handcuffs, and deducing that he was an escaped convict, immediately gave chase.

Realising that his pursuer was gaining on him, Shaw doubled back towards the station, eventually jumping into a ditch where he was recaptured by his two escorts.

When Shaw appeared at the Assizes before Mr Justice Wills on 18 November, he was more heavily guarded than the other defendants facing trial that day, his hands shackled behind him and no fewer than five men surrounding him. The contemporary newspapers reported that Shaw had gained a considerable amount of weight during his incarceration, commenting on his pale, bloated face and his red eyelids, which twitched constantly.

It was suggested by the counsel for the prosecution, Mr Sills, that Albert may have been killed while trying to defend his younger sister from Shaw's indecent assault on her. Failing that, the boy might have seen his uncle committing the assault, forcing Shaw to kill the only witness to his perversion. Sills conceded that the motive for Albert's murder was a matter of conjecture, adding that he wondered if a defence of insanity might be appropriate.

Little Alice was the first witness to be called and a medical examination had already confirmed that her claims that her uncle had assaulted her were true. She was adamant that her brother could not have seen what Shaw did to her, saying that she had sat down to have a rest and her uncle had continued walking with Albert before returning alone.

Sarah Hobbs told the court that, on 10 July, her brother had announced that he was going to visit the Smiths at Sulgrave. He returned earlier than expected, and when she questioned why, told her that the house had been locked and there was nobody at home, hence he hadn't seen the children. Sarah also told the court that her brother had suffered from fits as a child and that prior to enlisting in the army, aged fifteen, he had experienced an illness that affected his brain, leaving him stupefied for almost three weeks.

She stated that her brother had been under the care of a doctor, but when the doctor was brought to court, he claimed to have no record of Shaw's illness, or of him having suffered from fits as a child.

Having left the army, Shaw had destroyed his leaving papers, not realising that he would need them to get his outstanding pay. According to his sister, this had left him very depressed, and he had complained of dizziness and nausea, sometimes laughing to himself out loud for no apparent reason. Sarah concluded her testimony by stating that their father had attempted suicide several times.

Defence counsel Mr Hammond Chambers did indeed rely on an insanity defence. He suggested that Shaw's father's suicide attempts showed a family history of insanity and reminded the jury that his client had suffered from childhood fits and an illness that left him unconscious for three weeks. Hammond gave examples of some of the strange behaviour that Shaw had exhibited over the years, which apparently included muttering and laughing to himself, beating his pillow with a poker because he believed someone was hiding in it, unexpectedly throwing things, putting his fist through a glass window, fighting imaginary enemies, and sitting for long periods without talking.

Richard Drake, a warder at Northampton Gaol, told the court that Shaw had been under constant observation since his arrival at the prison on 13 July. Drake said that Shaw behaved very much like a man who didn't know what he was doing, adding that on three occasions he had violently assaulted prison staff for no apparent reason. He had also torn up all his clothes and smashed the windows in his cell, cutting himself afterwards with a sliver of broken glass.

The defence called former army colleagues Alexander Milligan and James McIntosh, who both stated that Shaw was widely viewed as 'tapped', or mentally unsound. They cited incidents of strange and violent behaviour that they had observed over the years, with McIntosh going as far as saying that he was always afraid that Shaw might either harm himself or others. Nevertheless, Shaw was said to be well-liked among his colleagues.

Dr Lee F. Cogan, the prison surgeon, found that Shaw's mood varied from confused to amused, to sullen and incommunicative. Cogan believed that Shaw was insane, although he was unable to say with any certainty that he was insane on 10 July. A second doctor concurred, adding that he believed that Shaw's insanity was long standing, thus he was most likely suffering from homicidal mania and therefore insane when the murder was committed.

The jury debated the matter of Shaw's guilt and sanity at length, and after four-and-a-half hours they were ready to announce their decision. They returned to court to state that they unanimously found Shaw guilty, with no addition of insanity to their verdict. It was left to the judge to don his black cap and pass the death sentence on Shaw, who stared at the floor.

Due to continuing doubts about his sanity Shaw was not executed and his sentence was commuted to one of life imprisonment. In April 1898 he was taken to Broadmoor Criminal Lunatic Asylum, where he would spend the next forty-nine years, dying, aged seventy-five, on 14 February 1947. The cause of his death is not recorded.

Margaret Rees: 1863–1903

Farmer's daughter Margaret Davies was not even eighteen years old when she married James Rees, the tenant of the neighbouring farm. The couple moved into James's tiny, one-storey farmhouse, Ty'r Bwlch, near Brynberian, on the side of the Preseli Mountains in Pembrokeshire, which they shared with James's widowed mother, Mary. James's brother, William, lived in a neighbouring house with his family.

As the years passed, Margaret gave birth to six children, four of whom survived. The birth of Anne, her youngest child, coincided with James falling seriously ill, and by September 1893 Margaret herself consulted her doctor, complaining of extreme despondency, listlessness, dyspepsia and

Preseli / Precelly Mountains. (*Author's collection*)

insomnia. She also told Dr David Havard of Newport that her milk had dried up, leaving her unable to continue breastfeeding Anne. Towards the end of 1893 Margaret built a dam in the farm pond and was seen by William purposefully carrying Anne towards the water. When she noticed William watching her, Margaret quickly turned and went back into the house, but the implied threat on the baby's life prompted the family into action. Dr Havard was consulted again and recommended a change of air and scene, so Margaret was sent to Cardigan to rest and recuperate.

By February 1894 she had returned home, and her health had improved considerably, but she then gradually deteriorated until James's mother, Mary, noticed her making another attempt on her baby's life. Mary screamed to William, 'She is killing the little girl,' and William rushed into his brother's house to intervene. As he entered the kitchen, Margaret ran into another room, with William hot on her heels, demanding that she hand over the baby.

'I can do what I like with my own child,' retorted Margaret, angrily, forcing William to grapple with her for the baby, who was by then in a near fainting condition, her face red and her lips blue.

Dr Havard was again consulted but told the family that there was no place at the local asylum for Margaret, advising James to watch her carefully. Although she made no further attempts on Anne's life, in November 1894 James intercepted her heading for the cowshed carrying a rope. She told him that she was intending to kill herself. Once again, the family were told that the asylum was full and that they should keep a close eye on Margaret.

On 6 June 1895 James woke up at three o'clock in the morning and roused his son, Rowland, to go out with him and round up the sheep from the mountainside. His ten-year-old daughter, Mary, who shared a bedroom with her brother, woke briefly then went back to sleep, until woken by her mother to go and collect the farm's three cows for milking. Margaret then took the milk back to the house, before returning to the cow barn and asking Mary to go to her uncle William with a message. 'Tell him little Anne is dead,' Margaret instructed her daughter.

'Is it you that killed her?' asked Mary.

'No,' replied Margaret, before going to William herself and telling him, 'I have killed my little girl.'

William ran to check, finding two-year-old Anne dead in her cradle. He returned to his own house, where Margaret asked him, 'What will become of me?'

'You will be hanged,' William replied. 'You will be in the bottom of Hell and the little child in Heaven, making your Hell a hundred times worse.'

Margaret told him that she might bury Anne in the meadow before killing herself, adding that she would kill her other children first so that they didn't starve after she had gone.

William sent for the police then went to fetch James, who arrived home with Rowland shortly before seven o'clock to find his youngest daughter dead. Meanwhile, Margaret was very distracted, threatening to kill herself and everyone else in the family, then begging William to get out his shotgun and shoot her. She showed no remorse or sorrow for her actions, her mood swinging wildly from extreme agitation to stupor.

When PC Morgan arrived at the farm, Margaret told him, 'I have killed my child. You have come here to take me away to be hanged tonight.' Morgan checked Anne, noticing the presence of four bruise-like marks on her left cheek and a slightly larger one on the right cheek. 'I did it,' explained Margaret. 'I got out of bed, took no time to dress, went to the cradle where the baby was and placed my hand over its mouth until it was dead.'

When Morgan tried to arrest Margaret, she resisted, telling him, 'No, I shan't come with you. I am going to be hanged.' Morgan reassured her that he would take her to see Dr Havard, and after washing herself and changing her clothes, she willingly left with him, telling her family, 'Farewell, children, farewell all. You will never see me again.' As she passed a group of curious women standing on the road outside the farm, she called out, 'Lord keep you, dear women, from doing what I have done this day.'

Confined in the lock-up at Fishguard, Margaret remained sullen and impassive, expressing no apparent regret for her action and reportedly 'acting like an imbecile'. Meanwhile, a post-mortem examination carried out on Anne by Dr Harvard confirmed her cause of death as suffocation, although he also found some traces of heart disease.

Appearing before magistrates in Newport, Margaret wore a blue-black dress, a shawl with a wide, wavy stripe and a traditional Welsh hat. According to the contemporary newspapers 'the healthy rosiness of her once chubby cheeks had been worn away by care and pain and there was a somewhat unnatural sparkle in her slightly blue eyes.' The newspaper also noted that Margaret had large eyebrows and a pronounced black, downy moustache, 'a noticeable mark on many persons not responsible for their actions'.

The main witness against Margaret in court was her ten-year-old daughter, Mary, who was separated from her mother by a screen to minimize her distress. Although Margaret was committed to the local Assizes, she never stood trial, being certified insane on 10 June 1895. She was sent to the Joint Counties Asylum in Carmarthen and transferred from there to Broadmoor on 29 July 1895.

Her physical health remained poor and on 27 November 1903 she died from blood poisoning arising from an abscess on her arm. At the inquest on her death her attendant, Florence Scott, commented that she had been 'ailing' for many years.

Richard Edward Goodall: 1863–1913

Thirty-eight-year-old Richard Edward Goodall lived with his wife, Clara, and their four children at Archer Street, Camden Town, London. Sadly, 1901 was not a good year for the family as Richard, who normally worked as a coal porter, fell ill with bronchitis and acute pneumonia. As a consequence, he was hospitalised at Highgate Infirmary from 11 May until 1 July, when he discharged himself, preferring to be treated as an outpatient at Middlesex Hospital.

Because of his illness, Richard was unable to work, and when his condition worsened, he lost the use of his left arm. Although Clara's work provided for the family, money was short, and the family's financial difficulties were increased when, towards the end of July, their lodgers, Willie Curtiss and his wife, gave notice of their intention to leave.

On 29 July Clara went to work as usual, leaving her husband in charge of the children: Florence (eleven), Edith Alberta May (nine), James Edward (three) and Mildred Catherine (twenty months). At around half-past nine in the morning, Richard asked Florence, 'Will you clear up for mother? I am going out with the children.' It was the last time the little girl was ever to see her siblings.

At around a quarter to eleven George Groom and Caleb Oram Hindness were working in a greenhouse near Chalbert Street Bridge when they heard a child's scream. When they went to investigate, they found Goodall standing in the middle of Regent's Canal with a little boy clinging to his back.

'Stick to him, boy,' called Hindness, to which Goodall responded by pointing to the water in front of him, saying, 'There's two gone down.'

While Hindness ran to get a rope, Groom rushed to Portland Town police station for assistance. When Hindness returned, he saw Goodall deliberately turn himself over so that the little boy fell into the water. As the child struggled to the surface, Goodall put his hand on his head and held him underwater until his struggles ceased. He then made his way to the towpath, before deliberately jumping back into the water and trying to drown himself.

Goodall's coat acted like a lifejacket and prevented him from drowning. After climbing out of the canal and jumping in again, Goodall eventually admitted defeat and scrambled onto the bank. 'You scoundrel! You cannot drown,' Hindness told him.

'No, I cannot,' admitted Goodall ruefully.

When police officer Stewart Milne arrived on the scene, Goodall walked towards him, dripping wet. 'Where are the children?' asked Milne and Goodall walked back a short distance before pointing to a particular spot in the water. 'They are there; they are my children; I threw them in,' he explained.

Milne hastily stripped off his clothes and dived into the murky water. Although he was unable to see any signs of the children, on his second dive he brought up Mildred, and on his third he managed to grab Edith and James. 'Thank God they are dead,' Goodall remarked, adding, 'I don't mind swinging for them.'

Goodall looked on dispassionately as Milne attempted artificial respiration for an hour, before the arrival of Doctor James Cooper, who confirmed that it was hopeless. The only comment that Goodall made was to policeman Walter Buckley, to whom he remarked, 'I did it because my wife has been out with my lodger. I tried to drown myself but could not.'

Goodall was taken to Portland Town police station and provided with dry clothes. He told policeman Frederick Fisher that he had been out of work for fourteen weeks. 'I done it and it can't be helped,' he admitted.

Dr Danford Thomas held an inquest on the three deaths, which Goodall declined to attend. His wife, Clara, told the coroner that her husband was a sober man and a good husband and father, who had never previously threatened to harm her or the children. Although money was tight, the family were surviving on her wages. However, since the onset of his physical illness, Richard had become a little strange. He was excitable and restless and had once run down the street gesticulating wildly. He resented being unable to work and provide for his family.

Doctor Cooper had performed post-mortem examinations on all three children, finding them all healthy, with no signs of any external injuries. Cooper told the inquest that Edith had died from syncope or heart failure, while the two youngest children had succumbed to asphyxia due to drowning.

The coroner's jury found a verdict of wilful murder against Goodall, as did magistrates at Marylebone Police Court. His case was forwarded to The Old Bailey, where he appeared before Mr Justice Bucknill on 13 September 1913 to face charges only for murdering James. (The other two murders and a further charge of attempting suicide were held in abeyance). Described as a 'strong, powerful man', Goodall remained calm and collected while in court, listening attentively to the evidence. However, it was noted that he had a wild look in his eyes and that he occasionally stared around vacantly, as if he didn't quite know what was happening.

Florence Goodall was the first witness, and after describing the events of 29 July, she was asked about her relationship with her father. 'My father was always kind to us,' she replied. 'He was a kind and affectionate father'.

Goodall had been confined in Holloway Prison while awaiting his trial and the medical officer, James Scott, was one of the chief witnesses. Having seen Goodall on the day of the murders, he described him as 'dazed and distressed'. He expressed regret for his actions but told Scott that he had come to the conclusion that it was better to drown the children and himself because he couldn't get work. Scott was convinced that Goodall didn't fully understand the enormity of his crime. He was depressed, suffering from melancholia, and in such an unstable mental condition that on the day of the murders he was undoubtedly insane.

Mr Justice Bucknill. (*Author's collection*)

It emerged that one of Goodall's sisters had spent time in an asylum and that one of his uncles had made repeated suicide attempts before successfully hanging himself.

The jury returned a verdict of guilty but insane and Bucknill sentenced Goodall to be detained until His Majesty's pleasure be known. On 26 September he was sent to Broadmoor Criminal Lunatic Asylum, where he lived until his death on 2 September 1913. He was found dead in bed, having cut his throat with a sharpened piece of metal, believed to have come from a tobacco tin. An inquest on his death returned a verdict of suicide while insane.

Agnes Dorcas Mould: 1866–1933

By the time twenty-one-year-old Agnes Dorcas Pollard of Tredworth, Gloucester, married William Mould on 27 March 1887, she had already shown some signs of mental instability. According to her brother, John, on at least one occasion she swallowed a large quantity of pins and needles, seemingly without feeling any ill-effects as a consequence. Nevertheless, Agnes and William seemed happily married and the couple went on to have several children.

In 1903 Agnes was expecting another baby – either her fifth or sixth, depending on which of the reports in the contemporary newspapers is correct. Although she was in good health, in the weeks leading up to the birth Agnes became very low in mood and depressed, complaining to her husband of dreadful pains in her head. A week before her confinement, William found her with a handkerchief tied tightly round her neck, which she explained was an attempt to 'do away' with herself. At around the same time, she also threw one of her children out of the window, luckily without causing any serious injury. Concerned, William consulted the family doctor and asked him if he thought his wife should be sent to the asylum, but Dr Bibby didn't feel that this was necessary. Although Agnes told the doctor that she was tired of life and wanted to go to the asylum, her answers to the rest of his questions were perfectly reasonable and rational, so he decided that she was better off being cared for at home.

According to Agnes's mother, Eliza Pollard, her daughter's mental state was very bad on the day she gave birth and on the day after. She was restless and agitated – so much so that the family took the baby away from her for fear that she might harm her. However, on the third day she seemed much calmer and quieter, so the baby was brought to her so that she might breastfeed it. Eliza believed that Agnes was very fond of her child and seemed completely at ease feeding her, so she left them alone in bed together and went to get on with some chores. Soon afterwards, Agnes wandered dreamily into the kitchen and announced, 'I've done something.'

Eliza ran to the bedroom, where she found the baby dead in bed. By that time, Agnes was hysterical and raving, and when Dr Bibby was summoned to attend her, he brought with him a magistrate and the local relieving officer, Mr Williams, who immediately committed Agnes to the asylum as 'a lunatic not under proper control'.

Throughout her stay in the county asylum, Agnes was described as 'being in a condition of extreme grief and melancholy'. She generally refused to answer when spoken to, but when Dr Bibby questioned her about what had happened to her baby, she told him that while giving it the breast she had held it close to her body until it couldn't breathe. Pressed further by the doctor, Agnes sobbed bitterly, telling him, 'I don't know why I did it,' and, 'I don't know what made me do it'.

While Agnes was still confined in the asylum, city coroner Charles Scott opened an inquest on the death of the baby, immediately adjourning it to allow Agnes more time to recover so that she might attend. However, when the inquest was reopened on 3 May 1903, although Agnes was physically present, she chose not to speak. After hearing the circumstances of the baby's tragic death on 19 May, the coroner summed up the evidence for the jury, instructing them that they must decide if the infant died by accident, by gross neglect, or as the result of an illegal act. If the jury came to the conclusion that the child's death was due to gross neglect or an illegal act, it was their duty to return a verdict of manslaughter. If they concluded that the baby was intentionally suffocated, then their verdict must be one of murder.

Scott advised the jury that should they return a verdict of manslaughter or murder it was not their job to take into consideration the state of the killer's mind – that would be the prerogative of a higher court. He reminded them that the evidence showed that the cause of the baby's death had been determined by Dr Bibby to be suffocation and that, when found, the baby was in the most dangerous position possible, such that if its mother fell asleep while feeding it could easily have been 'overlain.'

The jury decided that the baby's death was accidental, although they agreed that there was certainly evidence of neglect. The coroner decided that, at present, the law did not allow for a verdict of culpable homicide, although in his opinion England should follow the lead of other countries in making such a verdict possible. He berated both Agnes and her mother for placing the baby in such grave danger and asked the jury to clarify their verdict. Knowing as they did the woman's mental condition, did they believe that she had admitted to deliberately suffocating her child? If they did not believe that this was her clear meaning when speaking to the doctor at the asylum, then they were at liberty to give Agnes the benefit of the doubt and to state their opinion that she did not do it intentionally. If, however, they did believe that the death was intentional, then they must not shirk their duty.

The jury gave their verdict that the baby was not suffocated deliberately, and Agnes was returned to the asylum. However, William Mould not only worked as a tailor but he was also the licensee of a Gloucester public house, The Duke of Wellington. Left with children to care for, along with running a pub and working a second job, he urged authorities to let Agnes come home, something that she was equally eager to do.

Gloucester. (*Author's collection*)

On 14 December 1903 it was decided that Agnes was 'cured', and she was allowed to move back to the pub with her family. At first she appeared fine, but on the day after her release she complained of feeling unwell and spent the day sitting on a chair, refusing to speak to anyone, although on the following day she felt well enough to serve customers in the bar.

On 24 December sixteen-year-old William Mould junior accompanied his mother to do some last-minute Christmas shopping. After selecting dolls and toys for her younger children, Agnes handed over her money, asking her son to wait for the change. By the time he had collected it, his mother was nowhere to be seen.

William searched the streets for her, even asking policemen if they had seen her, but she seemed to have vanished and he was forced to return home alone. His father then began his own search, but to no avail. Agnes's brother, John Pollard, went out looking for her and found her wandering aimlessly on the Bristol Road in Gloucester. She refused to say how she got there and when John questioned her she eventually admitted, 'I have done something'. Naturally, John pressed her for more details until Agnes admitted 'I have drowned a little boy.'

John tried to persuade his sister to go back to the pub with him and she obediently began walking alongside him. John asked if she could show him where she found the little boy and she led him to a shop on the corner of Granville Street.

'Did he go willingly?' asked John, to which Agnes replied that he did.

Brother and sister continued towards The Duke of Wellington, until Agnes suddenly stopped and refused to go any further. John told her that she could either go home or go to the police station in Bristol Road and Agnes chose the latter option. However, they had scarcely started walking towards the police station when Agnes complained of being thirsty and asked her brother to buy her a drink.

John managed to distract his sister until they had reached the police station, where they spoke to a PC Hale, who told them that he had received no reports of a missing child and suggested to John that he take Agnes home. She arrived back at the pub, pale and dishevelled, her boots muddy. Her family took it in turns to sit up all night with her as she alternated between sullen silences and hysterical outbursts, during which she repeated her assertion that she had drowned a child.

Meanwhile, at the home of the Boulter family in Tudor Street, the dawn of Christmas Day heralded a tragedy. On Christmas Eve, Emily Boulter put her two youngest children to bed then left the house to do some shopping. When she returned home, only one of her children, Ernest, was still up. Mrs Boulter asked him if his brothers and sisters were in bed, and when he told her that they were, she went to bed herself without checking. When the family woke the next morning, they found six-year-old Hubert was missing.

John Boulter was working a night shift and wasn't expected home until later that day, so Emily first asked her neighbours if they had seen Hubert, before sending another of her sons to Bristol Street police station to see if they had any information. Given that Agnes Mould had visited the very same police station only hours earlier and tried to confess to drowning a child, Inspector Weaver went straight to The Duke of Wellington, where Agnes tearfully told him. 'I don't know what made me do it. I pushed him in [to the Gloucester and Berkeley Canal], just below where his cap is on the bank.'

Agnes was promptly arrested and taken by cab to the police station, where she refused to say anything further in response to police questioning. For two-and-a-half days, police and volunteers dredged the canal looking for Hubert's body, which was eventually recovered at a place called Two Mile Bend, almost a mile-and-a-half from his home. He was fully dressed apart from his cap and there were no marks of violence on his body. Tragically, the contemporary newspapers reported that one of the volunteers who found the body was the boy's father, John, who immediately identified his son.

As police began their enquiries into Hubert's death, it emerged that several people had seen a woman and child walking along the canal towpath on Christmas Eve. It was a bright, moonlit night and there were many boats on the canal. Their lights shone clearly on the woman, who was described as wearing black clothes and a distinctive black sailor hat. An identity parade was held at the police station, where all of the witnesses unhesitatingly picked out Agnes Mould as the woman they had seen with the now deceased child.

After the inquest on the death of Hubert Boulter returned a verdict of wilful murder against Agnes, she was committed for trial at the next Gloucester Assizes on the coroner's warrant. However, when Mr Justice Ridley opened the proceedings in February 1904, he informed the court that, by order of the Home Secretary, Agnes had been removed to the County Lunatic Asylum on 5 January and would therefore not be standing trial. On 3 March she was transferred to Broadmoor Criminal Lunatic Asylum, where she remained until her death from heart failure on 30 June 1933. She was sixty-six years old.

Interestingly, in the aftermath of his son's tragic death, John Boulter attempted to sue William Mould at the county court for the sum of £7, which he alleged were expenses necessitated by Agnes's actions in drowning the boy. This included £2 for the funeral and burial costs, 10s for refreshments for the bearers, £1 18s 6d for a black dress for Emily, along with the cost of mourning clothes for the remaining Boulter children. The claim also included ten shillings for Hubert's clothing, which was spoiled by his three-day immersion in the canal. Claims for all but the ruination of Hubert's clothes were disallowed by his Honour Judge Ellicott after Mould's solicitors agreed to this payment without admitting any liability.

John James Hitchens: 1867–1938

On the night of 28 February 1905 one of the patients in at Bodmin Asylum in Cornwall was proving difficult for staff to control. For the previous three or four days, thirty-eight-year-old John James Hitchens had struggled to sleep, frequently getting out of bed and wandering round at night, shouting and babbling incoherently. Alternatively described as a farm labourer and a gardener, Hitchens was said to be 'feeble-minded'. Normally a quiet, respectful and industrious patient, he was also severely epileptic, and both before and after suffering a fit, he became 'very excitable', although he was never considered to be dangerous or to pose a risk to other people.

After experiencing a succession of fits on 28 February, Hitchens was placed in the four-bed isolation unit at the asylum, along with two other unwell patients. John Thomas Williams suffered from delusions that the world was about to end, while Charles Rundle was suffering from severe melancholia and was also currently afflicted by scabies. As Hitchens was

Bodmin Asylum. (*Author's collection*)

so unsettled, it was decided to give him some medicine to help him sleep, but when night warder Harry Thomas approached him with the draught, Hitchens dashed it out of his hand, accusing Thomas of trying to poison him. 'Jack isn't having none, my boy,' Hitchens told Thomas. 'I know what that stuff is. That is that working medicine.'

Thomas reassured him that nobody was trying to harm him and that the medicine had been prescribed for him by Dr Dudley, the asylum doctor. Since Hitchens continued to refuse to take his medication, Dr Dudley was sent for. It was decided not to prepare another sleeping draught but instead to let Hitchens quieten down and hopefully go to sleep naturally.

Shortly before midnight Thomas heard a disturbance coming from the room where Hitchens was sleeping and rushed to see what the problem was. As he entered the room, he saw Hitchens with a bedside table raised over his head. 'Don't come near me!' he screamed at Thomas.

Thomas sent for reinforcements and day attendant Thomas Henry Retallick, who slept in an adjacent room, was quick to respond. Together the two attendants tried to rush Hitchens but were forced to draw back when he threatened them with the table. Retallick then held the door closed and Thomas telephoned for assistance, while Hitchens shouted and banged at the door.

When attendants Levy and Stephens arrived, the four men were able to subdue Hitchens, and having quickly dressed him, they took him away to another part of the asylum, leaving Thomas to examine the room, which was in a state of disarray. While Williams cowered in terror, Rundle lay

Centre Court, Bodmin Asylum. (*Author's Collection*)

with a washstand across his chest. Hitchens' bed had been turned on its side and there was broken furniture and crockery scattered everywhere. Most worrying was the copious amount of blood on Rundle's face and head and on the floor around him.

Rundle was put to bed and his multiple wounds were cleaned and dressed, but sadly he died at around half-past three on the morning of 1 March. A later post-mortem examination showed that Rundle had two deep cuts on his face, along with a large bump on the back of his head and numerous minor scrapes and abrasions. While Dr Dudley didn't believe that the wounds on their own were sufficiently serious to cause Rundle's death, he found that Rundle's heart was grossly enlarged, weighing almost 14oz, whereas it should have weighed no more than ten. In addition, all his major organs showed signs of degeneration. In 1873 Rundle suffered a fractured skull and lost his left eye and part of his face in an accidental explosion of dynamite. At the time it was thought highly unlikely that he would survive, and though he eventually pulled through, his extensive injuries contributed to his later diagnosis of insanity. Rundle was a married man with six children, and after his admission to the asylum, on 13 April 1897, he suffered from depression and refused food for some time. Hence, in Dudley's opinion, fifty-six-year-old Rundle was so feeble in body that the shock of the attack was enough to kill him.

The only two people present in the isolation unit besides Rundle were Williams and Hitchens. When Williams was questioned, he claimed to know very little about what had happened since it was dark in the room at the time. All Williams could say for certain was that Hitchens had become very excited and pulled Rundle out of bed, dragging him across the floor before throwing the washstand at him. (Williams was also pulled out of bed but was fortunately unhurt.)

When Hitchens was questioned, he again claimed that he was being poisoned. Lying in bed, he had imagined that someone was creeping up on him. Reaching out his hand, he claimed to have felt a face and punched it.

Coroner John Pethybridge held an inquest on Charles Rundle's death at which the jury found that his demise was 'caused by shock, consequent of a blow received from John James Hitchens and that said John James Hitchens did therefore feloniously kill him.' The coroner took this as a verdict of manslaughter and forwarded the case to the next Cornwall Assizes.

Mr Justice Bigham. (*Author's collection*)

However, once the case was placed before Mr Justice Bigham on 22 June 1905, prosecution counsel Mr R. E. Drummett was the first to raise concerns about whether or not Hitchens was fit to plead. The medical superintendent of the asylum, Mr H.A. Layton, was called to give his opinion and stated that, having treated Hitchens since 1901, he believed he was incapable of understanding the case against him. The jury accordingly found Hitchens unfit to plead and he was ordered to be detained until His Majesty's pleasure be known.

Hitchens was transferred to Broadmoor Criminal Lunatic Asylum on 26 June, remaining there until his death from bronchial pneumonia in September 1938. He was seventy-one years old.

Octavius Diaper: 1867–1938

Octavius Herbert Diaper of Suffolk was variously described as a farmer and a painter. He and his wife, Dorcas, had not had an easy life, having lost two of their three children, and Octavius was prone to bouts of depression. In September 1905 he attempted to commit suicide by cutting his throat but was found in time and made a full recovery from his physical injuries.

On 29 October 1917 Dorcas Diaper heard a loud bang from the kitchen at Jockey Farm, Earl Stonham, where the couple lived. When she went in to see what the noise was, she saw her fifty-year-old husband with his hand on his shotgun, which lay on the table. Knowing that her eighty-three-year-old father-in-law had been sitting by the fire in the kitchen moments earlier, Dorcas tried to take the gun from her husband, but he was too strong for her. He dragged her out into the farmyard, and hearing her desperate screams, the couple's farm labourer, Patrick John Hennessy, came to her aid.

Once he had disarmed Diaper, Dorcas asked Hennessy to check on her father-in-law. Hennessy went into the kitchen and found Prentice Diaper lying face down by the fire. The labourer turned him over, realising immediately that he was dead from a single gunshot wound to the right side of his neck.

Hennessy went back outside to tell Dorcas the sad news. By this time, her husband had run out of the yard into the road and was shouting unintelligibly. Hennessy brought him back into the house, then went for the police and a surgeon.

Dr Housefield was the Diapers' family doctor, and after a quick look at Prentice Diaper, he realised that the old man was beyond any medical assistance. Housefield turned his attention to Octavius, who was sitting on the couch babbling and shouting incoherently, with a man on either side, holding onto his arms. When he could be persuaded to speak, all that Octavius would say was that he wanted to go home, which he repeated over and over again. Housefield had previously treated Octavius for depression and later told the inquest on the death of Prentice Diaper that the farmer suffered from 'maniacal depressive melancholia'. According to the doctor, Octavius suffered bouts of depression every two years or so, yet between times he was quite well. Although Housefield believed that Octavius was more likely to injure himself than other people, he had previously warned the family to keep dangerous weapons away from him.

Octavius had recently been upset by a Zeppelin raid on the neighbourhood, after which he had trouble sleeping. About a week before the killing, he consulted Dr Housefield, claiming that his head felt queer, but the doctor didn't feel that he was as mentally unwell as he had been in the past. Even so, Housefield told coroner Mr G. E. K. Burns that he believed that Octavius was not responsible for his actions when he shot his father.

Dorcas Diaper told the inquest that her husband was normally on good terms with his father and that she had heard no quarrel between them on the morning of the shooting. This was confirmed by Patrick Hennessy, who added that his employer had seemed a little strange for a couple of days beforehand.

The inquest jury found a verdict of wilful murder against Octavius, who had already been certified insane and taken straight from Jockey Farm to the county asylum. His case was brought before Mr Justice Lush at the Suffolk Assizes in Ipswich on 18 January 1918. There, the medical superintendent from the asylum told Lush that he had seen Octavius every day since the killing. Dr James Whitwell was convinced that Octavius was unable to concentrate his attention sufficiently to take part in any trial or to instruct counsel. Lush told the jury that a man who was not fit to defend himself was not fit to plead, adding that Octavius must be detained in an asylum until His Majesty's pleasure be known.

Diaper was sent from Ipswich to Broadmoor Criminal Lunatic Asylum, where he was said to be suffering from 'acute melancholia'. He remained there until lapsing into a diabetic coma and dying in February 1938, aged seventy-one.

Sidney Stuart Lockhart: 1869–1952

Seventy-four-year-old post office pensioner Robert Lockhart was a man of meticulous and regular habits. In April 1916 his second wife was taken into an asylum, after which Robert could regularly be seen doing his housework, shaking out the mats on his front doorstep every day and polishing his brass door furniture. He was seen visiting a local shop to buy potatoes on the evening on 12 April, so his neighbours in Richmond Road, Worthing, were surprised to find that his milk hadn't been taken in the next morning. When it got dark that night, people noticed that no lights were switched on in Lockhart's house, and when his milk was left on the doorstep again on 14 April, his concerned neighbours contacted the police.

When officers visited the house to check on Robert, they found all the doors securely locked. Eventually, after scrambling over walls in neighbours' back yards to gain access to the rear of the property, a ladder was placed against an upstairs window. Seeing a man lying on the floor of a bedroom, the police forced an entry through a skylight in the scullery, finding the downstairs of the house looking as if the occupants had just finished eating a meal. Upstairs, a fearsome struggle had obviously taken place in the bedroom in which the man's body lay. The walls and ceiling were splattered with blood and brain tissue, and the dead man, Robert Lockhart, was terribly maimed. His head had been battered almost to a pulp, exposing his pulverised brain. There were several dents in his skull, one eye was knocked clean out and an

Aerial view of Worthing. (*Author's collection*)

ear was missing. The deceased also had severe bruising on his hands, along with wounds to his face, chin, both forearms, and his left foot, indicating that he had tried desperately to fight off his attacker.

Police found a hammer near the old man's body on the bedroom floor, although its head was missing and was never located. A hatchet wrapped in paper was found under the bed in the attic bedroom in which Robert's son, unemployed telegraphist Sidney Stuart Lockhart, normally slept.

Since Sidney was not at the house, the West Sussex Constabulary immediately issued a description of him, stating that he was wanted on a charge of murder. He was described as 5ft 5in tall, with ginger hair, which he usually wore 'plastered down with grease', with a centre parting. The description continued to say that Sidney may have a slight moustache and that he had 'sharp features, a prominent nose and rather glaring eyes', and that he always had a smile on his face. He was said to walk with a very swift, upright gait and to have a habit of looking behind him every few steps. Finally, having described Sidney's clothing, the appeal mentioned that he had been an inmate of Claybury Asylum eight years previously.

While searching the house, police found some letters that had been delivered on the morning of Friday 13 April, suggesting that the murder had taken place on the evening of 12 April. Among the letters was one from Robert Lockhart's other son, saying that he would be coming to visit his father on 14 April. Cuthbert Robert Whomes Lockhart, who worked in a bank in London, was later to tell the police that he hadn't seen his father for

Claybury Asylum, where Lockhart was a patient. (*Author's collection*)

years but had recently received a letter from him asking him to visit, saying that he would explain why he wanted to see him when his son arrived.

Meanwhile, Mrs Fuller, the landlady of a lodging house in Brighton, read the description of the missing man in her newspaper and was immediately suspicious of a man who had taken a room on 14 April. She contacted the police, and two constables immediately went to arrest him on a charge of murder, subsequently passing him into the charge of Worthing officers Superintendent Pennicott and Inspector Bristow. On his arrest, Sidney Lockhart was found to be carrying around £7 in cash, along with some photographs and items of jewellery that had come from the house on Richmond Road. Referring to the murder, he told the arresting officers, 'I know all about it,' before asking 'Is my poor father dead?' Her added that Robert Lockhart had intended to have him confined to an asylum, and having spent a year in Claybury, he didn't want to go back. 'You will find the papers at home, either in his pocket or in a drawer,' Sidney told the police.

An inquest on Robert Lockhart's death was opened by coroner Mr Alfred W. Rawlinson and almost immediately adjourned to allow for the analysis of stains found on Sidney's clothes. Dr Bernard Henry Spilsbury, the noted pathologist who was later to become Sir Bernard Spilsbury, was tasked with the analysis, finding extensive human blood on Sidney Lockhart's jacket, shirt, tie, socks and shoes. When the proceedings resumed, the inquest jury found a verdict of wilful murder against Sidney Lockhart, who was committed for trial at the Assizes on the coroner's warrant.

County Hall, Lewes, site of the Assizes. (*Author's collection*)

Sidney Lockhart appeared before Lord Reading at the Lewes Assizes on 5 July 1916. However, it was the opinion of Mr Benton, the acting medical officer at Lewes Prison, where the defendant had been confined since the murder, that he was not in a fit state to plead. It was therefore determined that Lockhart was insane, and Lord Reading ordered him to be detained during His Majesty's pleasure. After the trial, Mrs Fuller was given an award of three guineas for her part in Lockhart's arrest.

Lockhart was sent directly to Broadmoor, where he remained until his death on 6 September 1952. He was eighty-three years old, and the cause of his death was ruled as old age and natural causes.

Alice Keeling: 1873–1931

Thirty-four-year-old Alice Keeling worked as a servant at The Portland Arms Hotel in Church Street, Longton in Staffordshire, living in lodgings close by. On 3 April 1907 she went to work as usual but had not been there long when she complained of feeling unwell. She told Mrs Beatrice Turney, who ran the hotel with her husband, William, that she was going to take a headache powder. By lunchtime she claimed to be feeling much worse and suffering from pains in her legs. She asked for a glass of gin, and having drunk it, Alice then asked if she might go upstairs and lie down for a little while on the barman's bed.

Alice stayed upstairs until just after five o'clock in the afternoon, when she came downstairs and drank a cup of tea in the kitchen. Mrs Turney noticed that she looked unusually pale, and when Alice claimed that she didn't feel any better, Mrs Turney suggested that she take some more gin home with her. She left Alice in the kitchen while she went to serve someone in the hotel bar and when she returned Alice had gone.

It wasn't until almost nine o'clock that evening that Mrs Turney thought to check the barman's room and it was there that she found Alice, still looking very poorly. Alice asked for some brandy, which was brought to her and which she downed in a single gulp. Mrs Turney helped her downstairs, then, deciding that Alice was too ill to go home alone, she organised a bed to be made up for her on the sofa. When Alice was called to the table for some food, she stood up and immediately collapsed.

Mrs Turney called for assistance and a customer in the bar rushed through to the kitchen. Mrs Ann Arkinstall took one look at Alice and asked her 'Where have you put it?' Alice claimed not to know what she was talking about, but under repeated questioning, she eventually admitted, 'I put it down the lavatory.'

A doctor was called to the hotel, and having examined Alice, he determined that she had just given birth. Alice was said to be a 'very stout' girl and thus nobody had any idea that she might have been pregnant. Mrs Turney and Mrs Arkinstall sat up with her all night, until she was sent to the maternity ward at the Stoke workhouse the following morning. They believed what she had said about putting her baby down the lavatory, until charwoman Mrs Emily Jane Williams found the dead body of a premature baby boy in the room opposite that of the barman. Concealed beneath some papers and an old quilt, the infant was swaddled in a counterpane, a strip of which had been ripped off and wrapped tightly twice around his neck and secured with a single knot.

A post-mortem examination later carried out by police surgeon Dr Joseph Dawes found that the child was approximately two months premature. Dawes found that he had drawn breath and that the cause of his death was strangulation. Yet, curiously, although he was prepared to say that the child had 'breathed', he was not prepared to say that it had 'lived' independently of its mother. He also stated that it was possible, although highly improbable, that Alice might have wrapped the ligature around the baby's neck before it was born, in order to help its passage into the world.

At the subsequent inquest into the baby's death, his body was passed around in a small box for the jury to examine. County coroner Mr H. W. Adams told the jury that they must consider whether there was a *prima facie* case against Alice Keeling. If they believed that she was responsible for the death of her child it was their duty to say so, in which case, Alice would be committed to the Assizes to be tried for murder. The coroner pointed out that, by law, a child had to be born to be killed and the police surgeon had deemed it possible for the baby to have been strangled before it fully emerged from its mother. There was, however, no doubt that this woman had had a child and the evidence appeared to suggest that she alone was responsible for tying the ligature around its neck.

The jury found a verdict of wilful murder against Alice Keeling, as did the magistrates. Alice took no interest in any of the proceedings against her,

Mr Justice Sutton. (*Author's collection*)

and when questioned, claimed to recall nothing whatsoever about the events of 3 April. She was sent for trial at the Stafford Assizes but, when Mr Justice Sutton addressed the grand jury before the start of the proceedings, he told them that he had been informed that the defendant was not in any condition to plead.

Alice didn't stand trial after all, as she was found insane by a jury especially empanelled to examine her and determine her mental state. She was ordered to be detained during His Majesty's pleasure and admitted to Broadmoor Criminal Lunatic Asylum on 15 July 1907. She remained there until her death, aged fifty-seven, from an unspecified illness in May 1931.

George Scriven: 1873–1934

On the morning of 18 May 1934 Sidney Charles Scriven of Saltley, Birmingham, returned home after his night shift to the familiar sound of his parents arguing. Sidney went straight to bed but got up and went downstairs again after he heard his father threatening to hit his mother.

When Sidney asked fifty-eight-year-old Sarah Ann Rosina Scriven what the problem was, she sighed and told him that his father was 'carrying on again' because he was convinced that she had got herself a 'fancy man'. The accusations of infidelity against his wife had persisted for more than twenty years, especially when George Scriven had been drinking, so Sidney advised his mother to ignore it. Scriven was unemployed due to ill health, leaving his wife to support their family, a situation that Scriven deeply resented. His lack of work made him depressed, and he often told people that he felt useless.

When his father left the house, saying that he was going to visit another of his seven sons, Sidney went back to bed thinking that the argument had run its course. Just over an hour later, he heard his mother calling him, begging him to come quickly. He was halfway down the stairs when she screamed again, 'Quick, Sid – he's cutting my throat!'

Sidney rushed into the living room, to see his mother lying on the couch, his father holding her head down with his left hand and sawing at her throat with a cut-throat razor. Sidney grabbed his father from behind, pinning his arms to his sides and shouted to his mother to run. Meanwhile, Scriven fought against his son, slashing him on the arm before Sidney was able to push him into the scullery and slam the door shut.

Bleeding heavily from the cut on his arm, Sidney ran outside to his mother, finding her lying in the back yard in a pool of blood. As he and his neighbours tried to help her, sixty-one-year-old Scriven came out of the house, his eyes glassy and blood gushing from his neck. 'Look, I've cut my own throat as well,' he announced, seeming almost proud of the fact.

Victoria Law Courts, Birmingham, site of the Assizes. (*Author's collection*)

Neighbours had gone to the Saltley Gas Works, which was almost opposite the Scrivens' house, and the works superintendent there called an ambulance. In the meantime, first-aiders from the works rushed to help the stricken family, rendering vital assistance until it arrived. Sadly, Sarah Scriven was beyond help, having died from loss of blood, but her husband and son were both taken to hospital.

Both Scriven and his son were fortunate enough to survive their injuries and Scriven was charged with his wife's murder. Police recovered a bloody cut-throat razor from the kitchen, and it emerged that he had bought it that very day, presumably for the express purpose of killing his wife and himself. Magistrates were told that in 1892 Scriven had been involved in an accident at his work as a furnaceman, receiving a severe head injury, after which he suffered from epilepsy. One of the other after-effects of the accident was that Scriven began to experience delusions – he became wrongly convinced that his wife was being unfaithful to him and believed that he was being poisoned and that something was being put in his pipe, causing him to choke whenever he smoked it. He suffered from depression and had made numerous attempts to commit suicide over the years, including throwing himself in the canal, swallowing iodine, and drinking a bottle of disinfectant.

Mr Justice Lawrence. (*Author's collection*)

On 22 November 1933 he was certified insane and spent four months in the city mental hospital. He was released at his wife's request but returned as a voluntary patient after just two weeks, spending a further month in the asylum, before being discharged into his wife's care. Sidney Scriven told the court that after leaving the mental hospital it only took a couple of weeks before he began to experience delusions again, and within six weeks he had murdered his wife.

Magistrates forwarded Scriven's case to the Birmingham Assizes, where he appeared before Mr Justice Lawrence on 12 July 1934. He had been confined in Winston Green Prison since being released from hospital and the medical officer, Dr J. Humphrey, told the court that Scriven suffered from depression, melancholia, and unfounded delusions about his wife's fidelity. Humphrey told the court that he believed that at the time of the murder Scriven had no notion that he was doing wrong, and, in his opinion, was not in his right mind when he killed his wife. The jury did not need to deliberate long before finding him guilty but insane.

Scriven was sent to Broadmoor Criminal Lunatic Asylum on 19 July, where it was noted that the self-inflicted wound in his throat was not healing

Winson Green Prison, Birmingham, where Scriven was confined after his release from hospital. (*Author's collection*)

properly. The wound did not respond to treatment, so a consulting surgeon from outside the hospital was called in, recommending an operation. Scriven gave his consent to the surgery and a very light anaesthetic was administered while the surgery was performed. A piece of bone was found lodged in the wound, which was preventing it from properly closing and healing.

Within fifteen minutes of the end of the operation, Scriven collapsed. Surgeons immediately began artificial respiration and battled to save him, giving oxygen and injecting adrenalin directly into his heart. As a last resort, Scriven's abdomen was opened to allow his heart to be massaged but the doctors' efforts were in vain and Scriven could not be revived. A post-mortem examination cited heart failure as the cause of his death. An inquest later found a verdict of 'death by misadventure', the jury commenting that they were satisfied that everything possible had been done to save Scriven's life.

George Holland: 1876–1939

On 30 September 1894 John Upton noticed that there was a lamb missing from the flock he shepherded for farmer Charles G. S. Chapman Duke, at Angmering, West Sussex. The lamb was later found in a nearby field with its throat cut and suspicion quickly fell on twenty-one-year-old farm labourer George Holland from Burpham, near Arundel, who had been flint picking in that particular field on the previous day.

Holland had several convictions for committing similar atrocities on lambs and calves, but when questioned by PC Wood he initially denied the offence, before eventually admitting that he had killed the lamb. He could give no reason why he had done so, except to say that he wanted to see the blood run, adding that he felt much better afterwards.

Taken before magistrates at the West Sussex Michaelmas Quarter Sessions at Chichester on 18 October 1894, Holland was charged with 'feloniously killing a lamb of the value £1 5s'. One of the chief witnesses in court was surgeon Mr C. Evershed, who stated that he had known Holland from his early childhood. Evershed confirmed that the prisoner suffered from epileptic fits and also from 'blood mania', experiencing strong, uncontrollable urges to see blood flowing. It was stated that Holland had previously been sentenced to imprisonment with hard labour for killing calves and lambs in 1892, and at that trial it was suggested that this was his eighth similar offence.

Evershed told the court he felt very strongly that if Holland could not find a sheep or other animal to satisfy his blood lust when the urge came upon him, he would, in all likelihood, attack a human being, most probably a child. It was therefore Evershed's opinion that Holland should be confined to an asylum.

The Chief Magistrate asked the doctor why Holland had never been certified as a lunatic.

'I would not like to do it,' replied Evershed.

'Then, though not fit to be at large, he is, in your opinion, equally not fit to be in a lunatic asylum?' queried the magistrate.

'He is apparently sane on every other subject,' clarified the doctor.

The jury found Holland guilty, adding the rider that at the time of the offence he was not responsible for his actions. He was therefore ordered to be detained in Broadmoor Criminal Lunatic Asylum during Her Majesty's pleasure.

Holland was never to leave the confines of Broadmoor, dying there from natural causes following a stroke in February 1939. He was sixty-six years old.

Hannah Griffin: 1881–1948

Hannah Griffin of Binley, Coventry, was forty-six years old when she gave birth to her son, Ronald Allan Griffin, on 14 April 1927. Ronald was the eighth child born to Hannah and her husband, George, who worked as a laundry man. Seven of those children had survived, although one of them suffered from severe epilepsy and had consequently been hospitalised for seven of his nine years.

From the moment Ronald was born, Hannah worried about him endlessly, convincing herself that he was not receiving the proper nourishment, despite the little boy being quite a sturdy infant with no health problems apparent to anyone else but his mother. Hannah was so anxious about her baby that she was unable to sleep, and eventually her husband insisted that she consult a doctor. She saw Dr Phillips on 14 May, and after he reassured her that her concerns were ungrounded, she seemed much brighter.

On the morning of 18 May Hannah seemed more like her normal cheerful self as she prepared breakfast. At 8.15am she put Ronald in his pram, telling her family that she was taking him out for a walk and that she would bring something back for their dinner. Fifteen minutes later, a young woman named Jean Halliday Crombie was cycling along the Binley Road towards Coventry when she spotted an empty pram standing on a bridge over the River Sowe. Although Miss Crombie initially cycled on, the presence of the abandoned pram bothered her and she turned back to investigate further. Peering over the bridge to the river below, she spotted a woman floating on her right side in the water.

Miss Crombie immediately shouted for help, flagging down a passing car. William Arthur Thorpe and Cyril W. Mabey plunged into the river and managed to drag Hannah Griffin to safety. Only when she was hauled out of the water did they spot baby Ronald, cradled tightly in her arms.

While Miss Crombie took Ronald to a doctor, the two motorists performed artificial respiration on Hannah, eventually bringing her back from the brink of death. Summoned by Miss Crombie, PC Spooner arrived on the scene, finding Hannah sufficiently revived to be capable of accompanying him to the hospital. During the journey, she repeatedly complained about severe pains in her head, telling the policeman, 'It's my head. I couldn't stand it any longer. I've been thinking about it all night. I waited till my husband had gone to work and then came down here and threw myself and baby into the river. I wish I hadn't done it now but it is my head that made me do it.'

By now, baby Ronald had been seen by Dr C. E. Rice and pronounced dead. A later post-mortem examination showed him to have been a bonny, healthy baby, with no marks of violence on his body and no suggestion that he had been malnourished. Rice noted that the child's lungs were full of water and concluded that his death was due to asphyxia from drowning.

An inquest was opened by coroner Mr C. W. Iliffe under new rules, which stated that, in the event of the likelihood of a charge of murder, manslaughter or infanticide, any inquest must be adjourned until after the Assizes had been held and seven clear days had been allowed for an appeal. Thus, the only necessity for Iliffe was to hear sufficient evidence to issue a burial order, since, after the Assizes, any inquiry into the infant's death would simply be a matter of recording a formal verdict according to the findings of the court.

Hannah Griffin appeared before magistrates at Coventry County Police Court, charged with wilful murder and attempting to commit suicide (which was still a criminal offence in the United Kingdom until the passing of the Suicide Act in 1961). One of the chief witnesses was Hannah's twenty-year-old daughter, Evelyn, who told the court that theirs had always been a happy and united family and that Hannah was a good and caring wife and mother. However, since Ronald's birth, Hannah had suffered from depression and had been convinced that the baby wasn't thriving. In 1923 Hannah had spent some time in Hatton Mental Hospital after a needle became lodged in her hand. The wound, which had left her with a deformed hand, and which still caused her considerable pain, had turned septic and Hannah had consequently suffered a nervous breakdown.

Magistrates committed Hannah for trial at the next Warwick Assizes and she appeared before Mr Justice McCardie on 5 July 1927, tried only on the charge of wilful murder. There, prosecutor Mr Allesbrook told the court that it had been brought to their attention that the prisoner's state of mind was abnormal. Dr Hamilton-Smith, the medical officer of Birmingham Prison, gave his opinion that on the day of her son's death Hannah Griffin had been living and acting under such a defect of reasoning that she was incapable of appreciating the quality and nature of her act. Having examined her, Hamilton-Smith found her to be intensely depressed and greatly confused mentally, having no memory whatsoever of the events of 18 May that had resulted in the death of her infant son.

Having heard this, the jury found Hannah Griffin guilty but insane and she was ordered to be detained until His Majesty's pleasure be known. Sent to Broadmoor Criminal Lunatic Asylum, she remained there until her death from cancer, aged sixty-six, in February 1948.

Benjamin Bradford: 1882–1958

On 27 September 1920 desperate screams were heard coming from the home of collier Benjamin Bradford in Baptist Lane, Measham, Leicestershire. When neighbours rushed to investigate, they found Benjamin's wife, Rhoda Lavinia Bradford, lying on the floor of the cottage in a pool of blood, her throat cut from ear to ear. The wound was five inches long and had severed the muscles and some of the large blood vessels in Rhoda's neck, including her jugular vein

Leicester Infirmary, where Rhoda Bradford was treated. (*Author's collection*)

Doctors Hart and Thompson were sent for, and they treated Rhoda, managing to staunch the bleeding, while waiting for an ambulance to take her to the Leicester Infirmary. Meanwhile, neighbours detained Benjamin in the garden of his home until the arrival of PC Holmes, who conveyed him to the police station at Ashby-de-la-Zouch. Holmes later told magistrates that Bradford seemed dazed and claimed to have no idea what was going on, a sentiment he repeated to magistrates later that evening when he was charged with feloniously wounding his wife with intent to kill and murder her.

Fortunately, Rhoda Bradford survived the attack and was later to give evidence against her husband before the magistrates at Ashby-de-la-Zouch. Her throat bandaged, she was described in the contemporary newspapers as 'a gentle looking woman, muffled in a black fur'. Obviously still very weak, she was allowed to sit down while testifying.

Rhoda told magistrates that she and her husband had been married for eleven years and had three children, who were fortunately at school when she was attacked. According to Rhoda, her husband had suffered three nervous breakdowns, the most recent about eleven weeks prior to the attack on her. Although Dr Hart didn't consider Bradford to be dangerous, after his latest breakdown he had nevertheless recommended that he went to live with his brother. However, Benjamin's brother wanted to get rid of him and Benjamin himself desperately wanted to return to the marital home. He had in the past, made several threats against his wife if she did not allow him to live with her again: he had chased her with a poker; threatened to set fire to her bed while she was sleeping; and had also threatened violence against the children. On occasions, Rhoda had seen him lurking in the garden at night and trying the door and windows to try to gain entry to the cottage. She was so afraid of her husband that she had sometimes asked her two brothers to stay with her.

On the morning of the attack Benjamin visited the cottage on the pretext of picking up some clean clothes. Rhoda left him there while she went out to her cleaning job, and was surprised to find him still in the cottage when she returned. She told Benjamin that his brother had sworn at her because she refused to take him back, then, as she turned to tend to the fire, she felt her husband's arm around her and saw a flash of steel. There had been no quarrel between them that morning and no warning of her husband's intentions, but Rhoda suddenly felt a sharp pain in her throat and screamed 'Murder!' at the top of her voice. Her neighbour, Arthur Dewsbury, rushed into the house and pulled Benjamin away by the collar, handing him to another man before turning to assist the injured woman, wrapping a towel around her throat. His presence of mind in doing so was later credited by doctors as having saved her from bleeding to death.

At this point in the proceedings, magistrates asked Benjamin Bradford if he had any questions that he wanted to ask his wife. 'Is that my wife?' Bradford responded pathetically, still appearing dazed and utterly bewildered at finding himself in court. When he was asked again if he had any questions, Bradford ran his hands over his head and replied wearily, 'I want to go home'.

Dr Hart, who had been the family's doctor for many years, told magistrates that Bradford had spent three months in the county lunatic asylum fourteen years earlier, since when he had suffered from frequent attacks of neurasthenia or weakness of the nerves. Describing these attacks as a mixture of mental and nervous disease, Hart said that Bradford was subject to outbursts, during which it was perfectly possible that he might do things without realising that he was doing them. The magistrates noted that Bradford obviously had very little idea of what was happening, although there was some doubt as to whether or not he was faking. However, once it was decided to commit Bradford for trial, he was heard to mutter that he didn't know what all the fuss was about.

When thirty-eight-year-old Bradford was brought before Mr Justice Sankey at the Assizes in Leicester, it was determined that he was not in a fit condition to plead. Having heard evidence from Dr Hart about Bradford's mental state, which the doctor understatedly described as 'not normal', Sankey ordered Bradford to be detained during His Majesty's pleasure.

Bradford was sent to Broadmoor in November 1920 and remained there until August 1958, when he died, aged seventy-six, two days after undergoing surgery for an unspecified 'internal complaint'.

John Edward Jones: 1887–1958

In the early hours of the morning of 30 April 1929 forty-two-year-old dock labourer John Edward Jones walked into Lawrence Road Police Station in Liverpool in his stockinged feet and told officers, 'I've done my wife in.' Police went straight to his house in Casterton Street, where they found thirty-five-year-old Mary Bridget Jones unconscious in her blood-soaked bed, the left side of her head smashed to a pulp and a deep wound over her right eye. The dead body of her ten-month-old daughter, Eileen Sheila, lay beside her, along with a blood-and-hair-covered hammer. At the end of the bed cowered Jones's three sobbing stepchildren, Mary Josephine (eight), John Edward (seven) and Veronica Elizabeth (four), at least one of whom had witnessed their stepfather beating their mother and half-sister with a hammer.

Mary and baby Eileen were taken to the Liverpool Royal Infirmary, where Eileen was officially pronounced dead and Mary underwent an operation to remove a broken piece of her skull, which was pressing on her brain. Although the operation itself was successful, Mary died from her injuries on 1 June. Jones had already been charged with the murder of his daughter and now the attempted murder of his wife was upgraded to a second murder charge.

At the police station, Jones had given a statement in which he admitted to hitting his wife with a hammer, adding that he had fully intended to kill her. Mary Taubman, a widow with three children, had married Jones in December 1927, but Jones told police that their marriage was far from happy. Jones had taken to drinking heavily, and, according to him, his wife had, for the past year, been insisting that he was nothing more than a lodger and kept telling him to leave. 'She thinks I know nothing. She has been treating me like a dog,' he complained. Jones told police that his wife refused to look after him, saying that she had enough to do caring for the children. He was frequently locked out of the bedroom and his wife often refused to speak to him.

A note was found in Jones's pocket, which read: 'My God! Murder's no wonder. Give me a dog's life after what I went through. I am only a lodger here. The only thing I have got to do is turn out to work. Starve me out. The ******* swine gave me hell to try and get me out. She found her mistake and a lot more. Irish swine.'

In November 1928 the couple got into a fight in the street outside their home and Mary called a policeman to deal with her husband. 'I only ever shook her. I never raised a hand to her,' Jones insisted.

On the Saturday prior to the murders, Jones was arrested for being drunk, and on his return home from the police station Mary told him to go to hell, calling him 'a worm' and 'a Welsh rabbit' and saying that she no longer wanted him.

Although Jones claimed to have hit his wife only two or three times with the hammer, his stepdaughter gave evidence against him at the Liverpool Police Court. Mary Josephine described waking up and seeing Jones holding the hammer in both hands then watching him hit her mother five times with it.' She cried at first then stopped,' said little Mary.

Mr Justice Charles. (*Author's collection*)

Jones was sent for trial at the Liverpool Assizes, where he appeared before Mr Justice Charles on 17 June 1929, trembling uncontrollably and barely able to utter his plea of 'Not Guilty'.

Since the murder had been witnessed by the defendant's stepdaughter, and in view of his confession to the police immediately after the murders, Jones's only defence was one of insanity. It was revealed in court that Jones had fought in the First World War and had suffered a minor shrapnel wound to his forehead. He had also spent a considerable period as a prisoner of war in Germany, during which time he was very harshly treated.

Jones's brother-in-law testified to the fact that Jones had very strange ways, particularly when he had been drinking, and that his grandmother had died in a lunatic asylum. Edward Ellis Jones also recalled numerous occasions when he found his brother-in-law out of bed in the early hours of the morning, apparently fighting imaginary Germans in his sleep. Even the police officers stated that the defendant had appeared at the police station after the murder as if he were sleepwalking.

Walton Prison, where Jones was incarcerated. (*Author's collection*)

However, Dr John Ahearn, the prison surgeon at Walton Prison, where Jones had been incarcerated pending his trial, gave his opinion that the defendant had shown no signs of insanity, although he had been very agitated when he arrived. The police also pointed out that Jones had been able to recall the time on the clock in his bedroom when he made his initial statement, even correctly saying that it was half an hour fast. Jones had told the police that before killing his wife he got up, dressed himself, and sat by the bed watching her sleeping for a while, thinking about what he should do. He had said more than once, 'I intended to do both of them,' and, 'I meant to do it.'

Defence counsel Mr Maxwell Fyfe tried to persuade the jury that the defendant carried a load that was too heavy for him to bear, claiming that Jones was of low intelligence and suffered from a combination of hysteria and 'quasi-epileptic emotion', committing the murders while in a dream-like state. However, Dr Ahearn gave his opinion that, had this been the case, Jones would have been horrified, or, at the very least surprised, on recovering his senses and realising what he had done.

Fyfe's contention was supported by Dr Robert G. Walmsley, who was called as a specialist in mental illnesses. Having examined Jones, Walmsley concluded that he suffered from a disease of the mind, similar to epilepsy, and at the time of the killings probably had 'a cloudy consciousness' of the physical quality of the act but no idea of its moral quality. He described Jones' state of mind when committing the murders as 'an epileptic dream state, somewhat akin to somnambulism'.

The jury, which included three women, retired for twenty-five minutes, before asking if they might be permitted to see the law book from which the judge had taken his legal definition of insanity. The book was sent into the jury room, and twelve minutes later the jury returned with a verdict that Jones was guilty but insane. Mr Justice Charles ordered him to be detained during the King's pleasure. Jones was sent to Broadmoor Criminal Lunatic Asylum, where he remained until his death from natural causes, aged seventy-one, in August 1958.

Thomas Percival Thomas: 1886–1937

In 1925 Thomas Percival Thomas, a schoolmaster from Dartmouth Boys' Council School in Devon, was staying with his wife's parents in Paignton while he recovered from the latest in a series of nervous breakdowns. In the early hours of 21 June his wife's brother-in-law, Ernest John Coyle, who was also living at the house, heard a muffled scream. A few seconds later there was a loud thud and second scream, followed by a desperate shout of 'Help!' from the bedroom shared by Thomas and his wife, Ellen Martin Thomas.

Coyle went to investigate. As he entered the room, which was illuminated by a night light, he saw Ellen lying on the floor at the foot of the bed, a gaping wound in her throat. 'Save me,' she whispered desperately, while her husband sat on their bed, calmly watching her bleeding to death.

Coyle wrapped a towel around his sister-in-law's neck and told her to hold it there, before leaving the room to summon a doctor and the police. When he returned, Thomas was still sitting on the bed in a dazed condition, making no effort to help his wife.

By the time Dr Clement Carlyon Kerby arrived, only a few minutes later, Ellen had already died. The doctor noted a deep, two-and-a-half-inch-long wound on the left side of her neck, along with several smaller cuts and fingernail marks, suggesting that her throat had been tightly gripped. Her husband also had a deep cut on the base of his thumb, which Kerby dressed.

The first policeman on the scene was PC Skinner, who found Thomas wearing blood-stained pyjamas, a bloody razor blade on the bed next to him. 'What have I done?' Thomas asked repeatedly 'Why did I do it? We have always lived so happily together. I did it with a razor blade. Can't you save her?'

As Skinner waited for reinforcements, Thomas asked to go to the lavatory, but Skinner refused to let him leave the room. Thwarted, Thomas became violent, although he had calmed down again by the time he reached the police station. Charged by Police Sergeant Babb, Thomas seemed like a man

The Assize Courts, Exeter. (*Author's collection*)

who had woken from a terrible nightmare. He continually asked if his wife was dead, and when assured that she was, he put his head in his hands and wept bitterly. 'I don't know what made me do such a thing,' he sobbed, telling the sergeant that he wished he had stayed in the nursing home where he had been convalescing after his breakdown. Thomas claimed that the diet of milk and stout he had been fed had badly affected his nerves. 'I suppose they will say that I wilfully planned it but I have been driven to it. Absolutely driven to it. I can't say more.'

An inquest was held on Ellen Martin Thomas' death by deputy coroner Mr T. Edmunds. Thomas and Ellen Thomas were said to be a devoted couple, who were very happily married and had no worries, apart from Thomas Thomas' rather indifferent health. Having detailed her injuries for the coroner, Dr Kerby conceded that it was possible – although highly unlikely – that Ellen Thomas' wounds may have been self-inflicted. However, as her husband had immediately confessed to having slashed her throat with a razor blade, this possibility could be discounted. The doctor felt that Ellen's injuries were so severe that her life could not possibly have been saved, even if a doctor had been present.

At the conclusion of the inquest the coroner told the jury that there was no doubt that Thomas had murdered his wife by cutting her throat; not only had he been caught red-handed, but he had also admitted the offence time and time again. It was not their business to consider the state of mind of the accused, Edmunds reminded them. Accordingly, after just three minutes' deliberation, the jury returned a verdict of wilful murder against Thomas, who was committed to take his trial at the next Devon Assizes in Exeter.

At his trial before Mr Justice Rowlatt on 31 October, Thomas was deathly pale, his eyes red and swollen from weeping. His defence counsel, Mr Percival Clarke, asked the court first to consider whether or not his client was fit to plead. Dr Roy Craig, a physician at the Centre for Nervous Diseases at Torbay Hospital, told the court that he had first seen Thomas in March of 1925, at which time he had come to the conclusion that Thomas was too unwell to be cared for in an ordinary nursing home and should instead be sent to a proper facility. Suffering from delusions and chronic insomnia, he was therefore sent to a mental nursing home at Paignton, but during his stay there he escaped twice. He seemed to have a fear of being parted from Ellen, whom he claimed to love dearly, and was convinced that people were trying to break up their marriage and so tried desperately to get back to her. Craig told the court that he had last seen Thomas on 8 October and that then, or indeed at any point throughout his treatment, he would have been prepared to certify him insane.

Since the murder, Craig had also visited Thomas at Exeter Prison and found that Thomas had not even accepted that his wife was dead, often asking how she was getting on and if anything could be done to help her. Craig told the court that Thomas suffered from severe delusions while in prison, claiming that gas was being pumped under his cell door to harm him. He also tried to devise hidden meanings for everyday occurrences, finding great significance in circles he observed in the prison exercise yard. Thomas often communicated with Craig by letters written on different coloured papers, each colour having a special meaning in Thomas' mind. He was convinced that the other prisoners were conspiring against him, particularly anyone who wore any black garment.

'He might object to a jury man who was wearing a black tie?' asked his defence counsel, and Craig agreed that this was highly likely. The doctor believed that Thomas was in no fit condition to understand the trial or the evidence, challenge jurors or make a proper defence against the charge of wilful murder.

'You are certain about that?' Mr Justice Rowlatt asked Craig.

'Absolutely, my Lord,' replied the doctor.

Counsel for the prosecution, Mr Casswell, countered by calling Dr Wayland Smith, the surgeon at Exeter Prison. Smith completely disagreed with Craig, and though he conceded that Thomas had an obsessional interest in colours, questioned on any other subject, he was quite rational. Whereas he agreed that Thomas was not sane, and would also be prepared to certify him, Smith believed that he was more than capable of understanding and following his trial.

Mr Justice Rowlatt addressed the jury, telling them that it was clear that Thomas murdered his wife and equally clear that he was mad. Thus, the question for the jury to decide upon was whether or not he was fit to plead and stand trial. The jury agreed that he was not, and Rowlatt sentenced him to be detained during the His Majesty's pleasure.

Thomas was sent to Broadmoor Criminal Lunatic Asylum, arriving on 10 November 1925. He died on 17 November 1937, aged fifty-one, from heart failure resulting from high blood pressure.

Phillip George Dickinson: 1896–1946 and John Llewellyn Phillips: 1923–1948

Twenty-four-year-old pub pot man Phillip George Dickinson of Bromley often tried to pick up men for homosexual relations. On 2 February 1921 nineteen-year-old George James Rowe was standing outside a cinema in Bromley High Street when Dickinson approached him. Rowe knew Dickinson to speak to, although he didn't know his name, and when Dickinson asked if he would like to go for a drink with him, Rowe gave an excuse that he didn't have any money.

Dickinson showed Rowe a pound note and a handful of silver, so Rowe agreed to go for a quick drink and the two men went to the Swan and

High Street, Bromley, where Dickinson met Rowe. (*Author's collection*)

Mitre public house. A little later Dickinson asked Rowe if he would like to accompany him to the cinema at Catford. Again, Rowe demurred but Dickinson was persuasive and the two men eventually reached Queen's Hall. However, there was a long queue to get in and Rowe told Dickinson that he really ought to be getting home. Dickinson accompanied him as he caught a train to Southend Pond, where they had more drinks at the Green Man public house, leaving together at around half-past nine to walk to Bromley.

As the two men walked up Bromley Hill, Dickinson made what was described in the contemporary newspapers as 'a certain indecent suggestion'. Rowe recoiled in horror, but Dickinson was persistent and continued walking with him, making ever more obscene suggestions and requests, which Rowe wanted nothing to do with.

As they continued towards Rowe's home in Plaistow Lane, Dickinson suddenly remarked out of the blue that there were not many stars out that night. Rowe stopped and tilted his head back to look. As he did, he felt Dickinson grab his coat collar from behind before running something sharp across his throat.

Immediately afterwards, Dickinson fled, with Rowe hot on his heels, repeatedly shouting 'Help! Police!' as he ran. Eventually his cries were heard by PC Ilsley (or Isley), who chased after Dickinson but was unable to catch him. As he fled, Dickinson dropped a mackintosh coat, which a passer-by picked up and handed to Ilsley. The constable then walked back to where he had left Rowe, finding him staggering about, weak through loss of blood. Ilsley took him to the nearest police station and summoned the police surgeon to attend to him. When Dr H. J. Ilott arrived, Rowe was lying on the floor of the police station, bleeding heavily. There was a two-inch-long gaping wound on the right side of his neck, extending downwards towards his chin. Ilott tied one vein and stitched Rowe up as best he could on the police station floor, before sending him to the Bromley Cottage Hospital. Although very seriously injured, Rowe managed to accuse Dickinson of cutting his throat, and during the course of their evening together, he had learned his attacker's name, address and place of work and was thus able to direct the police straight to Dickinson's door.

The police went to his home that evening, finding Dickinson in bed, apparently asleep. The Cambridge Road area where Rowe was attacked had already been searched and the police had found a blood-stained cut-throat razor and a coat button that was identical to the ones on Dickinson's mackintosh, which had one button missing off the back.

Dickinson claimed to have been in all evening until the police produced his coat, which was spotted with blood. He said, 'I don't know anything about it. I had some beer tonight and my mind is blank. I don't know what made me do it.' He was arrested and charged with attempted murder.

Although Rowe's injuries were severe, he eventually recovered and was able to act as a witness against his attacker when he appeared before magistrates at Bromley Police Court.

One of the first witnesses to testify was Dickinson's mother, Kate Annie Dickinson. She stated that Phillip suffered from tuberculosis, which could explain the stains on his mackintosh, as he sometimes coughed up blood. According to Mrs Dickinson, her son had enlisted in the West Kent Regiment during the First World War, and soon afterwards had fallen off his bicycle and sustained a severe concussion, remaining unconscious for a week. During the hostilities, he had been wounded three times, and having been gassed and blown up in France, was discharged from the army with a disability pension in April 1919 because of his tuberculosis. Since returning to England, he had once gone missing from home but was later found by his brother. He suffered from loss of memory and often seemed rather dazed and vacant looking – his mother referred to him in court as 'a very uncertain fellow'. Mrs Dickinson also revealed that her daughter had once been confined in an asylum due to anaemia.

Dickinson was already known to the police having attacked a young boy on Bromley Common. Officers were of the opinion that his mind was unbalanced, theorising that he may be suffering from dementia. Thus, his solicitor suggested that if the charge of attempted murder progressed to the Assizes, he intended to argue that Dickinson was insane at the time and did not appreciate the nature of his act. He reminded the magistrates that under the Mental Deficiency Act they had the power to bypass the Assizes and send Dickinson directly to an asylum. However, magistrates were keen to hear from Rowe and adjourned the proceedings until he had sufficiently recovered to make an appearance.

Having described the events leading up to the attack, Rowe told the court that, as far as he was concerned, Dickinson's actions were 'senseless, motiveless and a very foolish thing to do'. There had been no animosity between them that evening – it was as if Dickinson had suddenly lost control of himself. Rowe had known Dickinson for some time and had always regarded him as 'a foolish sort of fellow'.

After some discussion, the magistrates chose to forward Dickinson's case to the Kent Assizes, although, as the Assizes were due to open in just a few days' time, they granted permission for Dickinson's counsel to apply for the proceedings to be held over until the following Assizes if he couldn't be ready. This proved unnecessary, as Dickinson appeared before Mr Justice

Maidstone Prison, where Dickinson was held awaiting trial. (*Author's collection*)

Bray on 17 February 1921, charged with wounding Rowe with intent to murder him and do him some grievous bodily harm.

Prison surgeon Dr E. L. Martin Lobb from Maidstone Prison, where Dickinson had been confined since the offence, told the court that he had seen nothing that led him to suppose that Dickinson was of unsound mind. Yet, in spite of the surgeon's testimony, the jury found Dickinson guilty but insane and he was ordered to be detained during His Majesty's pleasure.

Dickinson was sent to Broadmoor Criminal Lunatic Asylum on 24 February 1921, where he was described as 'a mental defective of a rather bullying type'. However, during his stay at Broadmoor, there were no complaints about his behaviour from other patients, until 31 May 1946, when he clashed with another patient, John Llewellyn Phillips.

Phillips, a naval submarine detector from Llanelly, Carmarthenshire, was admitted to Broadmoor in January 1945 following the murder of a naval rating in Mombasa, Kenya, for which he was found guilty but insane. Prior to attacking the rating with a knife, Phillips was in solitary confinement for striking an officer, so he was known to be a violent man, said by the asylum medical officer to be a 'psychopathic personality, a physic inferior type, suffering from maniatic depressive insanity' (sic). Almost from the moment he arrived at Broadmoor, Dickinson began to pester him with homosexual advances, in spite of Phillips making it absolutely clear that he wasn't interested. Eventually, Dickinson's advances became ever more sinister, and he threatened to harm Phillips if he didn't comply with his demands.

On the afternoon of 31 May 1946 asylum attendant Frank Fowler was approached by Phillips and another patient, who asked him to go upstairs as there had been a row. When Fowler asked what the problem was, Phillips told him 'Dickinson is dying'.

Fowler stayed with Phillips while attendant Thomas Coles went to Dickinson's room, where he found Dickinson still alive, lying on the floor in a puddle of blood, a broken bottle nearby. When Coles took a closer look, he realised that Dickinson's throat had been almost completely gouged out. Coles sent for the medical officer while his colleague, principal attendant Joseph Lee, went to Phillips and asked him what was wrong. Phillips, who was washing the blood from his hands, replied 'I would rather not tell you.'

Medical Officer John S. Knox was unable to save Dickinson, who had lost a large volume of blood. A later post-mortem examination showed severe bruising to his head and two major wounds in his throat, which had severed his larynx and his gullet. Knox concluded that Dickinson had first been struck by the unbroken bottle, which broke over his head and was then used to slash at his throat, causing him to bleed to death.

In the aftermath of Dickinson's death, Phillips became depressed, tearful, agitated and confused. He eventually revealed that Dickinson had been persistently making homosexual suggestions to him and threatening him for many months and he couldn't take it any longer, so he went to his room and hit him with a bottle.

Phillips appeared before magistrates at Wokingham, and much to his surprise, was committed for trial at the next Assizes, due to take place on 11 July. Although Dr Joseph Hopwood, the asylum medical officer, told the magistrates that he believed that Phillips was insane at the time of the attack, notwithstanding the fact that he was confined in a lunatic asylum when he murdered Dickinson, Phillips had wrongly assumed that he would automatically be pronounced unfit to plead. Realising that this was not the case, he stood up and asked for permission to call witnesses. This was denied and he was told that he would be granted legal aid for the trial, where he would be able to call all the witnesses that he needed.

However, when the case reached the Assizes, Phillips was, not unexpectedly, found unfit to plead and was returned to Broadmoor. In January 1947 he attempted to commit suicide, after which he was placed under more stringent observation. In July 1948 these restrictions were still in force when he was found in his room, strangled with a pair of braces.

At the inquest on his death, a juror inquired why a suicidal patient was allowed possession of his braces. Assistant Medical Officer Dr Edward Spicer explained that Phillips worked in the asylum laundry and had obviously secretly appropriated a pair of braces belonging to another patient. The inquest jury found a verdict of suicide while the balance of his mind was disturbed, adding a rider that they were of the opinion that supervision of suicidal patients at Broadmoor should be improved.

Phillips's body was reclaimed by his family and he was buried in Llanelly on 3 August 1948.

William Jarvis Yeoman: 1896–1960

On 7 May 1932 thirty-five-year-old farmer William Jarvis Yeoman went into Kingsbridge, Devon, and bought a box of cartridges for his shotgun. From there he went to the Cottage Hospital at South Hams, where his nine-year-old son, William George Yeoman, (known as George) was undergoing treatment for blood poisoning, having cut his leg on some barbed wire. Told that visiting hours weren't until 2pm, Yeoman hung around in the town until then, before returning to the hospital at the appointed time.

When visiting hours were over, Nurse Ida Croucher went to tell Yeoman that it was time for him to leave and found him sitting by his son's bed, with something wrapped up in a raincoat on his lap. As he stood up to leave, he pointed the raincoat at George and Nurse Croucher immediately realised that the object that it concealed was a shotgun. She caught hold of Yeoman's jacket and tried to pull him away, but as she did, the farmer fired twice, the shots hitting his son on the forehead. Although he initially survived the shooting, George died from his injuries less than forty-eight hours later.

A woman who was visiting her sister heard a child's scream. Emma Jose Townsend went to investigate, and to her horror found Yeoman beating his son with the butt of his shotgun. Courageously, Miss Townsend tried to wrest the weapon from Yeoman, who turned on her, saying 'Now I will give you one'. With that, he hit her over the head with the gun, splitting open her scalp and rendering her semi-conscious.

Nurses chased Yeoman out of the hospital and he fled across the fields. However, when police went to his home at Lower Sigdon Farm in Buckland-Tout-Saints, near Kingsbridge, they found evidence of an even greater tragedy.

The farmhouse was locked, and when police forced an entry, they found the body of Yeoman's wife, Olive Alice Yeoman, in the farmhouse kitchen. Ten-year-old Kathleen Lucy lay dead in the chicken run, while the body of eighteen-month-old Alfred Charles was found between two outbuildings.

Police immediately began to scour the countryside for Yeoman, who was eventually arrested near the neighbouring village of Marlborough. An inquest on the four deaths was opened by coroner Mr. G. Windeatt and adjourned after the identity of the victims had been established. Yeoman had refused to attend the inquest, but as soon as it concluded he was charged with George's murder.

When Yeoman appeared at the Devon Assizes before Mr Justice Charles, he was charged with all four murders, as well as with wounding Emma Townsend with intent to murder her. He pleaded not guilty to all charges against him.

Yeoman sat calmly and attentively in court, although he occasionally buried his face in his hands and sobbed. His aunt, Eliza Ann Ford, told the court that her nephew was an only child and that his parents had been first cousins.

Nurse Minnie Higgins told the court that before the day of the shooting Yeoman had been a frequent visitor to the hospital and had always appeared devoted to his son. She recalled that he had greeted George fondly with the words 'Hello, my dear,' when he arrived at the boy's bedside on 7 May.

Emma Townsend spoke of wrestling with Yeoman in an effort to disarm him, claiming that he was more like a wild animal than a human being and that he seemed quite demented.

Other witnesses came forward to testify that on the morning of the shootings Yeoman seemed on the best of terms with his wife and family. He was a sober, church-going man, who was always believed to be a kind and affectionate father. However, he had suffered a nervous breakdown about ten years earlier and a second breakdown, accompanied by severe depression, in August 1931. On both occasions he was treated by Dr D. Twining, who told the court that the cause of his breakdown the previous August was severe strain due to worries about the financial condition of the farm.

Twining described Yeoman in court as a 'heavily mental defective, animal type.' At this, Mr Justice Charles asked the doctor why he had not taken steps to deal with Yeoman, and the doctor replied that he hadn't considered Yeoman to be sufficiently mentally defective to necessitate any such measures. 'He could do his farm work,' Twining explained.

Before the birth of the Yeomans' youngest baby, he had supposedly threatened his wife with a gun. A farm labourer employed by Yeoman had heard Olive calling her husband 'a blackguard' and 'a scamp' after he kicked her when she tried to get the gun away from him. According to the labourer, the cause of the argument was the fact that the couple were expecting another baby and Yeoman was afraid of what his father would think.

Dr Roy Craig, described in court as 'a mental specialist', had been called upon to examine Yeoman and stated that he had found no trace of insanity.

However, according to Craig, Yeoman had a mental age of eight years old and was therefore incapable of reasoning in an efficient manner.

William Jarvis Yeoman was found guilty but insane and ordered to be detained until His Majesty's pleasure be known. Sent to Broadmoor Criminal Lunatic Asylum, he remained there until his death, aged sixty-four, in 1960. The cause of his death is not reported. Emma Townsend was later awarded the Empire Gallantry Medal for her efforts to disarm Yeoman. At the time, she was one of only four women to receive the award, which was later exchanged for a George Cross.

Harry Grice: 1898–1934

Although apparently happily married, Harry Grice and his wife, Emily, both suffered from bouts of severe depression and both had been hospitalised due to their condition. In November 1931, after Harry suffered a nervous breakdown, the couple moved in with relatives at The Rock Inn, on Carlisle Street East in Sheffield. They shared a room at the very top of the inn with their two small children, Ronald and Ernest. On 28 November the other occupants of the inn heard a scream coming from their room. Grice's sister, Mrs Christina Lucas, ran to see what was happening and saw her brother standing on the bed, bleeding from a wound in his throat.

As Christina ran downstairs to telephone for the police, Harry stumbled out of the pub into a yard at the back of the inn, where he was found covered in blood by his wife's sister, Rosetta Horton, who laid him on the floor and supported his head until medical assistance arrived. Over and over again, Harry repeated 'I want to die', begging Rosetta to hit him on the head and kill him. In the meantime, the pub's charwoman, Sarah Ellen Gunn, had been sent to fetch Emily, only to find her lying dead on the floor in her room, her own throat slashed from ear to ear. (The couple's two children fortunately slept through the whole incident.) The room was in a state of disarray as though there had been a desperate struggle, and it seemed as if someone had tried to get out of the window.

Harry was taken to Sheffield Hospital, where he remained in a critical condition for about ten days. While hospitalised, he told doctors that there was a will hidden in the family Bible in his room and when this was checked a note was found written on two envelopes.

> Dear old mother, sisters and brothers. Please forgive me but if I don't do this it will be worse for me and mine. Don't trust ******. Whatever happens, keep my two children with the family and give them a decent

bringing up. God bless them. Let them know nothing about it. I leave all I have in trust with my sisters Phoebe, Ina and Chris and my brother George for my two kiddies but on condition that they are left with one of my sisters or [an]other member of family and they are brought up by them as Grices should be. Tell our George to cheer up and all of you forget. God bless Mother and all. See that Dr Kelly examines our little Ron and tell our George to go to him. I would not have hurt Emily, only she has helped them all in their dirty work. One wrong action I have done and that more than three years ago and then to be driven to this and classed as a pig. Please help me by forgetting and all of you cheer up. Tell Harry Woodhouse to forgive me and help cheer the family up and tell them that it's for the best.

Grice's throat was swathed in bandages when he appeared before the magistrates and was committed for trial at the next Leeds Assizes. During his stay in hospital, he had continually expressed an urge to die and tried to escape through the window, and the delusions that he had experienced during his nervous breakdown had reoccurred. Doctors reported that he was convinced that people were persecuting him and following him, adding that they often pointed at him and called him a 'puff' or a 'poof'.

It was suggested that Emily may have been injured while attempting to prevent her husband from harming himself, since her hands and arms were covered in cuts. Yet the contents of Grice's letter seemed to indicate that he had premeditated her murder, although the police conceded that it had probably been committed by 'a man not in his proper senses'.

After his release from hospital on 22 December, Grice was detained in Armley Gaol pending his appearance at the Assizes, where medical officer Dr John Humphrey noted that he suffered from delusions, paranoia and religious melancholia, continually asking for forgiveness for his actions and begging to die. He was suspicious of his fellow prisoners and often caused unrest among them. When it came to Grice's trial on 29 February 1932, Humphrey told the court that, in his opinion, Grice was not capable of understanding the nature of the charge against him, nor was he in a fit mental condition to instruct solicitors and counsel. After only a few minutes' deliberation the jury reached the conclusion that Harry Grice was unfit to stand trial.

He was sent to Broadmoor Criminal Lunatic Asylum, where he was found to be suffering from dementia. His condition gradually worsened until March 1934, when he began to lose weight and was confined to his bed, growing ever weaker. He died on 31 July 1934. His death was deemed to be due to natural causes.

George Trotter: 1902–1957

Coal miner George Trotter of Ashington, Northumberland, married his wife Jean on 23 December 1922 and the couple went on to have five children together: Joyce, Brenda, Elizabeth, Leslie and George. By 1931 the family were living at 137½ Hawthorn Road, Ashington, but there were problems within the marriage. On 11 February of that year Elizabeth died, and on 17 April Jean admitted to her husband that she had been unfaithful to him and believed that George was not his child. On 25 April Jean left her husband and moved in with her father and stepmother at another house in Ashington, taking George junior with her and leaving the other three children with their father.

In the early hours of the morning of 30 April 1931 PC Lothian was patrolling Station Road in Ashington, when he spotted Trotter crouching against the wall of a house looking distressed, his head hanging down. Lothian asked what he was doing, and receiving no reply, asked him if there was anything wrong. 'You'd better take me in. I have strangled my eldest girl, Joyce,' Trotter eventually replied, adding, 'My wife has left me and things are bad.'

Lothian took Trotter to the police station and placed him in the charge of Sergeant John Armstrong, who secured him in a cell before accompanying Lothian back to Trotter's address. On entering the bedroom, they found two children asleep in one bed, and on a second bed lay the body of six-year-old Joyce, dressed in a woollen vest and flannelette nightdress. The child's body

Station Road, Ashington, where Trotter was apprehended. (*Author's collection*)

had been covered by a rug and there was a knitted tie secured loosely around her neck with a single knot. In the kitchen the police also found four short notes reading: 'God will find a way'; 'I see a way now'; 'Jean, you are doing everything for the best. I didn't know it. The children are going to Jesus'; and 'God knows all'.

Having been cautioned at the police station, Trotter went on to make a full confession to the murder of his daughter. He told the police that he had intended to kill all three of the children, but after killing Joyce, one of the others had begun to wake up and he couldn't bring himself to go through with it. According to Trotter, he had initially strangled his daughter with his tie, before loosening it and using his hands to 'finish her off'. A post-mortem examination carried out by Dr William Muir revealed fingertip bruises to both sides of her windpipe, leading Muir to conclude that the cause of Joyce's death was indeed manual strangulation. When Trotter was informed of this, he commented 'She was just a weakling anyway.'

In the aftermath of Joyce's death, an inquest was opened by coroner Mr Hugh Percy, but following a recent Act of Parliament, which exempted jurors from making a full investigation into any deaths where charges of murder or manslaughter were to be brought, the inquest dealt only briefly with evidence of identity, which was given by a sobbing Jean Trotter. Joyce's body was released for a funeral, which was held at the home of her grandparents, the neighbours congregating on the streets outside to join in the hymn singing. Six little girls representing Joyce's school attended,

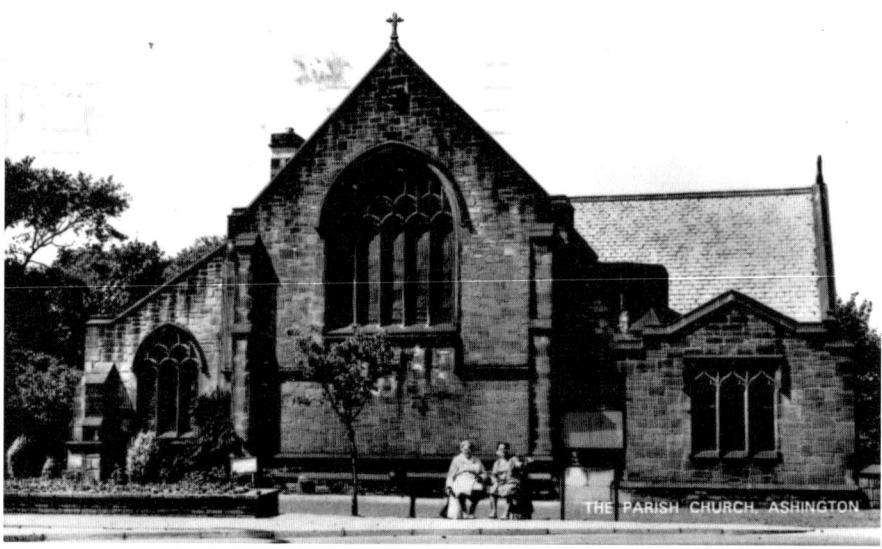

Ashington Church, where Joyce was interred. (*Author's collection*)

as did her brother and sister, Brenda and Leslie, who walked behind the coffin to Ashington Parish Churchyard, holding their grandfather's hands. Poignantly, one of the many floral wreaths bore the message: 'In loving memory of Joyce, the beloved daughter of George and Jean Trotter, died 30th April 1931. From her loving father and mother.'

After three adjournments, on 18 May George Trotter appeared before magistrates at the Police Court in Ashington, the first time in the building's history that it had ever been used to hear a case of murder. It was stated that Trotter was particularly fond of Joyce and that he may either have murdered her to spite his wife, in view of the unhappy relations between them, or that the succession of tragedies in his life may have affected his mind to such an extent that he had no idea what he was doing when he killed his daughter. As the hearing unfolded, the latter scenario began to seem ever more likely.

The magistrates were told that Trotter had not worked regularly since Christmas 1930 as he had been undergoing treatment for his nerves. However, Trotter was convinced that his bad health was due to the fact that wife was poisoning him, putting white powder in his food that was 'drying his blood' and making his eyes twitch. He told the police that his wife had injured him with a hairpin and that she had once taken him a bowl of porridge in bed and had kissed him – something she very rarely did. On arriving at the pit where he was working that morning after eating the porridge, Trotter claimed that he felt 'heavy and dull'.

Two days before Joyce's death, Trotter visited the police station at Ashington carrying some bread and a cardboard packet of tapioca. He told Inspector Mitchell that his wife was trying to poison him and demanded that the items of food should be analysed. Mitchell told him that he would not get the bread and tapioca analysed in Ashington but that he would have to take it to Newcastle. 'I will have it done if I have to walk there,' Trotter insisted. On the same day, Jean Trotter had also visited the police station to complain about her husband's strange behaviour. According to Jean, her husband had accused her of having had relationships with several other men, including his own father. Trotter had also threatened to kill himself and had actually cut his own throat, although the wound was minor and did not require medical treatment. On another occasion, Trotter had behaved like a dog, barking and growling while lying on the mat and gnawing at a bone.

The policemen and doctors who had seen Trotter after the murder recalled that he seemed quite calm and rational, although they acknowledged that he was delusional and genuinely believed that his wife was trying to poison him. He was aware that he had killed Joyce and had expressed sorrow at having done so, and the fact that he had killed a child that he undoubtedly loved was taken as further evidence of his insanity.

Magistrates committed Trotter for trial at the Newcastle Assizes, where he appeared before Mr Justice Finlay on 2 July 1931. After initially pleading 'Guilty', Trotter was persuaded by his counsel, Mr Harvey Robson, to change his plea to 'Not Guilty'. Prosecuting counsel Mr T.G. Talbot was adamant that all the evidence pointed to the fact that Joyce Trotter had been killed by her father. Talbot told the jury that the defence would probably claim that Trotter was insane, reminding them that everyone was presumed to be sane and so responsible for their crime unless it could be proven otherwise beyond reasonable doubt.

After Dr Weir had told the court that he believed that Trotter's delusions were indicative of insanity, Jean Trotter was called to give evidence. She told the court of her husband's strange behaviour, recalling his somewhat ineffectual attempt at suicide, his accusations of infidelity against her, and his periods of behaving like a dog. She also stated that her husband had suffered from terrible pains in his head and had, on occasions, poured boiling hot oil into his ears to try and alleviate them.

After hearing Jean Trotter's evidence, the jury did not need to hear from the defence counsel. Trotter was found guilty of murder but declared insane and ordered to be detained during the King's pleasure. He was admitted to Broadmoor Criminal Lunatic Asylum after his trial, where he remained until his death, aged fifty-five, in March 1957.

Amilia (or Amelia) Leach: 1917–1956

On the morning of 16 February 1950 thirty-three-year-old housewife Amilia Leach approached a policeman who was on traffic duty in the market place at Ramsgate, Kent. She was pushing a pram containing her two sons, aged ten months and twenty-three months, and was intent on making a complaint to the policeman about a coconut that she had bought, which she claimed was bad. PC Malcolm Gibson advised her to take it to the food office and she set off, as if intending to follow his advice. A short while later she returned, telling the policeman that the food office had directed her to another location on Newington Road.

She told the policeman that she had bought the coconut in a shop in Ramsgate but when she got it home and opened it up, she found that it was bad. She threw it in the dustbin, then decided to return it to the shop where she had bought it, but the shopkeeper insisted that it was not bad, and, according to Mrs Leach, 'got really nasty'. The policeman told her that her complaint was not really a police matter and she walked off.

Inner Harbour Ramsgate. (*Author's collection*)

Moments later, Frances Maryon Fincham, who lived on a yacht at the inner harbour at Ramsgate, was climbing down a ladder to board her yacht when she heard a loud 'plop'. Turning to see what had made the noise, she noticed a highly distressed woman with a pram, who was standing by some railings opposite the Royal Hotel sobbing hysterically and tossing bedding from the pram into the water. As Mrs Fincham watched, the woman suddenly picked up a baby and tossed it into the harbour.

Mrs Fincham shouted for help and her cries attracted the attention of bus driver Thomas Arthur Frederick Harris, who was standing next to his bus nearby. Harris ran to the edge of the harbour and looked over. To his horror he saw two children floating in the water, one roughly four yards from the quayside, the other six or seven yards away; one was face down and the other was on his back.

Harris stripped off his coat and shoes and jumped into the water, managing to grab one of the children, who was by now unconscious. He swam to a nearby rowing boat and handed the child over to the occupant, before turning to go back for the second. However, by that time postman Reginald George Mills had already jumped in and rescued the second child. A third man, Harry Bourne, who was disabled, got into a rowing boat and took both of the children to shore after they were pulled from the water, where Mrs Doris Evelyn Annie Britcher began giving them artificial respiration. By that time, someone had alerted PC Gibson, who sent for an ambulance and supervised the children's despatch to Ramsgate General Hospital.

He then approached Amilia Leach, who was still standing calmly on the harbourside watching the drama unfold, and told her that he was taking her to the police station for questioning. Once there, Mrs Leach launched into a litany of complaints about her life. She told the police that she had married her husband in 1947, since when she had been terribly unhappy. She claimed that she and her husband were always quarrelling and that he had hit her several times and was now 'going about' with another woman. The family occupied just one room, in which the four of them ate, lived and slept, and the children kept crying and were getting on her nerves. Their room was also very damp and she was unable to dry her washing, which was a real inconvenience with two children under two years old. 'I don't want to go back to those surroundings,' she told the police. 'I want a house where I can bring my children up. You can send me to prison if you want to,' she concluded, adding, 'I did not wish to murder them.'

Amilia Leach claimed that there were so many people about when she threw her sons into the water that she was confident they would be rescued, and though it was February and bitterly cold, would escape with nothing more than a chill. Yet even while discussing the attempted murder of two of her children, Amilia seemed more preoccupied with the bad coconut, which seemed to have acted as the catalyst for her tossing her children into the water that morning. Having interviewed her, Detective John Welsh came to the conclusion that she simply did not appreciate the seriousness of her actions.

Amilia Leach was brought before magistrates, and remained unmoved as Dr Basil L. Bisley, the house surgeon at Ramsgate Hospital, described the condition of the two boys when they arrived by ambulance. Both were blue with cold and exhibited very distressed breathing, but fortunately both responded to treatment and were discharged from hospital on 23 February. She didn't react as she was committed for trial at the next Sussex Assizes and remanded to Holloway Prison to await her trial. Meanwhile, Harris, Mills and Mrs Britcher were all given awards by the Royal Humane Society for their parts in rescuing and resuscitating the children.

By the time Amilia Leach appeared before Mr Justice Stable at the Sussex Assizes in March 1950, charged with attempting to drown her children with intent to murder them, she was judged unfit to plead. Dr Winifred Jaggers, the medical officer at Holloway Prison, stated that Mrs Leach was suffering from delusions and persecution mania, at which Mrs Leach, who was sobbing bitterly in the dock, interrupted by shouting out, 'I beg to differ.' Her protests made no difference to the outcome of the case, as she was sentenced to be detained during His Majesty's pleasure and sent to Broadmoor Criminal Lunatic Asylum.

Six years later, Amilia Leach was one of sixty Broadmoor patients to be stricken with food poisoning after eating some meat that had been improperly cooked. Mrs Leach was the only fatality from the outbreak, dying on 4 July 1956, aged thirty-nine. At the inquest on her death, Dr Norman Wood, director of Public Health Laboratory at Reading, said that her stomach had been poisoned by bacterial material, citing the cause of her death as gastro-enteritis. The inquest jury returned a verdict of death by misadventure.

John Lionel Raymond Rusdell: 1933–1955

On 2 March 1950 Harry Scott was talking to his neighbour, Reginald John Green, about seventy yards from his home in Marchwiel, near Wrexham, when both men heard a gunshot. They noticed a motorbike parked with its lights on just up the road, then heard footsteps, before the motorbike was started up and ridden away towards Wrexham. When Scott returned to his home a few minutes later, he found his thirty-year-old wife, Dilys Myfanwy Scott, lying dead from a shotgun wound to her back.

As the registered owner of a light motorcycle, eighteen-year-old soldier John Lionel Raymond Rusdell was interviewed by police the following morning and asked to account for his whereabouts at the time of the murder. Rusdell was said to be obsessed with crime and was an avid reader of whodunnit books and had recently bragged to his family that he could commit the perfect crime. He told the police that he had been to the cinema but said that it was possible that his bike had been borrowed by someone without his permission while he was watching the film. Rusdell also denied owning a gun other than an air pistol.

When he was taken to the police station, Rusdell changed his story, this time claiming to have spent the previous evening in the company of a man named Lionel Wynn Wilbraham. He told police that he had walked around Wrexham with Wilbraham, agreeing to go poaching with him that night. Rusdell then went to the cinema, before he and Wilbraham set off on his motorbike in search of rabbits.

After a somewhat stop and start journey, the two reached Marchweil, where, according to Rusdell, Wilbraham decided he wanted a drink of water and got off the bike, taking the gun with him. Rusdell then heard a shot and went to see where it had come from. He met Wilbraham running down the drive of the Scotts' home. Rusdell described walking to the rear of the house and seeing Mrs Scott lying face down on the floor. He panicked and rushed back to his motorbike, then he and Wilbraham made a quick getaway. Rusdell told police that he had not reported the shooting because he didn't want to get involved, seeing as he had been out poaching. 'I decided not to say anything as I might be putting a rope around my neck,' he concluded, adding that until he was apprehended by the police, he had believed that he was 'covering up' for his friend. 'I am assuming that, at that point, Wilbraham had already made up his mind to commit a murder and had established an alibi.'

Wilbraham was interviewed by the police but had an unshakeable alibi for the time of the murder, being at a choir practice with numerous witnesses. The house where Rusdell lived with his uncle and aunt was then searched. Police found a sawn-off shotgun that had recently been fired and cartridges, along with a notebook in which Rusdell had written directions to Marchwiel, the note ending with the words 'and then kill as you go back'.

When the shotgun was shown to Rusdell at the police station he explained, 'I went poaching. Am I under arrest?'

Magistrates at Wrexham committed Rusdell for trial at the next Denbighshire Assizes in Ruthin, and on 19 May 1950, before Mr Justice Jones, he pleaded not guilty to murder. His uncle and guardian, Wilfred Ewart Odgers, told the court that Rusdell's father had committed suicide in 1934 and his mother had died from tuberculosis. In July 1949 Rusdell suffered serious head injuries in a motorcycle accident. (At this, Rusdell shouted 'Liar' across the courtroom.) Later, after Wilbraham had given evidence, Rusdell leaned over the dock towards him and asked, 'How is it that that vampire there is not locked up? This is his second victim in four years.'

During the course of the trial Rusdell stated that he had not intended to kill Mrs Scott. 'I ordered her away,' he explained, and since she did not go, he was compelled to shoot her to avoid recognition. He later stated that he had intended to take Mrs Scott's body home with him and cut her up. 'I failed in the whole thing. It's got me,' he said, before becoming hysterical and having to be removed from the court by a number of policemen and warders.

Rusdell returned to court ten minutes later in a much calmer state to hear the judge pronouncing him guilty and sentencing him to death. Immediately afterwards, Rusdell claimed to have committed another murder when he was only fourteen years old. 'I killed Mrs Evans four years ago at Coedpoeth, near Wrexham,' he declared. 'Regarding the motive, I will tell you it was sex.' With that, he began to laugh and scream hysterically, waving his arms and trying to grab a woman in the courtroom, before being overpowered by warders.

Although insanity was never mentioned in court as a defence, Rusdell was reprieved by the Home Secretary and sent to Broadmoor Criminal Lunatic

Asylum. His stay there was far from trouble free. In July 1954 he made an attempt to escape. Rusdell had been playing the cello at a dance, and as he and other inmates were being escorted back to their quarters, Rusdell made his bid for freedom. Staff Officer Kingdon tried to stop him and was stabbed twice in the back with a homemade knife. Staff Nurse Fraser went to his colleague's assistance and received minor injuries before the two men were able to overpower Rusdell. Fortunately, neither of the staff members were seriously injured and it was announced that no disciplinary action would be taken against Rusdell, other than putting him under closer supervision and taking away some of his privileges.

As well as playing the cello, Rusdell was a keen painter and was allowed to keep some art supplies in his room. On 1 January 1955 he was found dead, having ingested a green paint stick which contained arsenic and copper. An inquest on his death was told that each paint stick contained around twenty-seven grains of arsenic oxide, which equated to between five and ten fatal doses. The cause of twenty-two-year-old Rusdell's death was recorded as suicide.

Thirty-eight-year-old schoolteacher Caroline Evans of Coedpoeth was murdered on 6 October 1945 while she was walking to the pub run by her mother, as she did most Saturday nights. Her body was found in a thicket beside her usual path, in a spot known locally as Dark Hollow. A nearby resident said he heard a piercing scream shortly after 10pm. Caroline was raped and strangled. Her clothing was torn, and she had obviously fought her killer tooth and nail. A witness reported seeing an airman lurking in bushes about an hour after Caroline's murder but all the RAF personnel in the vicinity were subsequently eliminated from the police inquiries. Although the case was re-examined in the light of Rusdell's confession, the police eventually determined that he could not possibly have killed her. Her murder remains unsolved.

Bibliography

Aris's Birmingham Gazette
Barnsley Chronicle
Bath Chronicle and Weekly Gazette
Belfast Morning News
Bell's New Weekly Messenger
Berkshire Chronicle
Birmingham Gazette
Blyth News and Ashington Post
Bognor Observer and West Sussex Recorder
Bromley Mercury
Buckingham Advertiser
Buckingham Express
Bury Free Press
Cambrian News
Cambridge Independent Press
Chelmsford Chronicle
Coleshill Chronicle
Coventry Evening Telegraph
Coventry Herald
Daily Independent
Derby Mercury
Devon and Exeter Gazette
Dundee Courier
Eastern Daily Press
Eddowes's Shrewsbury Journal and Salopian Journal
Essex County Chronicle
Essex Newsman
Essex Standard
Exeter and Plymouth Daily Telegrams
Exeter and Plymouth Gazette
Freeman's Journal
Frome Times
Gloucester Citizen
Gloucester Journal
Halstead and Colne Valley Gazette
Hampshire Advertiser

Hampshire Independent
Hertford Mercury
Herts Guardian
Illustrated Police News
Illustrated Weekly News
Kentish Gazette
Kentish Independent
Lancaster Gazette
Langport and Somerton Herald
Leeds Mercury
Leicester Daily Post
Leicester Evening Mail
Lincolnshire Chronicle
Liverpool Echo
Lloyds Weekly
London Evening Standard
Manchester Courier and Lancashire General Advertiser
Manchester Evening News
Midland Daily Telegraph
Morning Advertiser
Morning Post
Northampton Mercury
Norwich Mercury
Nottinghamshire Guardian
Nuneaton Advertiser
Pall Mall Gazette
Preston Chronicle and Lancashire Advertiser
Reading Mercury
Reading Observer
Reynolds's Newspaper
Royal Cornwall Gazette
Rugby Advertiser
Sheffield Daily Independent
Sheffield Daily Telegraph
Shepton Mallet Journal
Sleaford Gazette
Soulby's Ulverston Advertiser
Southern Times and Dorset Herald
Staffordshire Daily Sentinel
Stamford Mercury
Sunday Dispatch
Sunday Sun
Thanet Advertiser and Echo
The Cornishman

The Cornish Telegraph
The Diss Express and Norfolk and Suffolk Journal
The Era
The Examiner
The Royal Leamington Spa Courier
The Scotsman
The Shields Daily News
The Sketch
The Stamford Mercury
The Taunton Courier
Western Flying Post
Western Gazette
Western Times
West Sussex Gazette
Winchester Journal and General Advertiser
Witney Express
Wokingham Times
Worthing Gazette
Worthing Herald
York Herald
Yorkshire Evening Post
Yorkshire Post

https: //nla.gov.au/nla.obj-502233668 A Statement of Facts in evidence of the cruel injustice endured by Mr J.D. Shelley, an emigrant to South Wales

Index

Adams, Mr H.W. 182
Adams, Dr W. F.102
Adams, Mr Sergeant 6
Adelphi Theatre 131–132
Adkins, Ryland 150–151
Ahearn, Dr John 194
Allesbrook, Mr 189
Alliston, Mr 134
Ambler, William 108
Angmering 186
Ansell, Joseph 35
Archer, Harry 134
Archer, Mrs 134
Archer, Richard Millar / Prince, Arthur 131–135
Arkinstall, Ann 181–182
Armley Gaol 87, 206
Armstrong, John 207
Ashby-de-la-Zouch 190
Ashington, Northumberland 207–209
Ashman, Police Sergeant 8
Aspinall, Mr C. 78
Austin, Jane 61–62
Australia 3, 81

Babb, Police Sergeant 195
Bagshaw, Mr 86
Baker, W. 12
Banbury 157–159
Barber, Amy 89–90
Barker, Alfred 41
Barker, Sidney Albert 58–60
Bastable, Eliza 'Blanche' 117–119
Bastable, Elizabeth 117–119
Bastable, John 117
Bastian, Dr Henry Charles 134–135
Baumgartner, Dr John Richard 74–77
Bayley, Joseph 143
Beard, Charles Izard 57–61
Beard, Emily 57–60
Beatrice, Princess 122
Beckwith, Inspector 35
Benton, Joseph Franklin 48–49
Benton, Mr 181
Best, George 7–9

Bethlem (Bedlam) Hospital 2, 6, 13, 26, 30, 36, 39, 66
Bibby, Dr 168–169
Bigham, Mr Justice 175
Bignold, Edward S.75–77
Billinghay 47–48
Bingham 63
Binstead, Freda 101
Binstead, Sarah Ann 101–105
Birmingham 56, 183–186
Birmingham Prison / Winson Green 186
Bisley, Dr Basil L. 212
Black, David 59
Bland, Charles Henry 141
Bland, George James 140–144
Bland, Mary 143
Bland, Mary Ann 140–144
Blatherwick, Surgeon Major Thomas 95
Bodmin Asylum 173–175
Bones, Joseph 47–51
Bonsey, Mr 92–94
Boston 89
Boulter, Emily 171–172
Boulter, Ernest 171
Boulter, Hubert 171–172
Boulter, John 171–172
Bourne, Harry 211
Bournemouth 144
Bow Street Magistrates Court 28, 133
Brackley 159–160
Bradford, Benjamin 189–192
Bradford, Rhoda Lavinia 189–191
Bragg, John 133
Bramwell, Mr / Lord Justice Baron 56, 109
Brantham 125
Brany, Dr 94
Bray, Mr Justice 200–201
Brett, Mr Justice 63
Brider, John 136–139
Brider, Mrs 136–140
Brider / Kelly, Sarah 136–138
Bright, Dr 26
Brighton 57–60, 123, 179
Brislington Asylum 117
Bristow, Inspector 179

Britcher, Doris Evelyn Annie 211–212
Broadbent, Edward Fox 50–51
Broadmoor Criminal Lunatic Asylum 11, 13, 23, 30, 37, 39, 43, 47, 51, 54, 57, 61, 63, 65, 66, 70, 71, 74, 77, 79, 81, 89, 94, 96, 98, 101, 105, 109, 113, 116, 118, 119, 122, 125, 128, 130, 135, 139, 144, 147, 153, 156, 162, 167, 172, 175, 177, 183, 185, 187, 189, 195, 198, 201, 205, 206, 210, 212–214
Bromley 198–200
Brooks, Robert 80
Brown, Elizabeth 70–71
Brown, Susan 76
Brown, William 70–71
Brynberian 162
Buckley, Walter 166
Bucknill, Mr Justice 166–167
Bull, George 97–99
Bull, Florence Kate 97–98
Bull, Sarah Ann 97–99
Bullen, Mr 147
Burchell, Peter Lodwick 12–13
Burns, Mr G. E. K. 176

Caird, Mr 74
Calcraft, William 18
Camberwell Asylum 53–54
Carew, Harriet 79–80
Carew, William 79–81
Carruthers, Dr William Hodgson 63
Carter, Mr (Exeter) 73–74
Carter, Mr (London) 120
Cassidy, David 96
Casswell, Mr 197
Central Criminal Court / Old Bailey 12, 29, 68, 69, 88, 129
Chambers, Hammond 161
Channell, Mr Justice Baron 10–11, 50–51, 134
Chapman, Florence Elizabeth 114–115
Charing Cross Hospital 104
Charles, Mr Justice 193, 195, 204
Charminster Lunatic Asylum 119
Chelmsford 39–42, 104, 155–156
Cheshire Asylum 83
Chester 83–84
Clarke, Alfred 75–77
Clarke, Fanny 'Ann' Pleasant 125–128
Clarke, Mr H.C. 56
Clarke, Percival 197
Claybury Asylum 178–179
Clegg, Mr W. 49
Clements, Elizabeth 16–17
Clerkenwell Prison 121, 138
Cobb, Mr W. 41

Cobham 37–38
Cockrill, Robert John 153–156
Cogan, Dr Lee F. 161
Colchester 125–127, 153
Cole, Mr 34
Coleridge, Lord Chief Justice 124–125, 128
Coles, Police Constable 158–159
Coles, Thomas 202
Collier, Mr 33
Collins, Inspector 111
Collins, Mr 46–47
Collis, John 153
Collis, Samuel Bentall 153–156
Collis, Susannah 153–154
Collyer, Joseph 141
Colman, Joseph 75
Colney Hatch Asylum 53
Compton 7
Cook, Frederick 100
Cook, George Allen 44–45
Cook, Harry C. 154–156
Cooks, Mr 52
Cooper, Dr James 166
Cory, Dr Samuel 31–32
Cottingham, Police Sergeant 159
Coventry 147–148, 187–189
Coyle, Ernest John 195
Craig, Dr Roy 197, 204–205
Crawford, Matthew 128–130
Crawley, Elizabeth Ann (Betsy) 77–79
Crawley, Frederick 78
Crawley, William Thomas 77–79
Crombie, Jean Halliday 188
Crooks or Crookes, Mary 51–54
Croucher, Ida 203
Crowder, Mr Justice 12
Croydon, Ralph 131
Curme, Dr Decimus 117

Dadd, Richard 37–39
Dadd, Robert 37–39
Danbury 39–41
Darling, Mr / Mr Justice 112–113, 150–153
Darling, Sir Ralph 3–6
Dartmouth 195
Davey, Dr J. D. 10
Davidson, John 83–84
Davies, Police Constable 140
Dawes, Dr Joseph 182
Daws Heath 101–102
Dawson, Jane 107
Deavin, Walter 114–116
Deeson, Ann 13
Denman, Mr Justice / Lord 23, 145–147
Denmark, Hannah 75–76

Derby 13–17, 62
Devonport 72
Dewsbury, Arthur 191
Diaper, Dorcas 175–176
Diaper, Octavius Herbert 175–177
Diaper, Prentice 176
Dickinson, Kate Annie 200
Dickinson, Phillip George 198–202
Dobson, Mary Ann 53
Dommett, Charles 30–34
Dommett, Eliza 30–33
Dommett, Henry 30–35
Dommett, John 30–33
Dorchester Gaol 32, 46
Drake, Richard 161
Drew, Dr 85–86
Drummett, Mr R. E. 175
Drummond, Edward 28–30
Duckworth, Mr 82
Dudley, Dr 173–174
Duke, Charles G.S. Chapman 186
Dundee 131

Earl Stonham 127–128, 176
East Orchard 117
Edlin, Mr 10
Edmunds, Christiana 57–61
Edmunds, Mr T. 196
Edwards, Frances 81–83
Edwards, James 81–84
Edwards, James Henry 81–82
Edwards, Robert 74–77
Egham 111–112
Eliza 3
English, Felicia 44–45
Essex County Asylum 103
Essex, Henry 124
Evans, Caroline 214–215
Evershed, Mr C. 187
Exeter 146, 196–197
Exeter Prison 73–74, 197

Farnsworth, Thomas 48
Field, Abel 35
Fincham, Frances Maryon 211
Finlay, Mr Justice 210
Firman, Emily 102
Fisher, Frederick 166
Fisherton Asylum 13, 35, 43, 117, 134
Fishguard 164
Ford, Eliza Ann 204
Foster, James 50
Fouracre, Dr 100
Fowler, Frank 202
France 27–28, 38, 200
Fraser, Staff Nurse 215

Frost, Henry 75
Fryer, Louisa 114–115
Fulham Prison 130
Fuller, Mrs 179–181
Fyfe, Maxwell 194

Garrett, Isaac 57–60
Garrett, John 7–8
Gazelle 24
Gell, Mr 29
Gibson, Malcolm 210–211
Gilbert, Philip Francis 101
Gilmour, Henry 95
Gipson, Charles 41
Gipson, Elizabeth 39–41
Gipson, John 39–42
Gipson, John Rowland 68, 70, 98
Gisborne, Henry Francis 17
Glaisyer & Kemp 59–60
Glasgow 26–27
Glenelg, Rt. Hon Charles 5–6
Gloucester 168–172
Glover, William Edwin 16–17
Goddard, John 85
Goderich, Viscount 5
Godfrey, Mr 157, 159
Good, John 34
Goodall, Clara 165- 166
Goodall, Edith Alberta 165–166
Goodall, Florence 165–167
Goodall, James Edward 165–166
Goodall, Mildred Catherine 165–166
Goodall, Richard Edward 165–167
Goodson, Sarah 64
Gosney, Harriett 44
Graham, Margaret 75–76
Green, Inspector 13–14
Green, John 35–37
Green, Reginald John 213
Green, William 126–127
Greene, Dr 143
Greenwich 128–129
Greenwood, Mr 145
Gresty, Police Sergeant 62
Grey, Sir George 18
Grice, Emily 205–206
Grice, Harry 205–206
Griffin, Evelyn 189
Griffin, George 187
Griffin, Hannah 187–189
Griffin, Ronald Allen 187–189
Grimsdale, Annie 111
Grimsdale, George Henry 109
Gringburn, P.C. Alexander 52
Groom, George 165
Grosvenor Square 29

Guildford 139
Gunn, Sarah Ellen 205
Gunton, Revd. John 76–77

Hale, Police Constable 171
Hall, Harry 102–104
Hamilton-Smith, Dr 189
Hammond, Elizabeth 106–109
Hammond, Isaac 106–108
Hammond, John 106–109
Hampshire 94–96, 114–116, 145, 147
Hare, Superintendent 45–46
Harris, Thomas Arthur Frederick 211–212
Harris, Mr W.J. 70
Hart, Dr 190–191
Harvard, Dr David 164
Harvey, Dr Walter 8–9
Hatton Mental Hospital 189
Hawkins, Mr Justice 87, 112–113
Hayes, Superintendent 111, 123
Hayward, Ann 7–9
Hayward, William 7–11
Helmdon 157
Hennessy, Patrick John 176–177
Hewitt, Sarah 119–121
Higgins, Minnie 204
Higgs, Mr 29
Highgate Infirmary 165
Hindness, Caleb Oram 165–166
Hirst, Mary 84–87
Hirst, Wilfred 85–87
Hirst, William 84–86
Hitchens, John James 172–175
Hobbins, James 94–97
Hobbs, Sarah 157, 160
Hodgkinson, Mr 99
Holland, Dr 63
Holland, George 186–187
Holloway Prison 100–101, 134–135, 167, 212
Holman, Mr 126–127
Holmes, Police Constable 190
Holt, Jane 109–111
Hopwood, Dr Joseph 202
Horn, Police Constable 72
Horridge, Mr Justice 104
Horton, Rosetta 205
Hounsell, Dr John 32
Housefield, Dr 176
Hoxton House / Miles's Mad House 11
Hucker, Mr 124
Huddleston, Baron 125, 142–144
Huish, Acting Sergeant 80
Hume, Mary 107
Humphrey, Dr John 185, 206
Humphreys or Humphries, Ann 55–57

Humphreys or Humphries, Thomas 54–57
Humphreys, Travers 104
Hunt, James 52
Hurst, Hannah 83
Hurst, Mr J. 24–25
Hyslop, Theophilus Bulkeley 135
Hyson, Eliza 11–13
Hyson, Sophia 11–13

Iliffe, Mr C.W. 149, 188
Ilminster 8
Ilott, Dr H. J. 199
Ilsley / Isley Police Constable 199
Ingoldby, Mr P. B. 115
Ipswich 125, 127, 177

Jack the Ripper 140
Jackson, Emma/ Blown, Ellen 128-130
Jacobs, Police Constable 70
Jaggers, Dr Winifred 212
James, Forbes 138
Jarman, Samuel 141–142
Jennison (Tennison), Dr Edward Ryan 97–98
Johnson, Mr 79
Johnson, Police Constable 148
Johnstone, Alexander M.P .27
Joint Counties Asylum, Carmarthen 164
Jones, Edward Ellis 193
Jones, Eileen Sheila 192
Jones, John Edward 192–195
Jones / Taubman, Mary Bridget 192–194
Jones, Mr Justice 214
Joy, Mrs 80

Kay, Mr Justice 83–84
Keech, Esther 31–32
Keeling, Alice 181–183
Kelly, James 135–140
Kelly / Allen, Sarah 135
Kelmarsh 140–141
Kerby, Dr Clement Carlyon 195–196
Kerslaw, Superintendent 86
Kingdon, Staff Officer 215
Kingsbridge, Devon 203
Kirk, Ellen 89–94
Kirk, Fred 89–90
Kirk, William Enoch 89–94
Kirkdale Gaol 79
Knockhold, Dr William Stephen 98
Knowles, P.C. William 49
Knox, John S. 202

Lacy, John 75
Lancaster Castle / Prison 21–23
Laney, PC Thomas 110

Langham, Mr S. F. 138
Lantour, Dr 106–108
Lathbury, Mary 148–149
Lavender, Police Sergeant 32
Lawrence, Mr Justice 185
Layton, Mr H. A. 175
Leach, Amilia (Amelia) 210–213
Leach, Mr C. J. 118
Lee, Joseph 202
Lee, Mary 101
Leeds 84–87, 206
Leicester Infirmary 190
Leicestershire County Lunatic Asylum delete
Lester, Police Constable 16
Letheby, Professor 59
Levy, Mr 173
Lewes 60–61, 71, 180–181
Lewin, William Charles James / Terriss, William 131–135
Lewis, Mr C. E. 103
Lincoln 50–51, 91–94
Little, Mr 76–77
Littlewood, Police Superintendent 115–116
Liverpool 77–79, 135, 139, 192–193
Llanelly 201, 203
Lloyd, Detective Sergeant Francis 55
Lloyd, Mr 144
Lobb, Dr Martin E. 201
Lochwinnoch 23, 26
Lockhart, Cuthbert Robert Whomes 178–179
Lockhart, Robert 177–180
Lockhart, Sidney Stuart 177–181
Lodge, William 117–118
London 11, 24–25, 27, 36, 38–39, 51, 66–70, 97, 105, 123, 131–134, 135–136, 140, 165, 178
Longton 181
Lothian, Police Constable 207
Lowe, Edmund 52–53
Lowman, Dr 149
Lubbock, Edward 75
Lucas, Christina 205
Lush, John Henry 144–147
Lush, Mr Justice 46–47, 177
Lyme 9
Lyster, Abraham and Charles 37

Mabey, Cyril W. 188
MacDonald, Dr Finlay 103
Macnamara, Dr 104
Maddocks, Mr 150–152
Maidstone 88, 201
Male, Ann 9
Male, John 9

Manchester 24, 61–63, 87–88
Manning, Frederick 126
Marlin, Mr Henry A. 111
Marriott, John 64
Marshall Hall, Sir E 105
Marshalsea, Mary 31–32
Martin, Mr Baron 61, 79
Martin, William 75
Marylebone Police Court 166
Matcham, PC Thomas 99
McCardie, Mr Justice 189
McClean/ Maclean, Hector 124
McClean/Maclean, Roderick Edward 122–125
McEwen, Dr 84
McIntosh, James 161
McKinnon, William Alexander 94–95
McLeay, Alexander 4–5
McNab, Mr 36
McNaughten, McNaughton or M'Naghten, Daniel 26–30
McNaughten, McNaughton or M'Naghten, Daniel senior 26–27
Measham 189
Melmoth, Mr J.V. 45–46
Miller, Charles 58–59
Miller, Ernest 58
Milligan, Alexander 161
Mills, Reginald George 211–212
Milne, PC Stewart 166
Mitchell, Inspector 209
Mombasa, Kenya 201
Monckton, W.W. 8
Monroe, Dr Edward Thomas 29
Moore, Police Constable 82
Moores, Sarah 82
Morgan, Police Constable 164
Morris, Sarah 112
Mould / Pollard, Agnes Dorcas 168–172
Mould, William 168–172
Mould, William junior 170
Muir, Dr William 208
Munro, Dr 6
Mutton, John delete

Naseby 140
Nelson, Margaret 'Polly' 107–108
Netley Military Hospital 94–96
Nevill, Phoebe 40
New Brighton 135
Newcastle 131, 209, 210
Newgate Prison 12, 30, 54, 60, 68, 98
Newman, Florence 101–104
Newton-on-Ouse 106–107
Nicholson, Dr 94
Niles, Emily Albertina 71–72

Norcliffe, Angelina 74–76
Norfolk and Norwich Hospital 74–75
Normanby, Marquis of 7
Norris, Dr Edmund Stacey 111
Northampton Gaol 143, 160, 161
Nutt, Horace 45–47

O'Connor, Dr Thomas J. H. 78
Odgers, Wilfred Ewart 214
Ogilvy, Alexander 66–68
Orange, Dr William 139
Ore, William Beaton 66.68
Oxenden 141

Page, Frederick Ernest 125–128
Page, Henry and Mary 11–13
Page, Robert Everett 125–127
Paignton 195–197
Palmer, Mr 23
Parkhurst Prison 151, 153
Parr, Mary Ann 63–66
Payne, Alfred W. 148
Payne, Ann 80
Peacock, John 61–63
Pearce, Mr 42
Pebmarsh 153
Peckham Asylum 103
Peckham House 11
Peel, Sir Robert 24–29
Pennicott, Superintendent 179
Penton, Miss 144
Percival, Mr F. M. 159
Percy, Hugh 208
Peru 66–68
Petchell, Eyre 48–50
Pethybridge, John 175
Philbrick, Mr 127
Philips, Horatio 51–53
Phillips, Dr 149, 188
Phillips, John Llewellyn 198–203
Phillips, Sir Thomas 37
Pitfield, Superintendent John 118
Plant, George 62
Plant, John 61–63
Plymouth 71
Pollard, Eliza 168–169
Pollard, John 170–171
Portland Prison 151–153
Potter, James 13–18
Potter, Jemima 146
Potter, Sarah 13–18
Pratt, George 140–142
Preston 18–23
Preston Lunatic Asylum 23
Prestwich Lunatic Asylum 63

Price, Dr 87
Prior, Thomas William 112

Ramsgate 210–212
Randall, Agnes 64
Rawlinson, Alfred W. 179
Ray, Sidney Keyworth 94–96
Rayner, Hugh 138
Reading, Lord 181
Reading Prison 113
Redwell, Mr 36
Rees, Anne 162–164
Rees, James 162–164
Rees / Davies, Margaret 162–165
Rees, Mary (junior) 163–164
Rees, Mary (senior) 163
Rees, Rowland 163–164
Rees, William 162–164
Renfern, Samuel 85
Renshaw, Dr C. J. 82–83
Retallick, Thomas Henry 173
Rice, Dr C.E. 188
Richards, Dr D. T. 116
Richards, Dr W.A. 147
Ridley, Mr Justice 172
Ringrose, Odessa 140
Robertson, Police Inspector William 68
Robinson, Eliza 89–90
Robinson, Gertrude Lucy Brenner 72–73
Robinson, Henry 'Harry' William 89–94
Robinson, William Isaac 71–74
Robson, Harvey 210
Rochester 39
Roe, Sir Frederick 6
Rogers, Dr Arthur Anderson 115
Ross, Mr H.B. 127
Rowe, George James 198–201
Rowland, Charles 64–65
Rowlatt, Mr Justice 116, 197–198
Royal, Frances 13
Rudyard, Sergeant 45
Rugg, Dr Richard 59
Rump, Alfred 70–71
Rundle, Charles 172–175
Rusdell, John Lionel Raymond 213–215
Ruthin 214

Sale 81, 83
Saltley 183–184
Sankey, Mr Justice 191
Scott, Charles 169
Scott, Dilys Myfanwy 213–214
Scott, Florence 165
Scott, Harry 213
Scott, James 135, 167

Index 225

Scriven, George 183–186
Scriven Sarah Ann Rosina 183–185
Scriven, Sidney Charles 183–185
Senior, James 43–47
Senior Louisa Annie 43–46
Senior, Mrs 43–44
Sherborne 43–44
Shaw, James 156–162
Sheerness 70
Sheffield 205
Shelley, John Darby 3–7
Sherborne 43–44
Shill, Eleanor, Emily & Edith 109–110
Shill, Joseph 109–114
Shill, Maria 109–113
Shoreditch 11
Shrewsbury 54–56
Sidney, Samuel 3
Sills, Mr 144, 160
Silver, PC James 28
Skinner, Police Constable 195
Smith, Albert 156–160
Smith, Alice Sarah 157–160
Smith, Francis 156–160
Smith, George 157–158
Smith, James / Walker, John 87–89
Smith, Samuel 126
Smith, Dr Wayland 197–198
Solly, Ernest 146–147
Somerset and Bath Lunatic Asylum 124
South Petherton 7–8
Sparkford 79–80
Spencer, Ann 78
Spicer, Dr Edward 202–203
Spilsbury, Dr Bernard Henry 179
Spooner, Police Constable 188
Spurling, Jessie Charlotte 102–105
St Bartholomew's Hospital 137–138
St Luke's Hospital for Lunatics 11, 36
S.S. *Beechdale* 139
S.S. *Capella* 139
Stable, Mr Justice 212
Stephen, James Fitzjames 96
Stephen, Mr.17
Stephens, Mr 173
Stephenson, George 129–130
Stevenson, James 23–26
Stevenson, James senior 26
Stewart, Robert Bell 66
Stoke Workhouse delete
Stone, John 13–17
Sulgrave 156–160
Sutherland, Dr 6, 26
Sutton, Mr Justice 182–183
Swann, Mr 64–66
Sydney 3, 5
Sympson, Dr 92–94

Taubman, Mary Josephine delete
Taunton Prison 10, 81
Taylor, George 91
Terry, Mr W. 142
Thomas, Dr Danford 166
Thomas, Ellen Martin 195–198
Thomas, Emma 54–55
Thomas, Harry 173
Thomas. Thomas Percival 195–198
Thompson, Dr 190
Thompson, Dr Ebenezer 48
Thompson, James Edward 129–139
Thompson, William 66–70
Thorp, John 41
Thorp, Revd. Gervais 41
Thorpe, Police Sergeant 14–16
Thorpe, William Arthur 188
Tomkins, Richard 55
Torbay Hospital 197
Townsend, Emma Jose 203–205
Treadwell, Oliver 138–139
Tredworth 168
Trotter, George 207–210
Trotter, Jean 207–210
Trotter, Joyce 207–210
Tuckman, Mary Ann 107
Tur Langton 141
Turner, Edward 45
Turner, Dr John 103
Turney, Beatrice 181–182
Turpin, Ellen 153–154
Turpin, Thomas 153
Tuxford, Dr Reginald 90–91
Twining, Dr D.204

Upton, John 186
Utting, Edward 6

Vallack, James 16
Vaughan, James 73
Victoria, Queen 24–26, 122–125

Wadsley Lunatic Asylum 85
Walker, Dr Westby 18–23
Walmsley, Dr Robert G. 194
Walton Prison 194
Ward, Joseph 32
Ware 35–36
Warren, Walter 154–155
Weaver, Inspector 171
Weaver, Martha Spencer 39–43
Weedon, Mr W. delete
Weedon, William 37, 96
Wells 81, 124–125
Welsh, John 212
West Allington 30–31

Westminster Bridewell 6
White, Alice 148
White, Annie 147–148
White, Inspector 159
White, John 147- 153
White, Mary Ann 148–153
White, Walter 144–147
Whittle, Mrs Ann 18–21
Whittle, Mary 18
Whittle, Peter 18–23
Whittle, Sarah 18–22
Whittle, Thomas 18–21
Whitwell, Dr Francis 55–57
Whitwell, Dr James 177
Whorlow, Eliza 99–101
Whorlow, Harold Ernest 99–101
Whorlow, Henry Thomas 99–100
Whorlow, Mary 99–100
Wilbraham, Lionel Wynn 213–214
Wilford, David 143
Willes, Mr Justice 16, 33
Williams, Emily Jane 182
Williams, John Thomas 172–175
Williams, Mr 168
Williams, Mr Justice 42
Wills, Mr Justice 87–88, 160
Wilson, PC George 129–130
Wilson, Laura, 119–121
Wilson, Mary-Ann 120–121

Wilson, William (Danbury) 41
Wilson, William (Woolwich) 110–120
Winchester 116, 145–147
Windeatt, Mr G. 204
Windsor 109–111, 122–123
Wokingham 202
Woking Prison 89
Wood, Dr Norman 213
Wood, Mr J. P. 107
Wood, Mrs 58–59
Wood, Police Constable 187
Woodforde, Dr Francis Henry 10
Woolston 114
Worthing 177–179
Worthington, Dr T. 147
Wrexham 213–214
Wright, Mr Justice 92–94
Wright, Police Constable 91
Wright, Revd. R. J. 77
Wrinch, Dr 94

Yeoman, Alfred Charles 203–204
Yeoman, Kathleen Lucy 203–204
Yeoman, Olive Ann 203–204
Yeoman, William George 203–204
Yeoman, William Jarvis 203–205
York 108–109
Youlton, Elizabeth 121